T0319861

High-growth Women's Entrepreneurship

High-growth Women's Entrepreneurship

Programs, Policies and Practices

Edited by

Amanda Bullough

Associate Professor of Management and Co-Director and Co-Founder of the Women's Leadership Initiative, University of Delaware, USA

Diana M. Hechavarría

Associate Professor, Center for Entrepreneurship, Muma College of Business, University of South Florida, USA

Candida G. Brush

Franklin W. Olin Distinguished Chair of Entrepreneurship and Vice Provost of Global Entrepreneurial Leadership, Babson College, USA

Linda F. Edelman

Professor of Management and Chair of the Management Department, Bentley University, USA

IN ASSOCIATION WITH THE DIANA INTERNATIONAL PROJECT

Edward Elgar
PUBLISHING

Cheltenham, UK • Northampton, MA, USA

© Amanda Bullough, Diana M. Hechavarría, Candida G. Brush and Linda F. Edelman 2019

All rights reserved. No part of this publication may be reproduced, stored in a retrieval system or transmitted in any form or by any means, electronic, mechanical or photocopying, recording, or otherwise without the prior permission of the publisher.

Published by
Edward Elgar Publishing Limited
The Lypiatts
15 Lansdown Road
Cheltenham
Glos GL50 2JA
UK

Edward Elgar Publishing, Inc.
William Pratt House
9 Dewey Court
Northampton
Massachusetts 01060
USA

A catalogue record for this book
is available from the British Library

Library of Congress Control Number: 2019951576

This book is available electronically in the **Elgar**online
Business subject collection
DOI 10.4337/9781788118712

ISBN 978 1 78811 870 5 (cased)
ISBN 978 1 78811 871 2 (eBook)

Printed and bound by CPI Group (UK) Ltd, Croydon, CR0 4YY

Contents

Figures

Tables

Contributors

Naomi Birdthistle Associate Professor Naomi Birdthistle has been an academic for over 20 years. Naomi has taught extensively at all educational levels and is a visiting Professor at Aalto University – Mikkeli campus, for over a decade. An award-winning teacher and researcher, Naomi has won a teaching excellence award, her PhD has won a worldwide award given by the Family Firm Institute and she won several awards from Emerald Literati Network. Her research includes entrepreneurship education, family business management and high-growth firms.

Christopher J. Boudreaux is an Assistant Professor of Economics at Florida Atlantic University and a research associate at the Phil Smith Center for Free Enterprise. His research interests include entrepreneurship and innovation, economic growth and competition, institutional analysis, and business economics. Dr Boudreaux is a prolific writer and has published articles in premier journals in the fields of economics, business and entrepreneurship. He received his PhD from Florida State University and his BS from Nicholls State University.

Zuzana Brixiová is Associate Professor at the University of Economics in Prague and Adjunct Associate Professor at the University of Cape Town, the School of Economics. She is affiliated with the Institute of Labor Economics (IZA). Previously, she worked for several international organizations including as the UNDP Economic Advisor in Eswatini. Her research interests are development economics, entrepreneurship, labor economics and applied microeconomics. She holds a PhD in Economics from the University of Minnesota and was a Fulbright scholar at the Addis Ababa University in Ethiopia from September 2007 to March 2008.

Candida G. Brush is the Vice Provost of Global Entrepreneurial Leadership and a Full Professor at Babson College, USA, and holder of the Franklin W. Olin Distinguished Chair of Entrepreneurship. She is well known for her pioneering research in women's entrepreneurship. She is a Visiting Adjunct Professor to the Nord University, Bodø Graduate School in Bodø, Norway. Professor Brush is a founding member of the Diana Project International and holds an honorary doctorate from Jonkoping University, Sweden for her contributions to entrepreneurship research. Her research investigates nascent entrepreneurial ventures, women's entrepreneurship and financing of growth-oriented ventures. She is an active angel investor and serves on the boards of several companies.

Amanda Bullough is an Associate Professor of Management and Co-Director of the Women's Leadership Initiative at the University of Delaware. Her research and teaching span organizational behaviour, global leadership, cross-cultural management, and entrepreneurship. She publishes in premier journals, has presented at countless international business and management conferences, consults for high-profile clients, has experience in approximately 40 countries, and is the Immediate-Past-President of the Women of the Academy of International Business. Dr Bullough has a PhD in Management & International Business and an MA in International Studies, from Florida International University, and a BS in Marketing from the University of South Florida.

Dilek Cetindamar is an Associate Professor in the School of Information, Systems, and Modeling at University Technology Sydney, Australia. She worked at many universities, including Case Western Reserve University (USA), Chalmers University of Technology (Sweden), and Sabanci University (Turkey). She has more than 80 publications, including nine books. She received an 'encouragement award' from Turkish Academy of Sciences in 2003 and best book award from International Association for Management of Technology in 2012.

Miguel Córdova is Professor of Management and Internationalization Leader of the Management School and Department in Pontificia Universidad Católica del Perú. PhD. Candidate in Strategic Management and MBA of Centrum Católica (Peru). He also did doctoral studies at Copenhagen Business School. His research is about Corporate Networks, Supply Chain Management and Entrepreneurship. He is Coordinator of NEO Research Interdisciplinary Group. Professor Córdova is member of the Executive Board at Teaching and Learning (T&E) SIG of the Academy of International Business (AIB). He is Deputy Director of *360 Management Sciences Journal*, and was visiting professor at INSEEC Business School (Paris), Universidad del Desarrollo (Santiago de Chile), and ESADE Business School (Barcelona). He got four research grants, a scholarship for International Teachers Program (ITP) of the European Foundation for Management Development (EFMD) and one teaching grant.

Linda F. Edelman is a Professor of Management at Bentley University. She received her MBA and DBA from Boston University and she studied at London Business School and was a Research Fellow at the Warwick Business School. Her research examines small firm internationalization and women and nascent entrepreneurs. She is currently a Research Fellow at Saint Petersburg State University, Russia. Linda is the author of over 50 scholarly articles and book chapters. She serves on three editorial boards, as an expert panel reviewer for the Belgium FWO, and she recently received a research grant from the Kauffman Foundation.

Robyn Eversole is Professor, Social Impact at the Centre for Social Impact, Swinburne University of Technology, Melbourne, Australia. She is an anthropologist known internationally for her practice-focused research on regional and community development. Her books include *Knowledge Partnering for Community Development* (2015), *Regional Development in Australia: Being Regional* (2016), and *Anthropology for Development: From Theory to Practice* (2018).

Blaž Frešer, MA, is a junior researcher, teaching assistant for the field of entrepreneurship and quantitative research methods, and member of the Institute for Entrepreneurship and Small Business Management at the Faculty of Economics and Business, University of Maribor. His main research field lies in analysing high-growth enterprises in relation to different growth determinants, especially financial resources.

Vinita Godinho After more than two decades experience as a senior banker, Vinita switched hats to academia, completing a PhD on Indigenous financial capability and well-being in Australia. In her current role as the General Manager Advisory at Good Shepherd Microfinance, she is responsible for undertaking action-focused research, programme design and impact evaluation, so that the microfinance charity can develop evidence-based, people-centred financial products and services to meet the needs of Australians on low incomes, particularly women and girls.

Diana M. Hechavarría is an Assistant Professor in the Center for Entrepreneurship at the University South Florida's Muma College of Business. Diana explores the various dynamics confronted in the different stages of launching a new firm. Predominantly, Diana explores the nascent entrepreneurship gestation window, or the timing of start-up outcomes. Her other research interests also include social start-ups and gender. Diana has a PhD in Business Administration from University of Cincinnati (Cincinnati, OH, USA), an MA in Liberal Studies from Florida International University (Miami, FL, USA), and a BA in Sociology from University of Florida (Gainesville, FL, USA).

Fátima Huamán is Junior researcher affiliated to NEO Research Interdisciplinary Group of Pontificia Universidad Católica del Perú, and teaching assistant for the field of academic research. Graduated from the

Management program of Pontificia Universidad Católica del Perú, with specialized studies in Management Control at Universidad de Chile (Santiago de Chile). Her main research focuses on entrepreneurship field and female entrepreneurship. She received one research grant for her undergrad thesis and she was a speaker in CLADEA international conference in Costa Rica (2018).

Elayn James is a research student at the University of Technology Sydney. She is investigating digital transformation leadership within large organizations. She has a professional interest in digital and technology innovation strategy, and has been a consultant with one of the world's largest technology firms. She has a lifelong interest in gender issues and a 15-year association with the start-up scene in Sydney, Australia, including working inside a couple that have successfully exited.

Thierry Kangoye is a principal strategy and policy officer with the African Development Bank Group. His research interests include financial inclusion, financial sector development, gender, entrepreneurship and infrastructure development. He has also worked on issues related to development finance, private investments and banking, and private sector development capacity building initiatives in various multilateral organizations such as the United Nations Economic Commission for Africa (UNECA), the United Nations Industrial Development Organization (UNIDO) and the World Bank Group. He holds a PhD in Development Economics from the Clermont School of Economics (University of Auvergne, France).

Thorsten Lammers studied Physics and Business Administration in Hamburg and Brisbane. He finished his PhD in Strategic Management with a study on complexity in logistics networks. After some time working with a BIG4 consulting firm on strategy and technology projects around Europe, he joined the University of Technology Sydney as a Senior Lecturer. Currently, Thorsten focuses his work on the effects of digital technologies on the workplace of the future.

Yaokuang Li is a Professor at the School of Management of Hefei University of Technology. His main research areas include entrepreneurship and finance, with a focus on venture capital, business angels, and crowdfunding. He presides over several national research projects and publishes his research work in many peer-reviewed journals, such as *Venture Capital: An International Journal of Entrepreneurial Finance*, *International Entrepreneurship and Management Journal*, *Entrepreneurship Research Journal*, and *Chinese Rural Economy*. Dr Li has a Doctor and a Master in Management from Tongji University and Hefei University of Technology, respectively. He also has a Bachelor of Science from Anhui Normal University and a Bachelor of Economics from Nanjing University.

Shakeel Muhammad is a PhD student at the School of Management of Hefei University of Technology. He has a diverse background of research in women entrepreneurship, venture capital and finance. He writes many working papers based on social networking, reputation, and the institutional and cultural environment of women-owned businesses. He has published several papers within his expertise in research journals. Shakeel Muhammad has Master's and Bachelor's degrees in Finance and Economics from well-reputed universities in Pakistan.

Boris Nikolaev is an Assistant Professor of Entrepreneurship in the Hankamer School of Business at Baylor University. His research interests include public policy, applied microeconomics, entrepreneurship, and mental health and well-being. Dr Nikolaev has published over 30 articles, many of which in premier journals in the fields of economics, psychology and entrepreneurship. He received his PhD from the University of South Florida and a BS (Economics, Mathematics, and Philosophy) from Manchester College.

Alicia Pearce implements the UTS Athena SWAN pilot and for four years, the whole of the institution plan for gender good practice in STEMM. Alicia has had a diverse career in policy and advocacy management, specializing in workforce policy and gender equity practice and legislative reform, and has a discipline background in industrial relations and gender. Prior to UTS, Alicia led industry research into gendered experience in STEMM workplaces, managed a pay equity test case and led many policy and legislative reform projects.

Karin Širec, PhD, is Professor of Entrepreneurship and Business Economics, head of the Department of Entrepreneurship and Business Economics, and member of the Institute for Entrepreneurship and Small Business Management at the Faculty of Economics and Business, University of Maribor. She carries out research in the fields of entrepreneurship, business economics, innovations, female entrepreneurship, establishment and growth of companies. Since 2013 she serves as a country expert for the European Commission/OECD project Inclusive Entrepreneurship.

Elizabeth Sullivan is a highly experienced University executive, public health physician and research leader who is nationally and internationally recognized for her outstanding contributions to public health particularly in the fields of maternal, sexual and reproductive health. She was the Assistant Deputy Vice-Chancellor (Research) and the academic lead for UTS's Athena SWAN Gender Equity Initiative from 2015–2018. She was also the Head of the Discipline of Public Health and inaugural Director, Australian Centre for Public and Population Health Research from 2016–2019.

Polona Tominc, PhD, is a Professor of Quantitative Methods in business sciences at the Department of Quantitative Economic Analyses at the Faculty of Economics and Business, University of Maribor. She is leading a research group 'Entrepreneurship for Innovative Society' within the Institute for Entrepreneurship and Small Business Management. Her research areas include entrepreneurship and innovation, female entrepreneurship, management and research of teaching and learning strategies in higher education.

Megerssa Walo is a Research Fellow at the Centre for Social Impact, Swinburne University of Technology. He is an expert in place-based development, value chains and enterprise ecosystems with a strong track record in developing quality research outputs in the field of social sciences and contributing to research translation through policy development. He was awarded his PhD in Regional Development from the University of Tasmania in 2017.

Juan Wu is a PhD student at School of Management of Hefei University of Technology. Her major research area is female entrepreneurship, with focus on the entrepreneurial ecosystem, institutions and finance. She publishes her research work in the *International Entrepreneurship and Management Journal*, *Journal of Chinese Women's Studies*, *Entrepreneurship Research Journal*, and others. Juan Wu has a Master's and a Bachelor in Management from Hefei University of Technology and Anhui University, respectively.

1. Introduction: programs, policies and practices: fostering high-growth women's entrepreneurship

Amanda Bullough, Diana M. Hechavarría, Candida G. Brush and Linda F. Edelman

Women's entrepreneurship is widely recognized as a source of economic and social development (Hechavarría et al., 2019). The 2016 Global Entrepreneurship Monitor (GEM) Women's Report in 74 economies noted 274 million women had new or established businesses contributing jobs and innovations (Kelley et al., 2017). Despite their participation and contributions, there is a persistent storyline that women entrepreneurs do not perform as well as their male counterparts, in terms of sales, employment growth, or profitability (Orser et al., 2006; Fairlie and Robb, 2009). While there is some research examining performance and growth, the results are inconclusive as to whether there are differences, and what the causes of these might be (Robb and Watson, 2012). Growth-oriented businesses are essential for all economies to succeed because they are more likely to create jobs, support communities, and achieve higher productivity, innovation and exports.

Interest in programs, policies and practices around fostering high-growth entrepreneurship has increased significantly over the past decade. Let us start by explaining what we mean by each of these terms: programs, policies and practices. Programs include entrepreneurial training and curriculum that are focused on facilitating entrepreneurial activity (e.g., university programming, accelerators, incubators, National Science Foundation I-Corps, etc.). Policies refer to measures undertaken to establish entrepreneur-friendly legal and regulatory frameworks that are intended to foster growth-oriented new businesses and the process of innovation. Examples include initiatives that incentivize entrepreneurial activity, thus minimizing the risk and uncertainty associated with the process, as well as activities that ensure access to finance for innovation and growth. Practices are *what is*—common behaviors and institutional conventions in a particular society or context (e.g., encouraging cultural actions that promote and reward entrepreneurship).

To support women's growth-oriented businesses, research shows that women-focused programs, policies and practices would address the under-representation of women, increase women's participation in the labor force, and promote women's economic independence. Many countries have government or NGO sponsored programs that provide training, finance, skill building, technology support and a variety of other initiatives that help women entrepreneurs to grow their businesses (The Women's Business Council, https://www.womensbusinesscouncil.co.uk; The Goldman Sachs 10k Women Program, https://www.goldmansachs.com/citizenship/10000women/; the Quadruple Helix Central Baltic Program, http://www.balticfem.com/quadruple/; and others). In addition, governments often enter into partnerships with organizations to target inclusion and diversity in high-growth entrepreneurship globally, as well as domestically. For example, the United States Department of State and Kiva.org partnered to extend access to capital for one million women entrepreneurs in 83 countries through the Women's Entrepreneurship Fund. Women[x] Pakistan is a World Bank funded program that helps women entrepreneurs across five regions of Pakistan grow their businesses through training in business and leadership skills, utilizing social media, expanding their professional networks, and identifying growth opportunities.

Likewise, many governments have created policies to support women entrepreneurs' business growth by providing financing, trade missions, grants, set-asides and childcare (Brush and Greene, 2016; http://www.oecd.org/gender/OECD-Report%20-to-G7-Leaders-on-Women-and-Entrepreneurship.pdf). For example, the Government of Canada recently announced the Action Plan for Women Entrepreneurs, led by the Status of Women for Canada, an agency that is mandated to promote equality for women in the economic, social and democratic life of Canada. The Action Plan provides $700 million CAD for women-owned businesses. Australia created a digital platform (WIGB) supported by the Australian Trade and Investment Commission (Austrade) to provide information, resources, support and connections for women entrepreneurs to compete locally and globally, while Korea provides industry-specific training through the Gyeonggi Women's Development Center to help women entrepreneurs use social media and marketing (Brush and Greene, 2016). Other recommendations for policies that support the growth of women's entrepreneurship include: coordinating between existing policies and agencies, ensuring that entrepreneurs have the same access to welfare benefits as waged earners, encouraging engagement in STEM (science, technology, engineering and math fields) for boys and girls, reducing discrimination and increasing access to equity capital and loans, offering loan guarantees for women entrepreneurs, removing barriers to education, and so on (Henry et al., 2017; OECD, 2017).

There are also best practices supported by NGOs, educational institutions and foundations. For instance, the Tory Burch Foundation has a best practice playlist for growth-oriented women entrepreneurs, and the Clinton Foundation and the Ernst & Young's Entrepreneurial Winning Women (EWW) program offer mentoring programs tailored for women entrepreneurs. In 2014, the European Union held a conference with representatives from 28 member states to identify and share best practices regarding women's entrepreneurship (EIGE, 2014). Similarly, the World Bank offers newsletters that suggest best practice for growth-oriented women entrepreneurs.

Academic literature notes that programs, policy and practices that support women's growth-oriented entrepreneurship involve interconnected and mutually reinforcing features of a fruitful entrepreneurial culture, including financial and human capital advancement and readiness, new opportunities for expansion, and an assortment of institutional and infrastructural provisions for innovation and business growth. There are many gendered aspects of regulatory (e.g., policies and laws) and normative (e.g., cultural expectations) institutions that are subtle and hard to detect at the surface level, but are nonetheless ingrained in commonly accepted rules, norms and practices (Brush et al., 2018). Policies and rules that affect the expenses and regulations of starting and running a business can significantly influence the appeal of entrepreneurship (Manolova et al., 2017). Normative practices associated with women's roles and behaviors in society have a tendency to place responsibilities related to the household and family disproportionally on women compared to men, and undervalue women's roles in the economy and leadership. This can render entrepreneurship a less desirable and feasible career choice, and make starting and running a business much more complex for women (Bullough et al., 2017).

To overcome these institutional obstacles and harness the growth potential of women's businesses, the business networks that women build and the ecosystem that supports and encourages them are paramount. Networks contribute to social adaptability and capital (Baron and Markman, 2003), access to cheaper resources, enhanced reputation, and customer contacts (Kuada, 2009). A productive and supportive entrepreneurial ecosystem for women entrepreneurs must include a fair commercial and legal infrastructure with reduced barriers, access to equitable financial capital, and cultural norms that support women in growing their businesses (Brush et al., 2018; Hechavarría and Ingram, 2018).

Despite the numerous examples of policies, programs and practices, there is little academic research that investigates how these facilitate or hinder the growth of businesses owned by women entrepreneurs (Jennings and Brush, 2013). Therefore, we set out to foster a provocative discussion about topics on growth-oriented women entrepreneurs, and in particular focus on how public policy frameworks, along with programs and practices, are influencing the high-growth potential of women entrepreneurs. The catalyst for this book was the 2017 Diana International Conference,[1] held in Kansas City, Missouri, and sponsored by the Kauffman Foundation. This is the ninth book associated with the Diana International Project and will build on the success of the first book (Brush et al., 2006). In addition, a special issue in the *Journal of Small Business Management* on high-growth women's entrepreneurship also resulted from the 2017 Diana International Conference in Kansas City (Hechavarría et al., 2019).

We contend that globally, for economies to remain competitive, stakeholders involved in entrepreneurial ecosystems need to employ programs, policies and practices that promote diversity and inclusion in high-growth entrepreneurial activity. A long-term, integrated regional action plan for bringing about cultural change and promoting women-led high-growth ventures, encompassing initiatives in education, training, mentorship, administration, society, businesses and the media is needed. Such programs, policies or practices— improved tax incentives for businesses to invest, creation and support of institutions to implement the upgrading of the business environment, cultural initiatives, launch and support of cluster initiatives, creation of technology parks, and aggressive participation in federally funded science and technology programs—are efforts that can advance the preponderance of women creating high-growth ventures.

The scholars in this book conducted qualitative as well as quantitative research in contexts around the world, including Eswatini (Swaziland), Australia, China, Slovenia, Peru, and one global study of 43 countries. We have identified key themes in the research produced by the collaborators in this book and organized the chapters accordingly as follows: the practice of building networks, programs and the support environment, and policies and regulations. These three themes comprise the elements of a framework of policies, programs and practices for high-growth women's entrepreneurship, shown in Figure 1.1. The practice of building networks involves helping women entrepreneurs to build social, professional and business networks, and facilitating opportunities for these connections to be made. Programs and the support environment for high-growth women's entrepreneurship include mentoring, education and training, and incubators and accelerators. And, finally, policies and regulation that support women's business growth potential include the regulatory environment, the accessibility of financial resources, and financial policies and debt financing.

THEME 1: THE PRACTICE OF BUILDING NETWORKS

Prior research shows that social adaptability and a high level of social capital help entrepreneurs achieve financial success, because of having a favorable

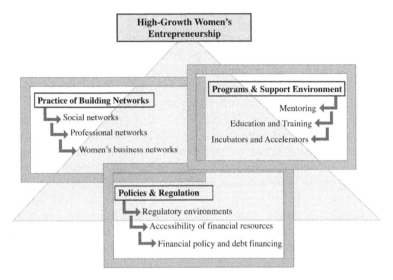

Figure 1.1   A framework for programs, policies and practices for high-growth women's entrepreneurship

reputation and extensive social networks (Baron and Markman, 2003). It is these social network ties that give entrepreneurs access to less expensive resources, as well as resources that would otherwise be completely unavailable, like a familiar reputation and customer contacts (Kuada, 2009). For firm survival, prior research suggests that networks are important, regardless of whether they are formal (e.g., lawyers, banks, trade associations, accountants) or informal (e.g., personal relationships, existing business contacts, family). However, for growth, formal networks are more important because they represent access to people that entrepreneurs do not already know and therefore build through acquaintances, indirect links, and unique connections among the entrepreneur's network (Watson, 2012). In fact, networks that are heavily related to family, and that are homogeneous, can actually be detrimental to small business owners. Breadth and heterogeneity of networks are critical for new ideas, resources and growth (Renzulli et al., 2000).

For entrepreneurial interest, while women have been found to have more positive attitudes toward networking (Dawson et al., 2011), they also exhibit fewer contacts to network with. More specifically, we know that people who personally know an entrepreneur are more likely to engage in entrepreneurship, but women have been found to be less likely to be acquainted with an entrepreneur, compared to men. This highlights the importance of access to people with entrepreneurial resources and role models in women's social networks (Klyver and Grant, 2010).

Chapters 2 and 3 in this book are both related to building networks. In Chapter 2, Brixiová and Kangoye examine the role of social networks—friends and family—and professional networks—career advisors, teachers and other entrepreneurs—in reducing gender gaps in access to formal financing and in entrepreneurial performance. They conducted their study with interview data collected by the United Nations in Eswatini, more commonly known as Swaziland, in Southern Africa. Their findings suggest that networks represent an important asset for women entrepreneurs in the start-up and operational phases of business development because of the role that networks play in generating capital. They point out that start-up capital is critical for generating sales, but women in Eswatini tend to start their business with less capital than their male counterparts. These authors recommend that policies aimed at women's entrepreneurship involve measures that promote network-building among female entrepreneurs and capital investors and funders, and financial literacy training. In Chapter 3, Córdova and Huamán examine how the absence of formal opportunities and state initiatives can generate high-growth behavior for a group of women entrepreneurs in Peru. By banding together and creating a network within a larger industry association, 11 entrepreneurial women created new opportunities for growth by sharing information and knowledge, and developing a mentoring program.

THEME 2: PROGRAMS AND THE SUPPORT ENVIRONMENT

An entrepreneurship ecosystem includes opportunities for new markets, access to financial capital, human capital, and a spectrum of institutional and infrastructural supports. The elements of the ecosystem are interconnected and mutually reinforcing, and influence a productive entrepreneurial culture that is innovative and has high potential for growth (Brush et al., 2018). A lack of access to talent, excessive bureaucracy, and difficulty acquiring financial capital are among the most commonly cited obstacles to start-ups and business growth (Isenberg, 2014). One response to these challenges is to build an environment that buttresses an entrepreneurial culture, skills, and support structures through universities (Fetters et al., 2010). Another way to resolve support challenges within the entrepreneurship ecosystem is through policy changes related to building a commercial and legal infrastructure, reducing barriers to entry, and fostering a culture with norms and expectations that support entrepreneurship (Hechavarría and Ingram, 2018).

Researchers have found that when it comes to many aspects of the entrepreneurship ecosystem, women do not have equal access to resources, participation and support, nor can they expect equal opportunities for success (Brush et al., 2018). Brush and colleagues explain that regulatory and normative institutions can all have gendered aspects that are usually less visible but ingrained in commonly accepted practices, rules and norms. The regulatory rules and policies, which are designed and enforced by government, and influence the expenses of setting up and conducting a business, can strongly influence the attractiveness of entrepreneurship. Normative expectations of women in society tend to place responsibilities related to the household and family on women rather than men, which can indirectly make entrepreneurship a less desirable career choice for women, and make starting and running a business much harder.

To address these challenges, recommendations for creating a culture of inclusivity include diversity initiatives accompanied with diversity and bias training that stimulate awareness and skill development, and are conducted over a significant period of time (Bezrukova et al., 2016). To assist women with building their competencies, women-only educational programs help women develop general business, and entrepreneurial and leadership skills they need to grow their businesses and allow women space to work through gender-specific issues (Bullough et al., 2015).

Chapters 4 and 5 of this book are related to programs and the support environment. In Chapter 4, Eversole, Birdthistle, Walo and Godinho look at the entrepreneurial support ecosystem in two very distinct regions of Australia to understand and map the support that is available for enterprising women. They find gaps in the current ecosystem that prevent women entrepreneurs from developing high-growth businesses. While mentoring, training, finance, incubators and accelerators, and peer networks are present in the support ecosystem, there are problems with their accessibility and appropriateness for women entrepreneurs. In Chapter 5, Cetindamar, James, Lammers, Pearce and Sullivan explore how Australia made progress in bridging a gap between alumni status of women who participated in a STEM program, to an entrepreneur status where those alumni actually start new technology companies. Their research is based on a case study of an institutional intervention in STEM education, known as the Science in Australia Gender Equity (SAGE) initiative. Their chapter highlights the importance of a gender-inclusive environment for STEM education and the workplace.

THEME 3: POLICIES AND REGULATION

Compared to men, women have been found to face significantly larger challenges with regard to securing capital for their businesses. Research has shown that the mere display of female-stereotyped behaviors often results in lower amounts of venture capital (VC) funding awarded to women (Balachandra et al., 2019). Women and men have also been asked different questions when delivering their pitches for funding, which has also led to lower levels of VC funding (Kanze et al., 2017). The discrimination women face in securing financial capital for their businesses does not only happen with venture capital. Commercial bank loans are also awarded to male entrepreneurs more than females (Marlow and Patton, 2005). While research has shown that quantifiable data is used in making bank loan decisions, gut feelings or hunches are also part of the loan decision equation, which leads to discrimination against female borrowers (Wilson, 2016). While microcredit is commonly associated with female entrepreneurs more so than males (Armendáriz and Roome, 2008), if microcredit is virtually the only financing available to women, it is easy to see why women do not grow bigger businesses (Kelley et al., 2017).

From a policy, programs and practices perspective, marketing existing financial products directly to women, as well as setting aside specific funds and designing financial products explicitly for women, can have a meaningful impact on women's abilities to successfully grow their business. Policies that incentivize programs and help facilitate these practices would include microcredit and commercial loan products and grants designed for, and marketed to, women and disadvantaged groups to help them overcome market, financial and social barriers, for example. Recruiting more female investors and advisors, and creating funds led by women and designed for investment specifically in women-owned businesses, could help rebalance VC and angel investment and would be particularly meaningful for women entrepreneurs with growth-oriented businesses (Halabisky, 2018).

Chapters 6, 7 and 8 of this book focus on the aspects of ecosystems that are related to financial awareness and accessibility. In Chapter 6, Boudreaux and Nikolaev propose that one factor—the regulatory environment—is a vital component that needs to be considered when understanding differences in early-stage growth aspirations between female and male entrepreneurs. By analyzing data from the Global Entrepreneurship Monitor and from the Economic Freedom of the World Index data, on 43 countries, they find that gender differences in the early-stage growth aspirations of entrepreneurs begin to disappear as the quality of the regulatory environment improves. Their initial results show that female entrepreneurs have lower growth aspirations than their male counterparts. When they add the quality of the regulatory environment into their analysis—credit market regulations in particular—they find a reduction in gender differences. Their important findings suggest that higher-quality credit market regulations can help equalize the early-stage growth aspirations of women and men.

In Chapter 7, Frešer, Širec and Tominc examine the gender gap in the accessibility of perceived financial resources in a sample of 125 Slovenian high-growth enterprises. They find direct gender discrimination from investors who prefer men-owned enterprises over women-owned enterprises. They offer policy recommendations, such as injecting entrepreneurial gender equality into the educational system, increased media attention on women's entrepreneurship and gender equality in business support from investors, and encouraging more women to become investors in business.

In Chapter 8, Wu, Li and Muhammad examine a financial policy that was implemented in June 2010 in China to reduce financial barriers for small- and medium-sized enterprises. Using national data from 293 Chinese women, they examine how women's awareness of this financial policy influences their debt financing activities. They find that as more women become aware of the policy, they become more likely to use debt financing, and in turn, tend to secure higher levels of debt capital.

CONCLUSION

In order for women to reach their full potential with regard to job creation, adding value to the economy, and building wealth and stability for themselves and their families, we need programs, policies and practices to support their work. Work in these areas has increased in recent years, in practice and in research. Women-focused programs, policies and practices have been found to tackle the under-representation of women, welcome more women into the workforce, and facilitate their economic independence. This has been done in the form of education and training, increased visibility and access to finance, technological support, and help with building business contacts and networks. Much of this work is supported by governmental intervention, NGO involvement, university collaboration and so on, and significant strides have been made.

Still, women are under-represented in the numbers of new start-ups, they invest lower levels of capital and utilize smaller amounts of financing, and they grow smaller businesses. This shows that work remains to be done in understanding why these realities continue to persist and what else can be done to help high-potential businesswomen grow bigger and more profitable businesses. This book helps advance our understanding about how to further coordinate policies and agencies, ensure awareness and access to financial capital, and encourage the advancement of women in STEM. We hope the research herein will also help reduce the bias that disproportionately affects women's access to loans, equity capital, education and so on (Henry et al., 2017; OECD, 2017).

With this book, we argue that economies and societies worldwide will need to continue and grow existing programs that are working well, and in many cases do more than is currently in place. To be competitive on the global stage, high-growth entrepreneurial activity among women needs to be a priority. To have a large portion of the world's population limited in their entrepreneur-ial potential, or sidelined altogether, is just bad business. A long-term and integrated strategy for cultural change and initiatives that promotes women's capacity to lead high-growth ventures is needed. This will include activities and projects around mentorship, business administration, the media, and diversity and inclusion training for program, policy and practice influencers.

NOTE

1. The Diana Project™ was launched in 1999 by Professors Brush, Carter, Gatewood, Greene and Hart to study the phenomenon of women's entrepreneur-ship in the United States. The Diana Project™ team, in partnership with ESBRI (Entrepreneurship and Small Business Research Institute, Sweden), inaugurated the Diana International Project (DIP) in 2003. DIP currently involves researchers from around the world and aims to provide a platform from which to develop, conduct and share a global research agenda dedicated to answering questions about women entrepreneurs and growth-oriented businesses.

REFERENCES

Armendáriz, B. and N. Roome (2008), 'Gender empowerment in microfinance', in S. Sundaresan (ed.), *Microfinance: Emerging Trends and Challenges*, Cheltenham, UK and Northampton, MA, USA: Edward Elgar Publishing.

Balachandra, L., T. Briggs, K. Eddleston and C. Brush (2019), 'Don't pitch like a girl! How gender stereotypes influence investor decisions', *Entrepreneurship Theory and Practice*, 43(1), 116–137.

Baron, R.A. and G.D. Markman (2003), 'Beyond social capital: the role of entrepre-neurs' social competence in their financial success', *Journal of Business Venturing*, 18(4), 41–60.

Bezrukova, K., C.S. Spell, J.L. Perry and K.A. Jehn (2016), 'A meta-analytical inte-gration of over 40 years of research on diversity training evaluation', *Psychological Bulletin*, 142(11), 1227–1274.

Brush, C., N.M. Carter, E.J. Gatewood, P.G. Greene and M. Hart (eds.) (2006), *Growth-Oriented Women Entrepreneurs and their Businesses: A Global Research Perspective*, Cheltenham, UK and Northampton, MA, USA: Edward Elgar Publishing.

Brush, C., L.F. Edelman, T. Manolova and F. Welter (2018), 'A gendered look at entre-preneurship ecosystems', *Small Business Economics*, Online First.

Brush, C. and P. Greene (2016), *Closing the Gender Gap in Entrepreneurship: A New Perspective on Policies and Practices*, Paris: OECD.

Bullough, A., M. Renko and D. Abdelzaher (2017), 'Women's business ownership: operating within the context of institutional and in-group collectivism', *Journal of Management*, 43(7), 2037–2064.

Bullough, A., M. Sully de Luque, D. Abdelzaher and W. Heim (2015), 'Developing women leaders through entrepreneurship training', *Academy of Management Perspectives*, 29(2), 250–270.

Dawson, C., N. Fuller-Love, E. Sinnott and B. O'Gorman (2011), 'Entrepreneurs' perceptions of business networks: does gender matter?', *The International Journal of Entrepreneurship and Innovation*, 12(4), 271–281.

EIGE (2014), *Good Practices in the Area of Women's Entrepreneurship: Report from a Consultation Meeting*, Luxembourg: Publications Office of the European Union.

Fairlie, R. and A.M. Robb (2009), 'Gender differences in business performance: evidence from characteristics of business owners survey', *Small Business Economics*, 33(4), 375–395.

Fetters, M., P.G. Greene, M.P. Rice and J.S. Butler (eds.) (2010), *The Development of University-Based Entrepreneurship Ecosystems: Global Practices*, Cheltenham, UK and Northampton, MA, USA: Edward Elgar Publishing.

Halabisky, D. (2018), 'Policy brief on women's entrepreneurship', OECD SME and Entrepreneurship Papers, No. 8, Paris: OECD Publishing. https://doi.org/10.1787/dd2d79e7-en.

Hechavarría, D., A. Bullough, C. Brush and L. Edelman (2019), 'High growth women's entrepreneurship: fueling social and economic development', *Journal of Small Business Management*, 57(1), 5–13.

Hechavarría, D.M. and A.E. Ingram (2018), 'Entrepreneurial ecosystem conditions and gendered national-level entrepreneurial activity: a fourteen-year panel study of GEM', *Small Business Economics*, Online First. https://doi.org/10.1007/s11187-018-9994-7.

Henry, C., B. Orser, S. Coleman and S. Foss (2017), 'Women's entrepreneurship policy: a 13 nation cross-country comparison', *International Journal of Gender and Entrepreneurship*, 9(3), 206–228.

Isenberg, D. (2014), 'What an entrepreneurship ecosystem actually is', *Harvard Business Review*, 5, 1–7.

Jennings, J.E. and C.G. Brush (2013), 'Research on women entrepreneurs: challenges to (and from) the broader entrepreneurship literature?', *The Academy of Management Annals*, 7(1), 663–715.

Kanze, D., L. Huang, M.A. Conley and E.T. Higgins (2017), 'Male and female entrepreneurs get asked different questions by VCs – and it affects how much funding they get', *Harvard Business Review*, June 27.

Kelley, D., B. Baumer, C. Brush, P. Greene, M. Mahdavi, M. Majbouri, M. Cole, M. Dean and R. Haevlow (2017), *Global Entrepreneurship Monitor 2016/2017 Report on Women's Entrepreneurship*, Wellesley, MA: Babson College.

Klyver, K. and S. Grant (2010), 'Gender differences in entrepreneurial networking and participation', *International Journal of Gender and Entrepreneurship*, 2(3), 213–227.

Kuada, J. (2009), 'Gender, social networks and entrepreneurship in Ghana', *Journal of African Business*, 10(1), 85–103.

Manolova, T.S., C.G. Brush, L.F. Edelman, A. Robb and F. Welter (2017), *Entrepreneurial Ecosystems and Growth of Women's Entrepreneurship*, Cheltenham, UK and Northampton, MA, USA: Edward Elgar Publishing.

Marlow, S. and D. Patton (2005), 'All credit to men? Entrepreneurship, finance, and gender', *Entrepreneurship Theory and Practice*, 29(6), 717–735.

OECD (2017), *2013 OECD Recommendation of the Council on Gender Equality in Education, Employment and Entrepreneurship*, Paris: OECD Publishing. http://dx.doi.org/10.1787/9789264279391-en.

Orser, B.J., A.L. Riding and K. Manley (2006), 'Women entrepreneurs and financial capital', *Entrepreneurship Theory and Practice*, 30(5), 643–665.

Renzulli, L.A., H. Aldrich and J. Moody (2000), 'Family matters: gender, networks, and entrepreneurial outcomes', *Social Forces*, 79(2), 523–546.

Robb, A. and J. Watson (2012), 'Gender differences in firm performance: evidence from new ventures in the United States', *Journal of Business Venturing*, 27(5), 544–558.

Watson, J. (2012), 'Networking: gender differences and the association with firm performance', *International Small Business Journal*, 30(5), 536–558.

Wilson, J. (2016), 'Making loan decisions in banks: straight from the gut?', *Journal of Business Ethics*, 137(1), 53–63.

2. Networks, start-up capital and women's entrepreneurial performance in Africa: evidence from Eswatini

Zuzana Brixiová and Thierry Kangoye

1. INTRODUCTION

Despite recognition of the potential role of entrepreneurship as an engine of inclusive growth, women's entrepreneurship in developing countries remains an under-researched topic in social sciences in general, and in economics in particular. While no unified theory of entrepreneurship exists, social science research on entrepreneurship has typically centered around three dimensions: (i) the institutional environment; (ii) sociological factors; and (iii) personal characteristics of the entrepreneurs (Djankov et al., 2005). This chapter focuses on the first two dimensions, namely the credit constraints as well as professional and social networks as important determinants of entrepreneurial behavior and performance. Given the lower rates of opportunity entrepreneurship among women than men, professional networking is important for women entrepreneurs who are not able to rely on peers as much as their male counterparts.

Considerable research has been undertaken on limited access to credit as a key constraint to entrepreneurship for the poor (Banerjee and Newman, 1993; De Soto, 2000), but research on the role of networks in the performance of women entrepreneurs in Africa has been limited. This chapter addresses this knowledge gap by exploring the networks–initial capital–firm performance nexus among women entrepreneurs in Eswatini,[1] a small landlocked country in Southern Africa where female unemployment approaches 30 percent of the labor force.[2] The novelty of this research is two-fold: first, the chapter empirically explores the role of networks as a success factor for women entrepreneurs both at the inception and operation phases of their firms; second, it provides the first systematic evidence on Eswatini, where high unemployment rates are coupled with very low growth rates and limited trade opportunities, making the case relevant for other lower middle-income countries.

More broadly, interest in entrepreneurship as a source of inclusive growth has risen in emerging and developing countries (Amin, 2010; Hallward-Driemeier, 2013; Brixiová and Kangoye, 2016). Entrepreneurship and small and medium enterprises (SMEs) have also received attention in global policy forums such as the G20.[3] In parallel, policy makers and researchers have also become increasingly interested in supporting women's access to credit and to investor networks, training, information services and technical assistance. Women in low- and middle-income countries continue to face challenges in landing jobs in the formal wage sector, making productive entrepreneurship an escape avenue from low-paid jobs. Besides economic benefits and empowerment, entrepreneurship also presents women with opportunity for shaping their identity and further integrating into the society (Blomqvist et al., 2014).

An extensive literature has discussed gender gaps in entrepreneurship in developed countries (examples include Hisrich and Brush, 1984; Fairlie and Robb, 2009; Minniti, 2009; Brush et al., 2017). Some studies have covered factors such as limited access to finance as a barrier to women starting and growing a business while others have analyzed gender-based impediments such as family and cultural burdens, limited mobility, and education. Yet, only a few studies have explored these factors in developing countries, where legal frameworks are weaker and hence softer factors, such as networks, play a critical role (Bardasi et al., 2009; Sabarwal and Terrell, 2009; Brixiová and Kangoye, 2016; Baliamoune-Lutz and Lutz, 2017). At the same time, sub-Saharan African countries have the highest share of women's entrepreneurship globally and the number of women entrepreneurs in the region has been rising (GEM, 2017). This trend underscores the need for research on constraints to high-growth entrepreneurship in the region.

Against this background, this chapter focuses on factors, including networks, that contribute to easing financial constraints on female start-up capital and their links with entrepreneurial performance in a middle-income African country, a topic which has received limited attention. Regarding conceptual underpinning, similar to the GEM (2017), the definition of entrepreneurship in this chapter emphasizes nascent entrepreneurship, and focuses on firms that have been running for 60 months or less. Further, as Bardasi et al. (2009) posit, gender barriers to entrepreneurship are likely to be more pronounced during the entry stage of the entrepreneurial process. We center on start-up capital, since its availability, and access to finance more broadly, is considered critical for a firm's creation, size and performance.

Based on the empirical analysis, we also discuss resources other than start-up capital that are associated with well-performing women-headed firms. We are especially interested in the effects of networks that women access on generating the initial capital and on the firm performance in the start-up phase. We include both social network (friends and family) and professional networks (namely career advisors, teachers and other entrepreneurs). Since this chapter focuses on the role of networks against other limited resources of women entrepreneurs, our research also contributes to the literature on the entrepreneurial bricolage (Senyard et al., 2009; Fisher, 2012). This topic is particularly unexplored in the African context.

The empirical analysis in this chapter confirms the importance of start-up capital for entrepreneurial performance, measured in sales, for both men and women. Moreover, gender gaps in start-up capital are associated with gender gaps in performance. In line with other studies, we found that women entrepreneurs in Eswatini have smaller start-up capital and are less likely to fund it from the formal financial sector than men.[4] Ties with professional support also matter for female entrepreneurial success, as women who receive such support are more likely to finance their start-up capital from the formal financial sector. Finally, women entrepreneurs with college education and adult women on average start their firms with higher amounts of start-up capital than their less educated and younger counterparts.

The rest of the chapter is organized as follows: section 2 reviews the literature; section 3 discusses data sources and some stylized facts, while Section 4 presents the empirical strategy and results. Section 5 concludes.

2.   REVIEW OF LITERATURE

Social scientists typically put forward three perspectives about the reasons for gender differences in entrepreneurial performance: (i) differences in entrepreneurs' personal characteristics, including different skills and attitudes toward risk (Lazaer, 2005); (ii) social factors such as cultural values and social networks (Renzulli et al., 2000; Kristiansen, 2004; Witt, 2004); and (iii) the institutional and business environment (Aidis and Estrin, 2014). Among social factors, links between demographic trends and entrepreneurship have been gaining increased attention. For example, Dutta and Mallick (2018) found that the impact of higher fertility rates on women's entrepreneurship is negative, but can be mitigated by factors such as women's increased tertiary enrollment and female labor force participation rates.

On the business environment side, access to credit as a barrier to entry and expansion of existing firms is a topic of continued interest, reflecting the lack of conclusive answers and effective policy solutions. Earlier research on the topic includes Aghion et al. (2007) for selected Organisation for Economic Co-operation and Development (OECD) advanced and emerging markets and Baliamoune-Lutz et al. (2011) for African countries. More recently, Fowowe (2017) examined subjective measures of financing access in 30 African countries and found that financing is key for firm growth. Quartey et al. (2017) showed that the SME access to finance in West Africa is impacted by firm size, formality, ownership, strength of legal rights, depth of credit information, managerial experience and firm's export orientation.

Research on gender gaps in access to start-up capital in Africa has been sparse. Exceptions include Asiedu et al. (2013), who examined empirically gender gaps in access to finance of firms in Africa and across developing regions. According to the authors, the gender of the firm's owner is an important determinant of financing constraints for SMEs, especially in sub-Saharan Africa (SSA). Drawing on cross-sectional financial data from firms in the Middle East and Africa during 2006–2014, Baliamoune-Lutz and Lutz (2017) found that (i) the availability of equity and/or debt capital and higher leverage have significant positive effects on firm performance, and (ii) women-owned firms have lower levels of equity and debt capital and also a lower leverage. However, when female-owned firms acquire more financing, their performance improvement exceeds that of other firms, pointing to access to finance as a binding constraint.

Several earlier studies on developing and emerging market countries also found gender differences in the amount and composition of start-up capital, with women facing greater constraints than men (Malapit, 2012). Women entrepreneurs face challenges in accessing formal sources of funding during the start-up phase and end up drawing on their personal sources or borrowing in the informal financial sector. In contrast, in their study on the Netherlands, Verheul and Thurik (2001) found gender gaps in the amount of start-up capital, but not in its composition (debt-to-equity ratios).

Regarding differences in attitudes of entrepreneurs toward risk, an influential stream of literature on entrepreneurship builds on the observation that relative to wage-workers, entrepreneurs tend to have lower risk aversion (Kanbur, 1982; Kihlstrom and Laffont, 1979). This stream suggests that in small firms the level and structure of start-up capital reflects the owners' attitudes toward risk. In this vein, Singh and Belwal (2008) underscored that gender differences in start-up capital are linked to variances in the risk appetite. In contrast, Baumol (1990) stressed that the risk attitude is not the key determinant of entrepreneurship. Rather, the important factor is that only some segments of the population have entrepreneurial inclinations and are able to seize effectively business opportunities. Recent evidence has suggested that gender differences in risk attitudes are smaller than previously thought (Nelson, 2015).

Another stream of literature links entrepreneurial networking with firm performance, where performance indicators can include the level or growth of sales, profits, survival, etc. (Witt, 2004). Within this literature, an influential paper by Renzulli et al. (2000) posited that the extent to which networks have a positive effect on performance depends positively on their heterogeneity and negatively on the share of friends and relatives they contain. A more recent view on the network success hypothesis posits that social and professional networks constitute a mechanism that helps create and pursue new opportunities (Leyden et al., 2014). The hypothesis assumes that networks allow the entrepreneurs to obtain resources at lower cost or gain access to resources they could not reach otherwise. Along these lines, Markussen and Roed (2017) posited that gendered peer effects contribute to persistent gaps between male and female entrepreneurship rates that persist in most industrialized countries. They found that peer effects operate both through role models and learning opportunities and access to important networks. Shahriar (2018) found, in a simulated environment, that gender gaps in entrepreneurial propensity are outcomes of socialization, with men in patriarchal and women in matrilineal societies investing more in new venture creation.

Several researchers explored the role of networks in entrepreneurs' access to finance and performance. Baron and Markman (2003) provided evidence that entrepreneurs' ability to build or be part of networks plays an important role in securing venture capital and increasing sales performance. In connection with gender-related gaps in access to start-up capital for entrepreneurs, the findings of Kuada (2009) suggest that women entrepreneurs rely more on their relationships and social capital than men to offset the limited access to bank financing. This chapter advances this research stream by seeking answers to the following questions: are women entrepreneurs who gather support outside of their social network (friends and relatives) starting their firms with higher initial capital? Do they post better sales performance than women entrepreneurs who rely mostly on the strength of close ties such as friends and family?[5]

3.   DATA SOURCES AND DESCRIPTIVE STATISTICS

The analysis utilizes the 2012 UN Eswatini survey of 640 small and medium-sized enterprises (SMEs) in the urban areas of the country (UN Eswatini, 2013). The sampling frame consisted of all SMEs listed in the 2011 SME directory of the Ministry of Commerce, Industry and Trade (provided by the Ministry's SME Unit). Using this frame, all firms listed in the major six cities that provided their full addresses were contacted for interviews. Among 640 business persons interviewed, 246 were firm owners, 169 directors, 121 managers, and the rest (104) were employees.

This chapter focuses on start-up capital. In that vein, it defines a start-up firm as a venture that is 60 months old or younger. Among 246 firm owners interviewed, 161 enterprises met this criterion, of which 93 had a female owner and 68 a male owner. Figure 2.1 illustrates the distribution of these respondent-owned enterprises by age for enterprises that were younger than 250 months. It shows that the majority of these fall into our definition of start-ups, that is, they are five years old or younger. Nevertheless, for robustness of the empirical analysis, we also examine links between networks, start-up capital and firm performance (sales) of all interviewed firm owners.

The initial sampling frame for the survey comprised all SMEs listed in the 2011 SME directory of the Ministry of Commerce, Industry and Trade (provided by the SME Unit). Using this frame, all firms listed in the six cities that provided their full addresses were selected for interviews. This choice implied that new and small firms as well as those that outgrew the 'SME status' or were not listed in the directory and operated more informally were not represented. To partly correct for this and also to replace firms that were no longer operating, about 100 enterprises that were not listed in the directory were interviewed. Overall, a large number of enterprises were interviewed relative to the population in selected areas.

2.1a. Women   **2.1b.** Men

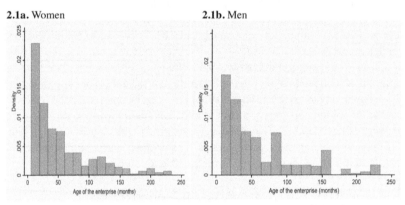

Source: Authors' calculations based on 2012 UN Eswatini survey.

Figure 2.1   *Distribution of enterprises by age, since their establishment (in months)*

The survey was conducted via face-to-face interviews. It was undertaken in Mbabane (capital) and other cities (Manzini, Ezulwini, Matsapha, Nhlangano and Siteki) in the Hhoho and Manzini regions. These regions were selected because of: (i) high entrepreneurial activity, and (ii) the potential to become a growth corridor of Eswatini, i.e., because of the potential to generate positive spillovers to the rest of the economy. With the exception of two, all SMEs employed less than 20 employees. Among sectors, services were the main area of activity.

The survey included questions that explored three perspectives on entrepreneurship that social scientists typically focus, including: (i) institutional environment; (ii) social and family networks; and (iii) personal characteristics

2.2a. Start-up capital (log), by gender   **2.2b.** Sales performance (log), by gender

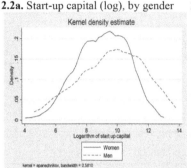
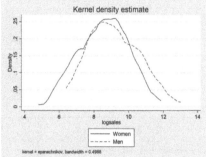

Note: Sales are for a typical month.

Source: Authors' calculations based on 2012 UN Eswatini survey.

Figure 2.2   *Kernel density estimate of sales and start-up capital among new business owners*

of the entrepreneurs. The interviews aimed at obtaining information on the background of the entrepreneurs, the objectives of the firms they run (profit or other motive) and the constraints they most frequently encountered. Gender was measured with a dichotomous variable, taking value 1 for female and value 0 for male respondents.

The survey also collected data on the main characteristics of the enterprise (sector, size, sales) as well as family background and network support for the entrepreneurs. Utilizing descriptive statistics and kernel density estimates, the paragraphs below examine the main demographic characteristics of men and women entrepreneurs. As Table 2.1 shows, men were on average slightly older, had higher education attainment, and were more likely than women entrepreneurs to have a nationality other than Eswatini. Men also spent on average several hours a week more than women in their firms and ran their business on full capacity for one month longer than women. Importantly, their average start-up capital was on average more than triple that of women while their firms were larger. Monthly sales of men-owned firms were more than double and more likely to grow than those of women. Men entrepreneurs were also more likely to be single and have more entrepreneurial and work experience than their female counterparts.

The kernel density estimates of probability function of monthly sales (expressed in log) (Figure 2.2a) show that in these nearly uni-modal distributions, men outperform women almost throughout the entire sales range. Women entrepreneurs have lower start-up capital than men for the entire

Table 2.1   Demographic characteristics of interviewed male and female entrepreneurs (in 2012, in % unless otherwise indicated)

Characteristics	Men (N=68)	Women (N=93)
Education		
High school or less	63.2	65.6
Tertiary	36.8	34.4
Age		
Youth (35 years or less)	54.4	49.5
Adult (above 35 years)	45.6	50.5
Marital status		
In traditional marriage	20.6	29
Modern marriage	27.9	26.9
Unmarried	51.5	44.1
Work efforts		
Weekly hours at work	44.1	42.6
Searching for job	30.9	14.6
Months last year at full capacity	10.6	9.7
Nationality		
Eswatini	77.9	91.4
Other	22.1	8.6
Start-up capital and sales		
Initial capital (mln. E)	74.6	23.2
Monthly sales (mln. E)	28.1	11.6
Sales stable or growing	53.4	48 ?
Firm size (employees)	2.09	0.84
Work history		
First-time business owner	88.6	95.5
Previous work in the formal sector	58.5	47.8

Note: E stands for Emalangeni (local currency).

Source: Authors' calculations based on 2012 UN Eswatini survey.

range, with some women starting their firms with almost no capital (Figure 2.2b).

Table 2.2 illustrates differences in reliance of men and women entrepreneurs (business owners) on their networks for support and start-up capital. This overall picture in the Eswatini context does not indicate that women entrepreneurs look more for support and sources of finance to their social network (family, friends) than men. In fact, women entrepreneurs in urban Eswatini

Table 2.2   Sources of entrepreneurial support and start-up capital

	Men (%)	Women (%)		Men (%)	Women (%)
Sources of encouragement			*Sources of discouragement*		
No one	35.3	31.5	No one	44.1	53.9
Social network	47.1	43.8	Social network	51.5	37.1
Professional network	5.9	14.6	Professional network	2.9	3.4
Other (e.g., media)	11.8	10.1	Other (e.g., media)	1.5	5.6
Sources of start-up capital			*Sources of influence*		
Own savings	55.9	61.8	No one	18.5	16.8
Social network	22.1	19.1	Social network	46.7	46.3
Bank	8.8	0	Professional network	31.9	33.6
Informal lenders	13.2	19.1	Other (e.g., media)	3	3.4

Note: Social networks comprise family and friends while professional networks consist of career advisors, teachers and other entrepreneurs.

Source: Authors' calculations based on 2012 UN Eswatini survey.

reported having received relatively more encouragement to pursue entrepreneurship from their professional networks (advisors, other entrepreneurs) and less discouragement from their social networks (family, friends) than their men counterparts. Women relied on social networks as sources of initial capital only marginally less than men, but provided it more often from their own sources, which was also reflected in lower levels of the initial capital. Overall, sources of financing for start-up capital in terms of debt and equity ratio are similar for men and women, as also found in Verheul and Thurik (2001), with women relying marginally more on equity from a combination of their own savings and social networks. While the higher share of women entrepreneurs contributed to start-up capital from personal sources, the amounts of such contributions were much smaller than among men. Finally, a larger share of women than men applied for credit from the informal sector and no women in the sample received bank credit.

4.   EMPIRICAL STRATEGY AND RESULTS

This section tests whether start-up capital and social factors (e.g., networks) are significant for firm performance in terms of the level of sales. It examines gender differences in (i) entrepreneurial performance (proxied by sales), accounting for entrepreneurs' start-up capital, networks and other factors as well as (ii) access to and composition of the initial capital. Differently put, the section analyzes if women entrepreneurs have on average lower start-up capital and sales than men and if they seek support from different types of network than men.

Our main hypothesis is that women entrepreneurs who gather support outside of their social network (friends and relatives) will start their firms with higher initial capital and will post better sales performance than women entrepreneurs who rely mostly on friends and family.[6]

The main findings for both male and female entrepreneurs are that higher levels of initial capital are associated with higher sales. In contrast to their male counterparts, women entrepreneurs start their firms with lower levels of start-up capital, which they fund mostly from their own savings. On a positive side, women with higher education tend to start their firms with more capital than their less educated counterparts. Specifically, women with tertiary education have higher initial capital than women who have lower educational attainment. Similarly, women who receive support from professional networks start their firms with higher initial capital than those who rely for support on social networks or no one. Moreover, women trained in financial literacy more often access external funding sources (including from social networks).

Two estimation methods have been applied to reach these findings: ordinary least square (OLS) regressions and (ii) probit regression (PR). The OLS measures the effects of the explanatory variables (networks, education, personal characteristics) for the (average) sales performance, and assumes a well-shaped distribution around the mean. The PR estimates the effect of the explanatory variables on the probability that women will fund their start-up capital from external sources. We estimate these equations for men and women:

$$log(Sales\_lev_i) = \gamma.Business\ char. + \delta.\ Networks + \upsilon.Entr.Char + \varepsilon_i \qquad (2.1a)$$

$$log(Init.Cap_i) = \alpha + \gamma Fund.Source + \sigma.\ Networks + \upsilon.Entr.Char + \varepsilon_i \qquad (2.1b)$$

$$Pr(External\ Funds) = \alpha + \sigma.Networks + \pi\ Entr.Char. + \varepsilon_i \qquad (2.1c)$$

where i stands for entrepreneurs. In the OLS regressions (2.1a), the dependent variable (Sales_lev) is a logarithm of the amount of sales in a typical month, in Emalangeni (local currency). In (2.1b), the dependent variable (Init.Cap) is a logarithm of the amount of start-up capital, also in Emalangeni. The probit model (2.1c) estimates the probability that the entrepreneur raises start-up capital from other than its own sources and takes on value 1 if that is the case and 0 otherwise. The '*Networks*' category includes the sources of start-up capital, sources of encouragement to become an entrepreneur, and also sources (professional or social networks) that demotivated the entrepreneur. Finally, '*Entr.Char*' (Entrepreneurial characteristics) captures the entrepreneur's age,

Table 2.3   *Networks, start-up capital, and sales: OLS regressions, new and all owner samples*

	Men	Men	Women	Women	Men	Women
		(new owners)			*(all owners)*	
	(1)	*(2)*	*(3)*	*(4)*	*(5)*	*(6)*
	Networks					
Start-up capital from social networks	−0.261	−0.323	−0.887	−0.915	−0.102	−0.523
	(0.292)	(0.299)	(0.304)***	(0.341)***	(0.299)	(0.261)**
Professional influence at start-up	−0.280	−0.396	−0.017	0.012	−0.151	0.015
	(0.260)	(0.261)	(0.244)	(0.270)	(0.230)	(0.199)
Based in Manzini	0.121	0.084	−1.037	−1.060	0.039	−0.596
	(0.234)	(0.235)	(0.269)***	(0.267)***	(0.280)	(0.238)**
	Business characteristics					
Initial capital (log)	0.424	0.463	0.414	0.413	0.420	0.318
	(0.065)***	(0.090)***	(0.084)***	(0.084)***	(0.076)***	(0.068)***
Licensed	0.539	0.574	1.003	1.009	0.361	0.726
	(0.286)*	(0.316)*	(0.293)***	(0.286)***	(0.282)	(0.234)***
Firm size	0.101	0.113	0.249	0.244	0.105	0.282
	(0.023)***	(0.025)***	(0.120)**	(0.125)*	(0.034)***	(0.076)***
	Entrepreneur characteristics					
Youth (35 years old or less)	−0.454	–	−0.076			
	(0.241)*		(0.224)			
Traditional marriage	–	0.214		0.171	−0.057	0.140
		(0.322)		(0.253)	(0.302)	(0.187)
	Skills					
Tertiary education	–	−0.100	–	0.073	–	–
		(0.331)		(0.276)		
Perceive own skill gaps	–	−0.236	–	−0.070	–	–
		(0.595)		(0.286)		
Intercept	4.884	4.282	4.484	4.401	4.771	5.151
	(0.587)***	(0.830)***	(0.773)***	(0.710)***	(0.684)***	(0.570)***

	Men	Men	Women	Women	Men	Women
	(new owners)				*(all owners)*	
	(1)	*(2)*	*(3)*	*(4)*	*(5)*	*(6)*
R^2	0.66	0.64	0.56	0.56	0.52	0.44
N	63	63	85	85	98	122

Notes: *, ** and *** denote 10%, 5% and 1% significance levels respectively. The dependent variable is the level of sales in a typical month (log). New owners are owners of enterprises that are 5 years old or younger. Heteroskedastic-robust standard errors are in parentheses.

Source: Authors' calculations based on 2012 UN Eswatini survey.

marital status and type of marriage, education level, etc. The variables are listed in the appendix to this chapter.

Regarding factors impacting sales levels, which is our variable for measuring entrepreneurial success, a larger amount of start-up capital (and bigger firms) is associated with better sales performance in enterprises run by both men and women entrepreneurs (Table 2.3). For entrepreneurs of both genders, having license to operate is also positively linked with sales, but to a larger extent for women than for men. Relying on social networks (friends and family) for funding of start-up capital has a negative and statistically significant impact on sales levels of women-run firms, and so does the Manzini location, which is the main industrial city of the country. This could, in part, reflect the type of sector that women entrepreneurs are involved in. Specifically, only 14 percent of women operate in manufacturing-related sectors relative to 20 percent of men. Finally, for firms with a male owner, being young (e.g., 35 years old or younger), was associated with lower sales levels. We did not find a similar impact for women entrepreneurs.

Given the importance of the amount of start-up capital for firm performance in terms of sales, we now turn to analyzing drivers of the initial capital, including funding sources. We first ran OLS regressions on determinants of the amount of start-up capital for new firm owners (owners of firms that are 60 months old or younger) as well as for a full sub-sample of men and women and summarize the results in Table 2.4. The results show that for both women and men entrepreneurs, funding their start-up capital from external sources, specifically through borrowing from formal and informal lenders, is associated with higher levels of initial capital (Table 2.4, all columns).

Another interesting finding from the policy perspective is that tertiary education (that is completing some or all university schooling) is positively linked with higher amounts of start-up capital for both genders (Table 2.4, all columns). For all women business owners, running their first business has a negative impact on their sales (Table 2.4, columns 1 and 4). Manzini location and age are positively associated with sales of male entrepreneurs, pointing to

Table 2.4   *Networks, human capital and the level of start-up capital: OLS regressions*

	Men (new owners)	Women (new owners)	Men (all owners)	Women (all owners)
	(1)	(2)	(3)	(4)
	Coeff (SE)	Coeff (SE)	Coeff (SE)	Coeff (SE)
Networks				
Professional support at start-up	0.288	0.453	−0.103	0.622
	(0.568)	(0.372)	(0.478)	(0.336)*
Debt funding from formal and informal lenders (outside family & friends)	1.655	0.723	1.909	0.649
	(0.497)***	(0.372)***	(0.452)***	(0.327)*
Working in Manzini	1.459	−0.177	−0.656	−0.167
	(0.546)**	(0.887)	(0.462)	(0.345)
Human capital				
Tertiary education	1.359	1.425	1.736	1.397
	(0.546)**	(0.445)***	(0.474)***	(0.398)***
First business	−1.057	−0.883	−0.613	−1.190
	(0.771)	(0.887)	(0.759)	(0.644)*
Personal characteristics				
In traditional marriage	−1.516	−0.451	−0.448	−0.423
	(0.614)**	(0.418)	(0.519)	(0.391)
Age	0.067	0.22	0.025	0.001
	(0.029)**	(0.027)	(0.023)	(0.016)
Intercept	6.65	8.39	7.88	9.10
	(1.460)***	(1.419)***	(1.185)***	(1.016)***
R^2 adjusted	0.51	0.17	0.34	0.14
Number of observations	44	66	77	100

Notes: Dependent variable is level of start-up capital (log). Regression coefficients reported. Heteroskedastic-robust standard error in parentheses. *, ** and *** denote significance at 10%, 5% and 1% respectively.

the likely role of clusters and experience in entrepreneurial performance. In sum, while professional supports do not seem to play a direct role in obtaining the initial capital, the access to external sources of funding does.

Table 2.5   *Networks and composition of start-up capital (new owners):*
             probit regressions

	Men (new owners)	Women (new owners)
	(1)	(2)
	Coeff (SE)	Coeff (SE)
Networks		
Social network support at start-up	−0.416	0.008
	(0.440)	(0.356)
Working in Manzini	−0.586	0.469
	(0.426)	(0.341)
Human capital		
Received financial literacy training	1.272	0.667
	(0.488)***	(0.392)*
Received business training	0.407	−0.091
	(0.592)	(0.383)
Personal characteristics		
Own contribution to start-up capital	−1.013	−0.778
	(0.438)**	(0.345)**
Intercept	−0.003	−0.771
	(0.452)	(0.341)
Pseudo R^2	0.27	0.16
Number of observations	68	87

Notes: Dependent variable is the external funding of start-up capital (=1 if from bank or informal lenders or family and friends and =0 if from own savings). Regression coefficients reported. *, ** and *** denote significance at 10%, 5% and 1% respectively. Heteroskedastic-robust standard errors in parentheses.

As a robustness check, we included entrepreneurial motives in the OLS regression; the qualitative results of Table 2.4 are unchanged. Interestingly, having a profit motive as the main driver of starting a firm is positively linked with sales levels of both new and all men owners but only with sales levels of all women owners. This is consistent with the view that women are more often than men driven to entrepreneurship by necessity or considerations such as greater time flexibility.

Regarding composition of funds, entrepreneurs—both men and women—who received financial literacy training were more likely to finance their start-up capital from sources other than their own savings, that is from funding from social networks and borrowing from either the formal or the informal financial sector than entrepreneurs without such training. However, the impact is stronger for men entrepreneurs. Making personal contributions to the start-up capital is associated with lower probability to receive funding from external sources for both men and women entrepreneurs. Finally, regional differences in access to external funds for start-up capital are not statistically significant for either women or men entrepreneurs (Table 2.5).

5. CONCLUSIONS

This chapter contributes to the literature on the role of networks in accessing start-up capital and firm performance among women entrepreneurs in Africa with evidence from Eswatini. By illustrating how other scarce resources impact firm performance, the chapter is also related to the emerging literature on entrepreneurial bricolage in developing countries.

The empirical analysis confirmed the critical role of start-up capital for sales performance of both men and women. The results also showed that, on average, women in Eswatini start their business with less capital and are more likely to fund it from their own sources than men. At the same time, education acts as a mitigating factor as women with higher education gather higher start-up capital than their less educated female counterparts. Moreover, women who receive support from professional networks have higher initial capital, while those trained in financial literacy more often access external funding sources, including through their networks.

The results are consistent with those of Renzulli et al. (2000) who found that high share of relatives and network homogeneity are key weaknesses of networks of women entrepreneurs in advanced economies. By documenting that women entrepreneurs in Eswatini rely more on their relatives and social capital than men when trying to access capital, the results are also related to those of Kuada (2009) who examined the role of social capital for women's entrepreneurship in Ghana. We add to this literature stream by illustrating that in Eswatini funding the start-up capital by borrowing from formal or informal lenders is linked positively with the amount of start-up capital and firm performance of both men and women entrepreneurs.

The results suggest that policies toward women's entrepreneurship need to go beyond strengthening the business environment and include proactive steps such as building networks among women entrepreneurs and funders as well as financial literacy trainings. The chapter gave evidence on the positive role of networks in obtaining start-up capital and firm performance; further research is needed on the causal links, to identify mechanisms through which the network effects are achieved. For example, it would be useful to explore if gendered peer effects contribute to persistent gaps between men and women entrepreneurs in their choice of sectors of operation and funding sources.[7]

NOTES

1. In April 2018, Swaziland changed its name to Eswatini. While in most places the chapter reflects this change, several documents and reports issued prior to this change still refer to 'Swaziland'.
2. Given the high poverty rates in Eswatini, we measure the entrepreneurial performance in terms of sales level, so as to reflect the potential of entrepreneurship to be a sustainable source of livelihood.
3. China listed entrepreneurship in the top ten priorities emerging from the G20 Hangzhou Summit in 2016: www.g20.org/English/Dynamic/201606/t20160601_2294.html. The Turkish G20 Presidency in 2015 already prioritized access to finance by small and medium enterprises in the area of financial inclusion: www.gpfi.org/news/key-gpfi-dates-priorities-2015-announced (links were accessed on June 30, 2016). In 2018, the Argentinian G20 Presidency put sustainable and fair development at the center of its agenda and identified empowering women as essential (https://g20.argentina.gob.ar/en/overview-argentinas-g20-presidency-2018).
4. For example, Chaudhuri et al. (2019) find significant underperformance in the size, growth, and efficiency of firms owned by women, utilizing a 2006–2007 dataset of registered and unregistered firms in India. They also illustrate that women-led businesses are less likely to obtain finance than men-led firms.
5. Conversely, reliance mainly on social networks for work resources, a practice which is more common among women, would be associated with reduced firm performance.
6. Conversely, reliance mainly on social networks for work resources, a practice which is more common among women, would be associated with reduced firm performance.
7. The authors thank Candida Brush, Amanda Bullough, Susumu Imai, Andreas Wörgötter, and two anonymous reviewers for helpful comments and discussions on earlier drafts. The views expressed are those of the authors and do not necessarily reflect those of the African Development Bank.

REFERENCES

Aghion, P., T. Fally and S. Scarpetta (2007), 'Credit constraints as a barrier to the entry and post-entry growth of firms', *Economic Policy*, CEPR; CES; MSH, 22, 731–779.

Aidis, R. and S. Estrin (2014), 'Institutions, incentives and entrepreneurship', in Z. Acs, L. Szerb and E. Autio (eds.), *The Global Entrepreneurship and Development Index 2013*, Cheltenham, UK and Northampton, MA, USA: Edward Elgar Publishing.

Amin, M. (2010), 'Gender and firm size: evidence from Africa', *Economics Bulletin*, 30(1), 663–668.

Asiedu, E., I. Kalonda-Kanyama, L. Ndikumana and A. Nti-Addae (2013), 'Access to credit by firms in sub-Saharan Africa: how relevant is the gender gap?', *American Economic Review Papers and Proceedings*, 103(3), 293–297.

Baliamoune-Lutz, M., Z. Brixiová and L. Ndikumana (2011), 'Credit constraints and productive entrepreneurship in Africa', IZA Discussion Paper 6193, Institute for the Study of Labor (IZA).

Baliamoune-Lutz, M. and S. Lutz (2017), 'Financing and performance of female-owned firms in Middle Eastern and African economies', Working Paper No. 1709, Universidad Complutense Madrid.

Banerjee, A.V. and A. Newman (1993), 'Occupational choice and the process of development', *Journal of Political Economy*, 101(2), 274–298.

Bardasi, E., S.M. Balckden and J.C. Guzman (2009), 'Gender, entrepreneurship, and competitiveness in Africa', in *Africa Competitiveness Report 2009*, Geneva: World Economic Forum; Washington, DC: World Bank; Tunis: African Development Bank.

Baron, R.A. and G.D. Markman (2003), 'Beyond social capital: the role of entrepreneurs' social competence in their financial success', *Journal of Business Venturing*, 18, 41–60.

Baumol, W.J. (1990), 'Entrepreneurship: productive, unproductive and destructive', *Journal of Political Economy*, 985(5), 893–921.

Blomqvist, M., E. Chastain, B. Thickett, S. Unnikrishnan and W. Woods (2014), 'Bridging the entrepreneurship gender gap: the power of networks', The Boston Consulting Group.

Brixiová, Z. and T. Kangoye (2016), 'Gender and constraints to entrepreneurship in Africa: new evidence from Swaziland', *Journal of Business Venturing Insights*, 5, 1–8.

Brush, C., A. Ali, D. Kelley and P. Greene (2017), 'The influence of human capital factors and context on women's entrepreneurship: which matters more?', *Journal of Business Venturing Insights*, 8, 105–113.

Chaudhuri, K., S. Sasidharan and R.S.N. Raj (2019), 'Gender, small firm ownership and credit access: some insights from India', *Small Business Economics*, forthcoming.

De Soto, H. (2000), *The Mystery of Capital*, London: Black Swan.

Djankov, S., E. Miguel, Y. Qian, G. Roland and E. Zhuravskaya (2005), 'Who are Russia's entrepreneurs?', *Journal of the European Economic Association*, 3(2–3), 587–597.

Dutta, N. and S. Mallick (2018), 'Enabling women entrepreneurs: exploring the mitigating factors for the negative effect of fertility rates on female entrepreneurship', *Kyklos*, 71(3), 402–432.

Fairlie, R. and A. Robb (2009), 'Gender differences in business performance: evidence from the characteristics of business owners survey', *Small Business Economics*, 33(4), 375–395.

Fisher, G. (2012), 'Effectuation, causation, and bricolage: a behavioral comparison of emerging theories in entrepreneurship research', *Entrepreneurship Theory and Practice*, 36(5), 1019–1051.

Fowowe, B. (2017), 'Access to finance and firm performance: evidence from African countries', *Review of Development Finance*, 7, 6–17.

Global Entrepreneurship Monitor (2017), Women's Entrepreneurship 2016/2017 Report. Smith College, Northampton, MA.

Hallward-Driemeier, M. (2013), *Enterprising Women: Expanding Economic Opportunities in Africa*, Washington, DC: World Bank.

Hisrich, R.D. and C.G. Brush (1984), 'The woman entrepreneur: management skills and business problems', *Journal of Small Business Management*, 22, 30–37.

Kanbur, S.M.R. (1982), 'Entrepreneurial risk taking, inequality, and public policy: an application of inequality decomposition analysis to the general equilibrium effects of progressive taxation', *Journal of Political Economy*, 90, 1–21.

Kihlstrom, R.E. and J.J. Laffont (1979), 'A general equilibrium entrepreneurial theory of firm formation based on risk aversion', *Journal of Political Economy*, 87, 719–748.

Kristiansen, S. (2004), 'Social networks and business success: the role of sub-cultures in an African context', *American Journal of Economics and Sociology*, 63(5), 1149–1172.

Kuada, J. (2009), 'Gender, social networks and entrepreneurship in Ghana', *Journal of African Business*, 10(1), 85–103.

Lazaer, E.P. (2005), 'Entrepreneurship', *Journal of Labor Economics*, 23(4), 649–680.

Leyden, D.P., A.N. Link and D.S. Siegel (2014), 'A theoretical analysis of the role of social networks in entrepreneurship', *Research Policy*, 43, 1157–1163.

Malapit, H.J.L. (2012), 'Are women more likely to be credit constrained? Evidence from low income urban households in the Philippines', *Feminist Economics*, 18(3), 81–108.

Markussen, S. and K. Roed (2017), 'The gender gap in entrepreneurship: the role of peer effects', *Journal of Economic Behavior & Organization*, 134, 356–373.

Minniti, M. (2009), 'Gender issues in entrepreneurship', *Foundations and Trends in Entrepreneurship*, 5(7–8), 497–621.

Nelson, J. (2015), 'Are women really more risk-averse than men? A re-analysis of the literature using expanded methods', *Journal of Economic Surveys*, 29(3), 566–585.

Quartey, P., E. Turkson, J.Y. Abor and A.M. Iddrisu (2017), 'Financing the growth of SMEs in Africa: what are the constraints to SME financing within ECOWAS?', *Review of Development Finance*, 7, 18–28.

Renzulli, L.A., H. Aldrich and J. Moody (2000), 'Family matters: gender, networks and entrepreneurial outcomes', *Social Forces*, 79(2), 523–546.

Sabarwal, S. and K. Terrell (2009), 'Does gender matter for firm performance? Evidence from Eastern Europe and Central Asia', IZA Discussion Papers No. 3758.

Senyard, J., T. Baker and P. Davidsson (2009), 'Entrepreneurial bricolage: towards systematic empirical testing', *Frontiers of Entrepreneurial Research*, 29(5), Article 5.

Shahriar, A.Z.F. (2018), 'Gender differences in entrepreneurial propensity: evidence from matrilineal and patriarchal societies', *Journal of Business Venturing*, 33(6), 762–779.

Singh, G. and R. Belwal (2008), 'Entrepreneurship and SMEs in Ethiopia: evaluating the role, prospects and problems faced by women in this emergent sector', *Gender in Management: An International Journal*, 23(2), 120–136.

UN Eswatini (2013), *Constraints and Opportunities for Youth Entrepreneurship in Africa: Perspectives of Young Entrepreneurs from Eswatini*, Mbabane: UN Eswatini.

Verheul, I. and R. Thurik (2001), 'Start-up capital: does gender matter?', *Small Business Economics*, 16, 320–345.

Witt, P. (2004), 'Entrepreneurs' networks and the success of start-ups', *Entrepreneurship & Regional Development*, 16, 391–412.

Table 2A.1   Description of variables

Variable	Description
Sales_level (log)	Log of the amount of sales (thousands of Emalangeni)
Initial capital (log)	Log of the amount of start-up capital (thousands of Emalangeni)
Initial capital from debt	Dummy variable taking the value of 1 if the initial capital was sourced from borrowing and the value of 0 otherwise
Profit motivation	Dummy variable taking the value of 1 if the person was motivated to become an entrepreneur by profits and 0 otherwise
Hours worked weekly	Average number of hours entrepreneur spends working in the establishment during one week
Personal contribution	Dummy variable taking the value of 1 if the entrepreneur made a personal contribution to the business at start-up and the value of 0 otherwise
Social influence	Dummy variable taking the value of 1 if friends influenced the entrepreneur to start up a business. The dummy takes the value of 0 otherwise
Professional influence	Dummy variable taking the value of 1 if the following influenced the entrepreneur to start up a business: teachers or lectures, career advisors, entrepreneurs, media. The dummy takes the value of 0 otherwise
Parents provided support	Dummy variable taking the value of 1 if the entrepreneur's parents provided financial support and/or mentoring and the value of 0 otherwise
Parents self-employed	Dummy variable taking the value of 1 if the entrepreneur's parents are self-employed and the value of 0 otherwise
Swazi citizen	Dummy variable taking the value of 1 if the entrepreneur has a Swazi citizenship and the value of 0 otherwise
From Manzini	Dummy variable taking the value of 1 if the entrepreneur is from Manzini and the value of 0 otherwise
Financial literacy training	Dummy variable taking the value of 1 if the entrepreneur received training in financial literacy and 0 otherwise
Business training	Dummy variable taking the value of 1 if the entrepreneur received any business training (including informal business training, introduction to business, formal business training and advanced business training) and 0 otherwise
Education	Dummy variable taking the value of 1 if the respondent obtained university education and 0 otherwise
Size	Number of employees
Age of business	Age of business (years)
First business	Dummy variable taking the value of 1 if the entrepreneur never owned/ran business before and the value of 0 otherwise
Licensed	Dummy variable taking the value of 1 if the business has formal license and the value of 0 otherwise

3. Absence of opportunities can enhance women's high-growth entrepreneurship: empirical evidence from Peru

Miguel Córdova and Fátima Huamán

1. INTRODUCTION

Ironically, the relevance of entrepreneurial efforts in terms of their benefit for developing countries is not always recognized in the development strategies of governments. Often, indeed, it appears that entrepreneurs' opportunities for development are undermined by their societies. Despite this, female entrepreneurs have something to teach us about resilience and perseverance. As Albert Einstein said, strong spirits emerge in time of crisis. So women in emerging markets are becoming stronger as they find themselves able to turn the tide and achieve high-growth performance, even when their context apparently conspires against them.

This study sheds light on how women overcome local difficulties and transform themselves into high-growth entrepreneurs, using a combination of formal and informal strategies. Our main contribution is to the female entrepreneurship literature, adding an empirical study in the Latin American region, which highlights the role of women in their countries' economy and how they can achieve high-growth levels by working together. Another theoretical contribution of this chapter is to the social networks literature, demonstrating the capability of female networks to diffuse knowledge and business practices. The managerial contributions of this study are focused on public policies enacting and guiding the business decisions of women entrepreneurs in difficult environments.

This chapter aims to answer the following general research question: How can the absence of formal opportunities generate high-growth behavior for women entrepreneurs? It will describe how some adverse characteristics of the environment, like the absence of state initiatives, prompted a group of women entrepreneurs in Peru to get together and establish an association that permitted them to keep up their tradition and boost their individual efforts. In addition to this, it will explore and describe their decision to apply for Nation's Cultural Heritage recognition, explaining how they improved their reputation, and then found new opportunities for growth, working as a network and developing an internal informal mentoring program. Using a case study in Peru called 'The *Picanterías* Society of Arequipa' (PSA), represented by a sample of 11 female entrepreneurs working together as a unique structure, this chapter describes in detail the composition, governance and main characteristics of this women entrepreneurs association, using primary information from extensive interviews. Second, some important issues are discussed, including how Nation's Cultural Heritage recognition by the state can influence and enhance women's opportunities for growth, enabling female entrepreneurship to overcome the limitations of the business environment, and finally, how women entrepreneurs could move forward by developing internal mentoring programs despite the lack of opportunities in an emerging market such as Peru.

Emerging economies are certainly severe contexts for entrepreneurs, who are often faced with weak institutions (Young et al., 2014) and a lack of support for organizational activities. As a result of this, firms tend to adopt various resource-search strategies that depend on the characteristics of each particular institutional context (Meyer et al., 2009). Moreover, due to this, managers' decisions and initiatives may face delay in implementation or are abandoned altogether (Hoskisson et al., 2000). Emerging markets also face high levels of uncertainty that hinder any organizational improvement process because of turbulent economic and political environments for doing business. Latin America is not an exception as it is a region with a highly complex business environment (Vassolo et al., 2011), often facing lack of opportunities for growth because of the absence of valuable resources which are necessary for organizational competitiveness (Jäger and Sathe, 2014), which forces firms to search for other informal but alternative and reliable sources of valuable resources (Musacchio and Read, 2007; Godfrey, 2011). Not just big firms, but small and entrepreneurial ones as well need to have a strategy and available resources to confront a turbulent business environment, and make important decisions under situations of uncertainty (Wiklund et al., 2018). The context in which entrepreneurs have to develop their activities represents both an opportunity and a constraint at the same time (Welter, 2011), therefore they need visibility of those resources, which will permit their survival and permanent growth. According to this, entrepreneurs seek to manage several strategic and valuable resources, which can be obtained from both internal and external sources (Ahuja and Morris Lampert, 2001; Hitt et al., 2001; Lazear, 2005; Yao et al., 2009). These resources will increase entrepreneurs' social capital (Adler and Kwon, 2002) as they mobilize the resources appropriately according to their needs (Kwon and Adler, 2014).

Entrepreneurship in Latin America is considered not just as an engine for economic growth, but also as a promising route to poverty reduction (CAF, 2013). Low education, high economic inequality, insufficient financial enhancement, and bad public health systems are indexes that represent some of the main concerns for Latin American countries, which regard entrepreneurship and small businesses as one possible way to solve these problems and achieve sustainable and healthy economic development (GEM, 2017). For these reasons, governments in the region have enacted several laws and regulations, all oriented to facilitate entrepreneurs' activity. However, entrepreneurs' challenges in transitional economies are not just related to solvency, access to credit or facilitating the generation of business ideas, but include other social, expectancy and cultural problems, embedded in their own environment, which can drastically impede their growth (Manolova et al., 2007; CAF, 2013).

Female entrepreneurship has to deal with a large gender bias when attempting to gain the trust of investors or other stakeholders (Kanze et al., 2018) or access to different opportunities for credit and loans (Brush et al., 2018). According to the characteristics of the local entrepreneurial ecosystem, women may find fewer or more institutional arrangements focused on leveraging or constraining their growth conditions (Brush et al., 2018). In Latin America, female entrepreneurs face this strong gender inequality and additional issues like local beliefs based on ancestral roots and an inappropriate level of education (Morrison, 2006). Furthermore, they usually suffer from limited access to sources of information and lack of opportunities for additional training or specialization in their jobs (Camarena and Saavedra, 2015).

Entrepreneurship in Peru has to overcome the regional constraints explained above, regarding lack of opportunities and limitations for growth. In Peru the state is incapable of being present in the whole Peruvian territory, highlighting its institutional weakness and the fragmentation of social interests in the country (Degregori, 2004; Grompone, 2009). Despite this, Peru presents high rates of entrepreneurial activity in Latin America (third after Mexico and Chile), but at the same time exhibits high indexes of failure. According to INEI (2017), new business creation in Peru has a daily average of 853, but on the other hand, 469 per day are closed. This is the reason the discontinuity rate is fixed at 8.3 percent, and the most common reasons are individual or family-related problems and an imprecise choice of business idea (Global Entrepreneurship Research Association, 2017). In addition to this, women entrepreneurs in Peru have to deal with many obstacles—for instance, domestic violence—that lead to poor performance results (Ponce, 2012). Female and male entrepreneurs show similar rates for entrepreneurial activity in Peru, but there is a prominent difference when comparing what motivates them for starting a business (GEM, 2017). While Peruvian women entrepreneurs have more presence in the service sector of the economy due to similarity with home tasks (more than 70 percent of them are located in this specific sector), men distribute their efforts in several sectors. Even more, in general terms, men find increased motivation for opportunity entrepreneurship than women, who are focused mostly in necessity entrepreneurship (GEM, 2017). According to GEM (2017), another difference is that men usually are better regarded in their jobs than women, who have to deal with gender biases which often prompt their desire to be an entrepreneur. In this chapter, using a social networks theoretical perspective, we aim to fill an important research gap in Peru about women entrepreneurs' alternatives for dealing with the hurdles they face and how some of them have achieved high-growth performance. Furthermore, our findings add valuable insights in terms of the female entrepreneurship literature, show the importance of social networks, and advance our knowledge about female networks' behavior in emerging markets. Our study also generates managerial recommendations to women in businesses, which are considered the roots for economic growth and social inclusion.

Despite the difficulties previously described, there are many examples of success in the Latin American region, and Peru is one of these. Female entrepreneurs find different alternatives to ensure their survival and growth over time, despite the adverse context that they have to deal with. If female entrepreneurship is hindered mainly by the inefficient presence of the local government, how do some high-growth women entrepreneurs successfully emerge from this adverse context? What reasons lie behind these successful experiences? How does the lack of state initiatives cause self-growth decisions of women entrepreneurs in Peru?

The next part of this chapter is focused on introducing the case study of the *Picanterías* Society of Arequipa, and explains in detail how the women initiated their businesses as individual efforts and then decided to together search for synergies and mutual benefits. The third part describes the methodology with which this study was conducted. The fourth section focuses on the Nation's Cultural Heritage recognition by the government and how the *Picanterías* Society of Arequipa was bestowed with it, enhancing several new opportunities for them as a formal mechanism for building reputation. The fifth part highlights how this group of women entrepreneurs found an informal mechanism for management knowledge and sharing of good operational practices. In the sixth section, we discuss some implications of the main findings of the study. Finally, in the seventh part we present the conclusions and new paths for further research.

2.   BEGIN USING INDIVIDUAL EFFORTS, THEN THINK AS A STRENGTHENED NETWORK

2.1   Arequipa's Traditional Food Restaurants: '*Picanterías*'

Arequipa is the second biggest city in Peru, based on its population size, and is located 1011 km south of the capital city, Lima. Also known as the White City, Arequipa was founded in 1540 and due to its cultural characteristics, gastronomic traditions, colonial architecture and historical legacy, was granted World Cultural Heritage recognition from UNESCO.

For more than 400 years, Arequipean women felt the necessity of feeding their families in a healthy manner, considering their poor economic conditions, but having a lot of different local ingredients at their disposal. This diversity and availability of ingredients boosted women's cooking innovation in the region. Hence, Arequipa's *picanterías* are considered 'the most significant expression of the traditional food practice that characterizes the city of Arequipa and its rural environment' (SPA, s.f.-b), and their ingredients' quality is considered as exceptional by many experts. The knowledge of their culinary techniques and procedures has been passed from generation to generation (SPA, s.f.-d). However, at the beginning of their existence, *picanterías* were not valued or well-recognized by the society. The women who ran them (*picanteras*) rarely knew each other and, before the establishment of the PSA, took little care in transmitting their knowledge and cooking techniques. They used to work individually, dealing with small local competitors which prepared unhealthy food (Huamán, 2018).

According to historical data, Arequipa's *picanterías* existed since the sixteenth century under the name of '*chicherías*', characterized by the selling of the traditional '*guiñapo chicha*'. This beverage is made through fermenting a ground black corn that only grows in the Arequipa region. Traditional food was also offered and this is the reason they began to be called *picanterías* (Fuentes, 2014). Nowadays, these restaurants are characterized for their rustic décor environments, having long tables that can be shared by more than one family or customer group. They have to sell *guiñapo chicha* and traditional food as well, being places where people of all economic conditions and professions can meet. Because of these characteristics, they are considered as an identity element of the Arequipa region, where people of all social strata converge (Ruiz Rosas, 2014).

2.2 The *Picanterías* Society of Arequipa

The *Picanterías* Society of Arequipa (PSA) is an association formed by professionals of the traditional food restaurant business, other food experts, and lovers of the culinary traditions of Arequipa (SPA, s.f.-a). It was founded on August 2012 by Alonso Ruiz Rosas in a gathering at the restaurant La Lucila Picantería, with a group of '*picanteros*' (traditional food experts) and friends of the *picantería*, having the purpose of recovering and preserving the traditional food and customs. However, its creation actually began in 2008 when Alonso Ruiz Rosas was writing the first edition of his book of recipes (Ruiz Rosas, 2009) and had the opportunity to learn more about the *picanterías* and how to fraternize with their owners. He was a lover of *picanterías* from a very young age. Due to several visits that he made, first with his parents and then with his friends, he was able to acquire a lot of related material to write his book. After that, he engaged in various personal activities from which arose the creation of an organization that would integrate the *picanterías* of Arequipa and prompt them to work together. Ruiz Rosas had foreseen their great potential in terms of the richness of tradition and culinary culture that their history represented.

From that time on, he worked in coordination with his partner Miguel Barreda, current General Coordinator of the PSA, to bring together the first *picanterías* who would be interested in being associated. Their original idea was to establish an organization in which not only traditional culinary chefs would participate, but also an organization which *picanteros* (both men and women) and other professionals, as well as lovers of the *picanterías* could all join, bringing a variety of contributions from different approaches, holding common objectives. The PSA strives to strengthen the idea of the cultural heritage of each *picantería*, since some of them are unaware of their legacy. It provides ideas to improve the quality of the *picanterías*, not by assessments, but by providing opinions.

According to the organization's executives, the PSA does not interfere directly in the economic or financial aspects of the *picanterías*. However, it is a feasible way of contacting professionals who can provide specialized services for their businesses. Nonetheless, the decision on whether to use these services depends on each *picantería* owner. Despite the fact that the PSA was created mainly to preserve and protect the traditional food of Arequipa, its achievements have also indirectly influenced the positive financial results of the *picanterías*.

The PSA fulfills the characteristics of being a collaborative network since it includes aspects such as intensity, extension, integrality, feedback, diversity and reputation (Huamán, 2018). Relationships among *picanteros* and the managers are strong, because these are based on trust and friendship (Granovetter, 1973), but that was not the case in the beginning. The network was initially weak because they did not know each other or had not interacted before. Currently, the possibility of integrating new partners is open and also working with different organizations and individuals in order to extend and strengthen the network is considered as a priority. The PSA's diversity and extended network offers the opportunity to promote the *picantería* tradition in order to continue generating benefits for its associates and its vicinity as well.

2.3   Members

Four types of associates are declared in the statutes of the PSA: professional, aspirant, active and honorary (SPA, s.f.-c), with the aim of promoting its objectives and values as the duty of all its members (SPA, s.f.-c).

This is a short description of the associate types:

- Professional associate: Owner and legal representative of a *picantería* already established, located in any of the districts of the province of Arequipa. They must have at least two years of foundation. The requirements for belonging to this category are: (i) capability for seven-days-a-week service, (ii) traditional *guiñapo chicha* preparation, and (iii) capability of production of different meal options every day.
- Aspirant associate: Owner and representative of the business. Service is given just on weekends or one day a week. They are usually new operatives in the *picantería* traditional activity.
- Active associate: Person who engages in other professional activity, but is emotionally linked with the culinary tradition in Arequipa and usually takes time to occasionally visit the *picanterías*, even if not resident in the region. This person contributes to *picanterías* with specific professional experience.
- Honorary associate: Person who has a good and proven reputation in culinary, civil, academic or other fields of knowledge and who is also emotionally connected with the *picanterías* tradition in Arequipa and whose membership honors the PSA, even if they do not live in the region of Arequipa.

2.4   Main Objectives

The main goal of the PSA was to protect and promote Arequipa's gastronomic and culinary cultural heritage embodied in the *picanterías*, which would involve taking care of all aspects of this heritage: raw materials and ingredients, habits and practices, forms of consumption and recipes. Thus, three main lines of action were established:

- Achievement of Nation's Cultural Heritage recognition by the Ministry of Culture: this objective was achieved on April 23, 2014, eleven months after Alonso Ruiz Rosas began the process (Fuentes, 2014).
- Realization of an annual event promoting the organization: this is how the *Fiesta de la Chicha* was born, held every first Friday of August in the Plaza de Armas (main square) of Arequipa. This idea arose because the founder had lived in Germany from a very young age, where he had the opportunity to work in the Beer Festival (Oktoberfest), and this prompted the question of why in Arequipa there was no drinking celebration with the traditional *guiñapo chicha*. Years later, the idea was proposed and well received by the association's members.
- Creation of the Center of the Culinary Culture of Arequipa: this challenge, which is still pending, would mean constituting an institution that would guarantee in the medium term that Arequipa be a very consistent space in culinary terms, more than what it is at present.

2.5 The *Picanterías'* Patrimonial Appropriation

Arequipa is considered one of the important cradles of Peruvian gastronomy because, approximately 400 years ago, women started to prepare different meals for their customers, first as *chicherías* and later as *picanterías* (Fuentes, 2014; Ruiz Rosas, 2014). Since then, women have always been in charge of *picanterías* in Arequipa; traditionally led by women, they can take care of their families' needs and also look for financial benefits at the same time. The SPA membership reflects this gender difference, having men as a minority group (Huamán, 2018). Therefore, women still play an important role conserving Arequipa's gastronomic patrimony (Fuentes, 2014); however, *picanterías* have become more diverse today, and many are now owned by men, lovers of their food, who are involved in the mission of contributing to the spread of the traditional food culture (Huamán, 2018).

The first objective of the PSA was to achieve recognition of the cultural heritage by the government, and this was accomplished after almost two years on April 23, 2014. The Ministry of Culture named the Arequipean *picantería* Cultural Patrimony of the Peruvian Nation, due to its considerable amount of culture and tradition that should be valued and preserved in order to be passed on to future generations (Huamán, 2018). This achievement makes Arequipa's *picanterías* a cultural product, so that traditional dishes, still prepared using the oldest recipes, have not only regained their validity at a regional level, but are also recognized throughout the country and the world (Fuentes, 2014).

Having achieved this goal, the PSA focused on strengthening the idea of cultural heritage of each of the associated *picanterías*, since at first many of them were unaware of all the wisdom and knowledge behind their historical legacy. On the other hand, after achieving Cultural Heritage status, the *picanteras* felt that this lent a special added value to their businesses—they now had a prestige which helped to strengthen and empower them (Huamán, 2018). It should be noted that of the existing *picanterías* in Arequipa, almost 50 percent belong to the PSA (SPA, s.f.-b).

Therefore, being part of a Cultural Heritage has positively affected their businesses, by generating new opportunities for them and strongly impacting their reputation. It is suggested that the PSA continue to position itself culturally, relying on the diversity of resources in the organization, where other people who are not owners of *picanterías* can speak, write and disseminate the existence of the Arequipa's *picanterías*, thus ensuring the continuity of these businesses and preserving the culinary tradition.

2.6   Mentoring in the *Picanterías* Society of Arequipa

Besides their reputation, another characteristic observed was mentoring. Many of the best infrastructures, customer services, relations with suppliers and their identity found in each *picantería* began thanks to the creation of the PSA. The most experienced and successful *picanteras* were those whose workers felt very happy to be able to help their companions according to the results of interviews carried out.

The opportunity to be a mentor has also been encouraged. Mentors have the opportunity to appear on local television demonstrating how traditional food is cooked. In addition, they give classes in institutions that teach gastronomy. Many of them were consulted about these activities during their interviews and they were very enthusiastic about educating new *picanteros*, arguing that by doing so, the *picantería* will not disappear over time.

3.   METHOD

The study has a descriptive focus and a qualitative research methodology, under a case study approach, using in-depth interviews of female entrepreneurs affiliated with the PSA in Peru. The sample consisted of 11 women entrepreneurs from 38 professional associates in the PSA. These women were appointed for the interviews after a classification according to their member condition and their availability for contributing in the study. Moreover, these female entrepreneurs of the sample were identified as high-growth entrepreneurs due to: (i) their long-term operation in the market, having run their businesses for more than 12 years, thus being considered as consolidated ones (GEM, 2017);

Table 3.1   *Classification of the information from interviews*

	Before PSA formation	After PSA formation
Information collected from interviews	Main challenges in the history of their businesses	Improvements in their businesses as a consequence of the network
Outcomes for the study	Identify the absence of opportunities for female entrepreneurs	Identify high-growth behavior of women in the sample

and (ii) the journey they have followed to turn into lifestyle entrepreneurs (Acs and Amoros, 2008; Díaz de León and Cancino, 2014), most of them starting as entrepreneurs by necessity, which was demonstrated by their growing sales and the balance between economic wealth and personal needs that they have found. As mentioned previously in this chapter, only professional associates were selected for the interviews, because of their service capacity and their cultural commitment to the tradition of the gastronomy activity. As professionals, selected members were not just the businesses' owners, but also the principal workers of their own entrepreneurial initiatives, so it was therefore not necessary to extend the interviews to include other restaurants' collaborators.

A research project timetable for the three visits from Lima to Arequipa was established in order to be able to complete the interviews, taking into account the availability of those women entrepreneurs, considering that their businesses attend to customers seven days a week, and the variety of meals they serve generate intensive activity in the kitchen.

Once the interviews were completed, their content was transcribed and separated into two different groups, according to the research purposes of: (i) identifying the main constraints of those women before PSA formation, and (ii) identifying the improvements they achieved after PSA formation (see Table 3.1).

Our methodological approach included that each of the 11 women entrepreneurs declared their availability and their commitment to this study, signing an information consent form and giving data use permission.

4.   FORMAL MECHANISMS FOR FEMALE ENTREPRENEURSHIP DEVELOPMENT

Governments are responsible for establishing appropriate legislation to ensure equal and fair market competition, and facilitate business activities and formal transactions for both established firms and new entrepreneurs. State-guided initiatives tend to support companies that are in a disadvantageous position or which represent a strategic opportunity for the country. Governments in Latin America usually look for a strong presence in market business activities, but inefficient bureaucracy and lack of quick response generate institutional voids in the environment (Khanna and Palepu, 1997) which could represent big barriers for organizational activity but enormous ones for entrepreneurs who are just in their early stages. The unpredictability and uncertainty of this kind of business environment could result in some successful regulations, but there are others that need a more complex structure in order to function successfully.

In Peru the government is attempting to establish formal mechanisms which could help the initiative of entrepreneurs, such as less documentation for new firms and a less expensive and shorter process for their setting up, low cost training centers, access to assessment and consultancy firms, quality certificates, and Nation's Cultural Heritage recognition, among others.

The Peruvian Cultural Heritage recognition was created to enhance the reputation of firms or associations which aim to preserve or divulge traditions, culture or legacy of a specific region or activity. In the case of PSA, they are focused on sustaining the ancestral cooking traditions of the Arequipa region, which was achieved by the Nation's Cultural Heritage recognition, awarded in 2014. Reputation is considered as a meta-resource that is capable of activating other valuable resources that firms or individuals already have in order to mobilize them to overcome environmental institutional voids (Gao et al., 2017). Furthermore, resource capital, guided by the organization's strategy, as well as institutional capital, including incentive and training public programs or nation's recognitions, are all considered necessary to achieve a sustainable competitive advantage (Oliver, 1997).

According to interview results, women in the PSA realized that they were committed together within a strong local movement, which seeks to keep up the ancestral cooking traditions of their region. They realized also their role in the society regarding the opportunity to enhance their influence and social recognition, using the Nation's Cultural Heritage recognition to participate in several official areas of cultural diffusion within the country and abroad. Therefore, they feel that this recognition allows them to incorporate into social discussion their objectives, procedures and results, in order to receive feedback or advice from different interested agents of the society or stakeholders who could participate as investors or consultants. At the same time, the local society legitimated their role inside PSA and supported it, due to their gender affinity to service and gastronomy traditional activities, which is perceived as women's terrain from an individual-level perspective (Brush et al., 2018).

Female entrepreneurs of the PSA, according to Figure 3.1, started moving together as a unique structure and effort, and through their Nation's Cultural Heritage statement the PSA has access to new spaces of diffusion and the opportunity to be recognized by a bigger part of the society as well. Moreover, their opportunities abroad have also increased, so long as they are part of a cultural movement supported by the government.

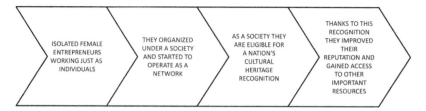

Figure 3.1   Formal mechanism for female entrepreneurship

5.   INFORMAL MECHANISM FOR KNOWLEDGE MANAGEMENT IN FEMALE ENTREPRENEURSHIP

There are formal mechanisms promoted by governments and available for entrepreneurs, and some organizations tend to seek opportunities in informal mechanisms, because these allow them to overcome the institutional voids existing in the environment. So, it is a common practice in emerging markets to look for alternative instruments or techniques which could be at the entrepreneurs' disposal and have the capability to attract important resources, which become critical and necessary for any business initiative (Barney, 1991; Pfeffer and Salancik, 2002) such as entrepreneurial activity and its long-term survival. As entrepreneurship represents new businesses, there are few possibilities to obtain these valuable resources from inside the organization. However, outside them, they would depend on their own capabilities to establish collaborative relationships with others and their level of participation as agents in the society or business community, managing and exploiting properly their business networks (Córdova, 2017).

One external, informal mechanism through which entrepreneurs can find new and valuable resources—and usually spontaneously generated—is a network. A network is a set of nodes that could be individuals or organizations as well, which are related by ties that represent different relationships between the nodes (Granovetter, 1973), generating also the appearance of empty spaces between non-linked nodes called structural holes (Burt, 1992) which are capable also of ensuring the flow of non-redundant information through network participants. Inside of this structure, individuals are linked to each other by some common interests or characteristics and start to participate or collaborate amongst themselves, in accordance with their commitment level. Networks represent reliable conduits for resources, capable of enabling the diffusion of information, knowledge, learning capabilities, and managerial practices among actors inside the entrepreneurial ecosystem (Brush et al., 2018). This represents an important factor for boosting female entrepreneurs' opportunities to achieve high-growth standards. In addition to this, according to Shipilov et al. (2010) and Shropshire (2010), establishing relationships that link two or more organizations facilitates the adoption process of practices and knowledge. Other resources such as trust and support come from family connections, which represent a reinforcement for entrepreneurial decisions (Welter, 2011). Furthermore, according to Martin et al. (2015) some specific networks become active just under a high level of uncertainty in the environment, which explains just how important network creation could be for entrepreneurs in emerging markets. Moreover, static networks such as the PSA, which do not have drastic changes in their structure and participants' role over time, are able to operate diffusion processes better than dynamic networks, creating a contagion effect of resources and knowledge inside the network (Herrera et al., 2015).

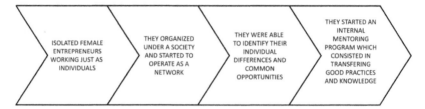

*Figure 3.2   Informal mechanism for knowledge management in female
                entrepreneurship*

So, once a female entrepreneurial network started to operate, following the process described in Figure 3.2, those women recognized their knowledge and individual differences, along with their opportunities to improve as a group. Finally, according to these particular findings, they decided to begin an internal mentoring program, in order to look for synergies between them, trying to balance their differences and work to enhance their opportunities. They used networks as reliable conduits for information, practices and knowledge, effectively demonstrating what the literature about social networks states, and opening new paths for research about how different kinds of entrepreneurship could take advantage of networks under many circumstances. Moreover, social network strength is visible when comparing Figure 3.1 and Figure 3.2, when the two first steps are related to collaborating as a network instead of just individuals.

6.   DISCUSSION OF THE RESULTS

Female entrepreneurs arose as a different type of entrepreneurial actor, capable of adapting to extremely adverse conditions of the environment in order to survive. In accordance with Morrison (2006), Ponce (2012), and Camarena and Saavedra (2015), female entrepreneurship exhibits some specific dis-advantages that may be profound depending on the characteristics of the environment. Furthermore, in our study, neither entrepreneurial strength nor professional skills are sufficient for female entrepreneurship to learn how to deal with the uncertainty of a turbulent business context, so they opted for a strategy to go beyond the few initiatives that the state could provide them, searching for new specific informal mechanisms which permitted them to confront institutional voids and continue operating.

According to our study results, female entrepreneurship showed evidence of resilience in some changing and unstable environments. The PSA did not act as an isolated participant, but as a very dynamic one, establishing rela-tionships with other agents in its environment and participating with cultural and gastronomic institutions in order to mobilize its resources in places where the government provided few opportunities, such as in the secondary cities. However, female entrepreneurs also were highly proactive when deciding to take advantage of its network and started to practice knowledge management in its internal mentoring program. This evidence of resilience and proactivity under hostile circumstances provides us an excellent example of how female entrepreneurship learnt to deal with an adverse context and bravely pursue their business objectives.

Figure 3.3 shows how the PSA started as some isolated and dispersed individuals in stage 1, trying to harvest resources in an adverse and complex business environment which does not offer the minimum requirements for economic growth or entrepreneurship opportunities. There are important resources like the Nation's Cultural Heritage offered by the government, but at that point, it was completely unreachable for them. However, in stage 2, they decided to unite in a network and establish an association. Then as a consoli-dated group, they were legitimated by the PSA society and had access to the Nation's Cultural Heritage recognition. In stage 3, the PSA started to exploit their reputation as a meta-resource that came from this cultural heritage recog-nition. Reputation began to activate several other important resources outside and inside the network, such as information flow, learning capabilities and motivation. Finally, in stage 4, the association established an internal mentor-ing program, taking advantage of the network as an informal mechanism for diffusion of good practices and knowledge.

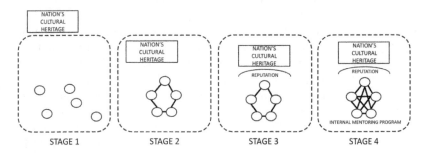

Figure 3.3   Female entrepreneurship process in the PSA

According to Figure 3.3, female entrepreneurs progressively learnt how to deal with the uncertainty in the environment—not just by taking advantage of what was institutionally available in the country, but by generating new collaborative opportunities from the inside as well. Despite individual entrepreneurial efforts, governments have to strengthen local institutions as active participants, facilitating the connections and business activities, and/or generating a strong base of opportunities through efficient regulations and control.

The whole idea of diversity within a specific group is evident in the PSA, as their associates are from different backgrounds and have traveled different paths in order to get there. As an association then, they are capable of sharing their knowledge and experience with each other, using the network mechanism to do so, and having access to new dimensions of growth. Their way to evolve and endure then is not just an individual task anymore, but also a common one, where the established network has the potential to stand firm against a lack of advantages in a business environment that is constantly changing.

7.   CONCLUSIONS AND FURTHER RESEARCH

To answer our main research question, we found that the lack of opportunities for female entrepreneurs in the business context promotes behavioral changes in these women, who persist against institutional weakness, and work towards achieving high-growth levels for their entrepreneurial activities. Traditional mechanisms for high-growth achievement, such as access to education or credit, must be challenged in order to be open to new alternatives where these traditional ones are not effective or are insufficient, depending on the conditions of the environment and other factors involved.

The PSA demonstrated, as a consolidated network, new capabilities to attract strategic resources that were unreachable as individual businesses. However, we state that those capabilities would not be necessary if the institutional context and business environment of the country was normally capable of offering and facilitating an appropriate framework for female entrepreneurship's development. This finding supports what was stated by Welter (2011), considering their family connections and support (social context), their traditions and cultural richness of a specific region (spatial context), and the constraints and opportunities offered by formal and informal institutions in the country and/or city (institutional context); as enablers for different responses of contextualized entrepreneurship. Hence, we have advanced the study of female entrepreneurship highlighting how a proper combination of advantages and constraints which were contextualized in our case study, turns female entrepreneurs into high-growth performers. Furthermore, female entrepreneurs tend to activate new undiscovered capabilities for their survival and growth, when the institutional voids in the environment oblige them to react. Without the presence of these obstacles, female entrepreneurs perhaps would never have discovered how to help themselves inside a network. So, the environment and its characteristics in a Latin American country such as Peru, are relevant complementarities, which have a strong power to enable disruptive ideas, practices and finally innovation for female entrepreneurial activity, which is also in accordance with Schneider's (2013) view when he referred to institutional complementarities as the glue for a whole economic system operation in a country.

In accordance with GEM's (2017) statements for Peru, even if our case study refers to a service industry, a common activity for Peruvian female entrepreneurs, our findings contribute to the entrepreneurship literature as a whole, shedding light on how contextualized the entrepreneurial activity is (Welter, 2011) and how women can find additional motivation from creating a network and taking advantage of an existing public policy in order to persevere with their entrepreneurships despite the difficulties and disadvantages in the business environment. According to this, an additional contribution of this chapter is focused on how network structures can prompt government programs, making them accessible for female entrepreneurs operating together.

The way public policies are designed and put into practice can enhance the ability of female entrepreneurship to exploit local available resources. This is in fact a new research path that promises to be extremely important and significant in emerging economies, not just because of what entrepreneurial activity means for a country's economic development, but also because of what it represents as a business option for a vulnerable group under vulnerable conditions. Our results follow the argument of Brush et al. (2018) that family presence supports the entrepreneurial activity and networks are important for female entrepreneurs in order to facilitate several valuable resources. We found that the PSA was able to overcome weak institutional arrangements in the Peruvian environment, which were hindering women's potential for growth; the PSA leveraged their strengths into an organizational level, using a network structure that allows them to share resources, while taking advantage of their individual experience through recognition from the local society of women's key role in culinary activity (Brush et al., 2018). This suggests that public policies need to recognize the nuances of the conditions for female entrepreneurs, supporting the arguments of Manolova et al. (2007) for different types of network-reinforced oriented policies from governments.

We want to encourage other female entrepreneurs around the world, especially in emerging economies, who may be confronting a difficult environment for their businesses, by taking as an example what the PSA did in Peru. We believe, following our findings, that female entrepreneurs have to deal with different and additional obstacles than their male counterparts do, but they also have the strength to find new roads for development and achieve high-growth businesses.

Finally, despite existing examples of successful female entrepreneurship growing and surviving within turbulent and adverse conditions, if positive change for enhancing entrepreneurial possibilities in emerging economies is to be achieved in the long term, governments have to lead the common effort of the different stakeholders who look for a stable business environment which permits the same business opportunities for everyone. Furthermore, we think that an efficient and effective action of the state, through institutional intervention and regulation, is crucial in order to permit the healthy development of local entrepreneurship. Institutions must be reinforced and regulations have to be implemented unhindered in order to allow new organizational ventures to find an environment operating according to efficient legal and economic systems. In addition to this, government initiatives have to facilitate strategic resources for local entrepreneurs, taking into consideration that these new businesses are extremely advantageous for emerging economies in terms of employment, economic development and social inclusion.

ACKNOWLEDGMENT

The authors want to thank the members of the *Picanterías* Society of Arequipa for their commitment and support in this research period that allowed them to capture useful information to complete this study.

REFERENCES

Acs, Z. and J.E. Amoros (2008), 'Introduction: the startup process', *Estudios de Economia*, 35, 121–132.
Adler, P. and S. Kwon (2002), 'Social capital: prospects for a new concept', *Academy of Management Review*, 27(1), 17–40.

Ahuja, G. and C. Morris Lampert (2001), 'Entrepreneurship in the large corporation: a longitudinal study of how established firms create breakthrough inventions', *Strategic Management Journal*, 22(6/7), 521–543.

Barney, J.B. (1991), 'Firm resources and sustainable competitive advantage', *Journal of Management*, 17(1), 99–120.

Brush, C., L.F. Edelman, T. Manolova and F. Welter (2018), 'A gendered look at entrepreneurship ecosystems', *Small Business Economics*, 50(3), 1–16.

Burt, R.S. (ed.) (1992), *Structural Holes: The Social Structure of Competition*, Cambridge, MA and London: Harvard University Press.

CAF (2013), 'Emprendimientos en América Latina: desde la subsistencia hacia la transformación productiva. Reporte de Economía y Desarrollo 2013', Banco de Desarrollo de América Latina, Corporación Andina de Fomento (ed.), Bogotá, Colombia.

Camarena, M.E. and M.L. Saavedra (2015), 'Retos para el Emprendimiento Femenino en América Latina', *Criterio Libre*, 13(22), 129–152.

Córdova, M. (2017), 'How entrepreneurs can use networks as a part of their business strategy in emerging economies?', paper presented at the CLADEA 2017 conference, Riverside Convention Center, October 18.

Degregori, C.I. (2004), 'Ilave: desafío de la gobernabilidad, la democracia participativa y la descentralización', Grupo Propuesta Ciudadana (ed.), Lima, Perú.

Díaz de León, D. and C. Cancino (2014), 'De emprendimientos por necesidad a emprendimientos por oportunidad: casos rurales exitosos', *Multidisciplinary Business Review*, 7 (December), 48–56.

Fuentes, C. (2014), 'La picantería arequipeña: patrimonio cultural de la nación', 1–11, Instituto de Investigación del Patrimonio Cultural (ed.), Lima, Perú.

Gao, C., T. Zuzul, G. Jones and T. Khanna (2017), 'Overcoming institutional voids: a reputation-based view of long-run survival', *Strategic Management Journal*, 38, 2147–2167.

Global Entrepreneurship Monitor (GEM) (2017), *Global Entrepreneurship Monitor – Perú 2016–2017*, accessed December 7, 2018 at https://www.gemconsortium.org/report/reporte-gem-peru-2016-2017.

Global Entrepreneurship Research Association (2017), *Global Entrepreneurship Monitor: Global Report 2016/17*, accessed December 10, 2018 at http://www.gemconsortium.org/report/49812.

Godfrey, P. (2011), 'Toward a theory of the informal economy', *The Academy of Management Annals*, 5(1), 231–277.

Granovetter, M.S. (1973), 'The strength of weak ties', *American Journal of Sociology*, 78(6), 1360–1380.

Grompone, R. (2009), 'Los movimientos sociales en el Perú y sus marcos explicativos', in R. Grompone and M. Tanaka (eds.), *Entre el crecimiento económico y la insatisfacción social. Las protestas sociales en el Perú actual*, Lima, Perú: IEP – Instituto de Estudios Peruanos.

Herrera, M., G. Armelini and E. Salvaj (2015), 'Understanding social contagion in adoption processes using dynamic social networks', *PLoS ONE*, 10(10), e0140891. doi:10.1371/journal.pone.0140891.

Hitt, M.A., R.D. Ireland, S.M. Camp and D.L. Sexton (2001), 'Strategic entrepreneurship: entrepreneurial strategies for wealth creation', *Strategic Management Journal*, 22(6–7), 479–491.

Hoskisson, R., L. Eden, C. Lau and M. Wright (2000), 'Strategy in emerging economies', *The Academy of Management Journal*, 43(3), 249–267.

Huamán, F. (2018), 'La Gestión de Redes en el fortalecimiento de emprendimientos femeninos: estudio de caso de la Sociedad Picantera de Arequipa', Lima, Perú: Pontificia Universidad Católica del Perú.

INEI (2017), 'El ABC de la Estadística: un día en cifras', accessed November 12, 2018 at http://abc.inei.gob.pe.

Jäger, U. and V. Sathe (2014), 'Sustainability for strategy', in U. Jäger and V. Sathe (eds.), *Strategy and Competitiveness in Latin American Markets*, Cheltenham, UK and Northampton, MA, USA: Edward Elgar Publishing.

Kanze, D., L. Huang, M. Conley and E. Tory Higgins (2018), 'We ask men to win and women not to lose: closing the gender gap in startup funding', *Academy of Management Journal*, 61(2), 586–614.

Khanna, T. and K.G. Palepu (1997), 'Why focused strategies may be wrong for emerging markets', *Harvard Business Review*, 75(4), 41–51.

Kwon, S. and P.S. Adler (2014), 'Social capital: maturation of a field of research', *Academy of Management Review*, 39(4), 412–422.

Lazear, E. (2005), 'Entrepreneurship', *Journal of Labor Economics*, 23(4), 649–680.

Manolova, T., N. Carter, I. Manev and B. Gyoshev (2007), 'The differential effect of men and women entrepreneurs' human capital and networking on growth expectancies in Bulgaria', *Entrepreneurship: Theory and Practice*, 31(3), 407–426.

Martin, G., R. Gözübüyük and M. Becerra (2015), 'Interlocks and firm performance: the role of uncertainty in the directorate interlock–performance relationship', *Strategic Management Journal*, 36, 235–253.

Meyer, K., S. Estrin, S.K. Bhaumik and M. Peng (2009), 'Institutions, resources, and entry strategies in emerging economies', *Strategic Management Journal*, 30(1), 61–80.

Morrison, A. (2006), 'A contextualisation of entrepreneurship', *International Journal of Entrepreneurial Behavior & Research*, 12(4), 192–209.

Musacchio, A. and I. Read (2007), 'Bankers, industrialists, and their cliques: elite networks in Mexico and Brazil during early industrialization', *Enterprise & Society*, 8(4), 842–880.

Oliver, C. (1997), 'Sustainable competitive advantage: combining institutional and resource-based views', *Strategic Management Journal*, 18(9), 697–713.

Pfeffer, J. and G. Salancik (eds.) (2002), *The External Control of Organizations: A Resource Dependence Perspective*, Stanford, CA: Stanford Business Press.

Ponce, J. (2012), 'Niveles de violencia contra la mujer emprendedora en el Perú : un análisis basado en la encuesta demográfica y de salud familiar – Endes 2011', *Revista de Ciencias Empresariales de La Universidad de San Martín de Porres*, 3(2), 7–56.

Ruiz Rosas, A. (ed.) (2009), *El recetario de Arequipa: 500 recetas de la gran cocina mestiza* (1ra. ed.), Arequipa, Perú: Cuzzi Editores.

Ruiz Rosas, A. (ed.) (2014), *El recetario de Arequipa: 600 recetas de la gran cocina mestiza* (2da. ed.), Arequipa, Perú: Cuzzi Editores.

Schneider, B. (ed.) (2013), *Hierarchical Capitalism in Latin America*, Cambridge: Cambridge University Press.

Shipilov, A., H. Greve and T. Rowley (2010), 'When do interlocks matter? Institutional logics and the diffusion of multiple corporate governance practices', *The Academy of Management Journal*, 53(4), 846–864.

Shropshire, C. (2010), 'The role of the interlocking director and board receptivity in the diffusion of practices', *Academy of Management Review*, 35(2), 246–264.

Sociedad Picantera de Arequipa [SPA] (s.f.-a), 'Sociedad Picantera de Arequipa', accessed November 15, 2018 at https://www.facebook.com/Sociedad-Picantera-de -Arequipa- 383898101684067.

Sociedad Picantera de Arequipa [SPA] (s.f.-b), 'Sociedad Picantera de Arequipa – La sociedad', accessed November 15, 2018 at http://www.sociedadpicanteradearequipa .pe/content/la_sociedad.html.

Sociedad Picantera de Arequipa [SPA] (s.f.-c), 'Sociedad Picantera de Arequipa – Los estatutos', accessed November 15, 2018 at http://www.sociedadpicanteradearequipa .pe/content/ls_estatutos.html.

Sociedad Picantera de Arequipa [SPA] (s.f.-d), 'Sociedad Picantera de Arequipa – Productos y platos', accessed November 9, 2018 at http://www .sociedadpicanteradearequipa.pe/content/productos_y_platos.html.

Vassolo, R., J. De Castro and L. Gomez-Mejia (2011), 'Managing in Latin America: common issues and a research agenda', *Academy of Management Perspectives*, 25(4), 22–34.

Welter, F. (2011), 'Contextualizing entrepreneurship: conceptual challenges and ways forward', *Entrepreneurship: Theory and Practice*, 35(1), 165–184.

Wiklund, J., W. Yu and H. Patzelt (2018), 'Impulsivity and entrepreneurial action', *Academy of Management Perspectives*, 32(3), 379–403.

Yao, X., W. Wen and Z. Ren (2009), 'Corporate entrepreneurship in the enterprise clusters environment: influence of network resources and entrepreneurial orientation on firm performance', *Frontiers of Business Research in China*, 3(4), 566–582.

Young, M., T. Tsai, X. Wang, S. Liu and D. Ahlstrom (2014), 'Strategy in emerging economies and the theory of the firm', *Asia Pacific Journal of Management*, 31, 331–354.

4. Towards a typology of supports for enterprising women: a comparison of rural and urban Australian regions

Robyn Eversole, Naomi Birdthistle, Megerssa Walo and Vinita Godinho

1. INTRODUCTION

Women entrepreneurs are one of the fastest growing entrepreneurial populations in the world making significant contributions to innovation, employment and wealth creation in all economies (Brush et al., 2006b). Yet a gender gap persists in women's and men's entrepreneurial participation, access to resources, and entrepreneurial outcomes. As local communities and regions around the world seek to support the development of entrepreneurs who will create the industries of the future, women's entrepreneurship remains an underutilised resource. The support structure for entrepreneurship, often theorised as the 'entrepreneurial ecosystem', creates the environment for enterprise emergence and growth. Research has shown that 'gender-blind' entrepreneurial ecosystems do not support women entrepreneurs to the extent they support men entrepreneurs (Global Entrepreneurship and Development Institute, 2013). Yet there has been little gendered analysis of how entrepreneurial ecosystems can better support women (Brush et al., 2018; Hazell, 2017; Huq and Tan, 2014). This chapter explores what a responsive support ecosystem to enable high-growth women's entrepreneurship could look like.

1.1 Focus and Aims

Australian women have a significantly lower entrepreneurial participation rate, and much lower growth ambitions than their male counterparts (Audretsch, 2012; Steffens and Hechavarría, 2015). This chapter begins with the question, how can a nation like Australia, with interlinked challenges of lower participation and lower growth ambitions for women entrepreneurs, support and encourage more women to become successful high-growth entrepreneurs?

Specifically, the chapter explores: What does the current support ecosystem for 'enterprising women'—women who are, or have the potential to become, high-growth entrepreneurs—look like in Australia; how well does this support ecosystem currently work to encourage women's entrepreneurship; and how can it be improved?

To answer these questions, we analysed the current 'support ecosystem' for enterprising women in two very distinct Australian contexts: Melbourne, Victoria (a major urban region) and North West Tasmania (a rural, island region). To define a 'support ecosystem' for entrepreneurship, the research initially adapted Lilischkis et al.'s (2013) typology of policy areas for supporting high-growth firms. Researchers then applied a regional development lens to assess policy and programme supports at regional scale, recognising that the nature of support ecosystems may vary significantly across regions within the same country.

In each of the two very different Australian contexts, we identified the supports available for women entrepreneurs locally. Supports are intentional mechanisms developed by governments and/or private providers to improve the environment for entrepreneurship; supports thus comprise a constituent element (Aulet, 2008; Brush, 2014; Brush et al., 2018; Fetters et al., 2010; Kantis and Federico, 2012) or pillar (Drexler and Eltogby, 2013) of entrepreneurial ecosystems. The 'support ecosystem' in each local region (Melbourne and North West Tasmania) comprised a range of different supports to encourage and enable entrepreneurial start-up and scale-up. This is in line with Feld (2012), Stam and Spigel (2016) and Brush et al.'s (2018) observation that in an entrepreneurial ecosystem, there are many actors and players that provide support, as well as Isenberg's (2010) observation that both government and private sector play an important role in nurturing entrepreneurship.

Previous studies suggest that without intentional action to create an ecosystem that fosters and supports start-ups to achieve size and impact, and stop the overseas exodus of its potential gazelles, Australia is at risk of being permanently relegated to a derivative economy (Kinner, 2015). Further, previous work emphasises that support ecosystems for entrepreneurship will need to be cognizant of the requirements of female entrepreneurs and designed to attract, include and support them (Hazell, 2017). According to Gender-GEDI (Global Entrepreneurship and Development Index) 2013, economic development on its own is not enough to encourage high-potential female entrepreneurs; we propose that a necessary condition for a vibrant entrepreneurial economy is the availability of an appropriate and accessible ecosystem of supports that enables and encourages enterprising women (Global Entrepreneurship and Development Institute, 2013, p. 7).

To enable analysis and comparison of support ecosystems across different local regions, the research team developed a typology of supports, based on desktop research supplemented by key informant consultations with enterprising women and service providers in Melbourne and North West Tasmania, who identified and categorised sources of support. The resulting typology of supports enabled support ecosystems to be mapped in each local region and compared across regions, with reference to the types of support that were present or absent in each, and what we know about the enablers of high-growth women's entrepreneurship internationally. Comparing and contrasting support ecosystems across very different regions of the same country revealed important differences and significant gaps in availability, accessibility and appropriateness of supports. The findings demonstrate the value of a regional-scale analysis of support ecosystems and highlight specific opportunities to improve support ecosystems for enterprising women.

2.　　　THEORETICAL FOUNDATION

2.1　　　A Profile of Women Entrepreneurs: The Australian Context

Australia is known as an innovation-driven economy and most entrepreneurship is driven by opportunity rather than necessity (Steffens et al., 2017). Audretsch (2012) highlights that Australia ranks third behind only Canada (13.3 per cent) and Estonia (11.7 per cent) in terms of female entrepreneurship among the innovation-driven economies. The Global Entrepreneurship Monitor (GEM) 2016 report shows that Australia's women entrepreneurs create, run and grow businesses across all industrial sectors. Australia also outperforms most other developed economies on various indicators of quality and economic impact of business start-ups, including growth aspirations, number of opportunity-driven start-ups and innovativeness (Steffens et al., 2017). Yet female entrepreneurial participation in Australia is only 65 per cent that of males (Audretsch, 2012), revealing a significant gender gap.

Australia's business environment is also good for women's entrepreneurship, with the Global Women Entrepreneurs Leaders Scorecard ranking Australia number two, following the United States (Aidis and Weeks, 2016). On the same scorecard Australia is ranked third (following Sweden and the UK) in women's access to fundamental resources such as finance and education. Further, Australia's GEM report for 2016–2017 (Steffens and Omarova, 2017), shows that three-quarters of female entrepreneurs are highly educated. The Global Women Entrepreneur Leaders Scorecard (Aidis et al., 2015), which incorporates a diagnostic tool for identifying the impediments to high-impact female entrepreneurship, also ranks Australia number one in 'Potential Entrepreneur Leaders', indicating a strong growth orientation among women entrepreneurs. Nonetheless, Australia performs poorly on the 'Pipeline to Entrepreneurship' criterion, ranking 14th out of 31 countries.

This signals that supports might be lacking at the early stages for potential high-growth entrepreneurs, leading to the need to understand how the support ecosystem is currently performing for women entrepreneurs, and how it can be improved.

2.1.1   Contrasting Australian contexts: Melbourne, Victoria and North West Tasmania

This research was conducted in the states of Victoria and Tasmania, Australia, to explore the different contexts for entrepreneurship in a metropolitan urban region (Melbourne) and a rural region (North West Tasmania). Prior research shows significant geographical differences in women's businesses and entrepreneurship motivations in urban and rural Australia (Vega, 2012). At the same time, this research has shown that women's businesses outside the major cities have similar annual turnover levels to those in the urban centres and are more likely to employ staff (Vega, 2012). A brief comparison of the two study regions, and the urban and rural environments, is presented in Table 4.1.

Melbourne is a large metropolitan urban area and the capital of Victoria. It is ranked as one of Australia's top start-up ecosystems, with strengths in the 'Late Activation' phase, meaning it creates a plethora of accelerators, co-working spaces, and other start-up support organisations (Startup Genome, 2018). Interesting, though, is the lack of availability of early-stage funding, with median funding round sizes smaller in Melbourne when compared to other cities (Kimmorley, 2018). In Victoria overall, 25 per cent of business founders are female (LaunchVic, 2017).

Tasmania is an island off Australia's south coast. The start-up ecosystem in Tasmania is still small but growing (Farrell, 2016). Tasmania is known as the most affordable place to do business in Australia and had the lowest entry and exit rates for businesses of all Australian states in 2016–17, and the highest business survival rate (Tasmanian Government, 2017a, 2017b). In 2016 the Tasmanian government injected $500 000 into creating start-up hubs in Launceston and the state capital, Hobart (Dias, 2016). This research took place in largely rural North West Tasmania.

2.2   High-Growth Businesses and Their Contribution to Australia

Research has shown that start-up businesses, especially high-growth start-ups, are the key to job creation and economic leadership in new industries. Differing definitions have emerged as to what constitutes a high-growth firm, depending on how growth is measured: in terms of profits, sales, book value, workforce or even future expectations (White and Reynolds, 1996). The OECD defines a high-growth enterprise as a firm with an 'average annualised growth in employees (or turnover) greater than 20 per cent a year, over a three-year

High-growth women's entrepreneurship

Table 4.1   *Comparing urban and rural entrepreneurial environments*

	Urban – Melbourne, Victoria	Rural – North West Tasmania
Location	The coastal capital of the South Eastern Australian state of Victoria.	Rural region of an island state off Australia's south coast.
Population	Over 4.8 million[a]	111 000[b]
Start-up ecosystem	One of Australia's top start-up ecosystems.	Small but growing start-up ecosystem.
Women's business characteristics	In urban Australia, women's businesses congregate in professional services, education and training, and healthcare and social assistance industries.[c]	In rural Australia, women's businesses congregate in agriculture, construction, retail, accommodation, and transport industries.[c]
Motivations of women entrepreneurs	In urban Australia, women start businesses primarily due to flexibility requirements, to escape corporate management and culture, having a great product/service idea.[c]	In rural Australia, women start businesses primarily due to a lack of other employment opportunities.[c]
Sources of start-up finance for women	Personal savings or credit card debt.[c]	Banks or credit union loans.[c]

Notes:
[a] Population Australia (2018), Melbourne Population 2018, accessed 23 July 2018 at http://www.population.net.au/melbourne-population/.
[b] ABS (2018), Data by Region West and North West, accessed 6 March 2019 at http://stat.abs.gov.au/itt/r.jsp?databyregion#/.
[c] Vega (2012).

period, and with ten employees at the beginning of the observation period' (OECD, 2008, p. 18). Other international studies use different definitions of high-growth. Rather than focusing on the firm, the Australian Government's definition focuses on the individual and is broad enough to capture all prospective high-growth firms that are 'formed by founders that possess high levels of human capital, based around innovative ideas and high technology' (Clark et al., 2012, p. 13). GEM also focuses on the entrepreneur rather than the firm as the unit of analysis and defines 'high-expectation entrepreneurs' as those 'nascent and new entrepreneurs who expect to have more than 20 employees in five years' (Autio, 2007, p. 5). This study adopts Autio's (2007) definition as the study focuses on enterprising women who are, or have the potential to become, high-growth entrepreneurs.

Australia displays a relatively positive climate for entrepreneurship, with an entrepreneurial participation rate of 13.1 per cent, amongst the highest of all developed economies (Steffens and Hechavarría, 2015). Nevertheless, those who create high-growth firms are a select subset of entrepreneurs: Hendrickson et al. (2015) found that a very small fraction of the total number of Australian start-ups (3.2 per cent) account for firms that grow dramatically over five years' post-entry; these firms account for the majority (77 per cent) of total post-entry job creation of all micro start-ups in their cohort. The Australian Innovation System Report 2017 estimated that while high-growth firms in Australia contributed 46 per cent of employment growth, they represent only 9 per cent of all firms with five or more employees (Department of Industry, Innovation and Science, 2017). Further, there is a worrying decline in the proportion of high-growth firms, from 18.6 per cent of Australian firms in 2005 to only 12.5 per cent in 2014 (Department of Industry, Innovation and Science, 2017). Understanding what drives firm success requires looking closer at the local contexts in which firms operate, and how local business environments may facilitate growth (Li et al., 2016).

From a female perspective, the GEM report for 2014 (Steffens and Hechavarría, 2015) highlights low growth expectations: only 25 per cent of Australian women entrepreneurs were considering growing their business to over five employees and only 6 per cent were aiming to penetrate international markets. Conway (2015) found that Australian women are significantly under-represented as founders of larger, fast-growth businesses; for instance, only about 4 per cent of high-growth technology businesses have female founders. Women are nearly half of the workforce in Australia, more than 30 per cent of business owners, and more than half of our university students, yet their failure in building high-growth firms has become a major economic deficit. The nation has fewer jobs—and less strength in emerging industries— than it could have if women's entrepreneurship were on par with men. Enterprising women may well be our greatest under-used economic resource.

2.3   Entrepreneurial Ecosystem

The concept of entrepreneurial ecosystems has recently become a 'hot topic' amongst both policy makers and academics. According to Stam (2015) the entrepreneurial ecosystem has been heralded as a 'new framework' to transition from entrepreneurship policy towards a policy for an entrepreneurial economy. But what is it? The concept itself does not have an agreed upon definition. For example, Mazzarol (2015, p. 2) explained an entrepreneurial ecosystem 'as a conceptualisation of an environment in which the right combination of elements helps to foster economic growth through enterprise and innovation'. Stam's (2015, p. 1765) definition somewhat reflects Mazzarol's views, through proposing 'the entrepreneurial ecosystem as a set of interdependent actors and factors coordinated in such a way that they enable productive entrepreneurship'. Stam (2015, p. 1764) emphasises that 'geographically an ecosystem could be a city, a region, a country and other systems, less strictly defined in space, such as sectors or corporations', Further, Brush et al. (2018) argue that while, in theory, all entrepreneurs have equal access to services the entrepreneurship ecosystem provides, practically this is not the case due to different ecosystem attributes. For example, evidence from the Global Entrepreneurship Monitor (GEM) Global Women's Report shows that there are substantial differences in start-up rates between men and women entrepreneurs (GEM Global Report, 2016/2017).

To examine a nation's ecosystem, the World Economic Forum (WEF) identifies that the ecosystem for entrepreneurship comprises eight pillars: accessible markets, human capital/workforce, funding and finance, support systems/mentors, government and regulatory framework, education and training, cultural support, and universities as Catalysts (World Economic Forum, 2011). The WEF (2013) ecosystem framework highlights several supports that are crucial to enabling an entrepreneurial environment to exist. One is the support system which includes mentors, incubators, accelerators and a peer network. Additionally, supports can be provided through institutions such as universities, and a culture with a positive outlook on entrepreneurship. Roper (2016, p. 157) posits that a key starting point for the encouragement of start-ups, which can ultimately lead to high-growth firms, is to have a 'business and entrepreneurship-friendly atmosphere in which business success is seen as positive and there are positive entrepreneurial role models'. Roper (2016, p. 157) also recognises that 'creating this type of environment is of course a relatively long-term project'.

There are three major differences between an entrepreneurial ecosystem and conventional economic development, innovation and cluster policies: (1) an entrepreneurial ecosystem focuses on entrepreneurial activity and on high-growth firms, (2) it emphasises local and regional environments and supports ambitious entrepreneurs, and (3) it emphasises the interactions between framework conditions and local/regional geographical environments (Mason and Brown, 2014). Thus, the entrepreneurial ecosystem provides an appropriate theoretical lens for examining the nature of support ecosystems (programmes and policies) for women entrepreneurs in different regions of Australia and comparing supports across local regions.

2.3.1   Policies to create entrepreneurial ecosystems

Government policy is one of the pillars needed for a strong entrepreneurial ecosystem (World Economic Forum, 2011), and public policy initiatives have a positive role in stimulating regional as well as national innovation and enterprise (Cooke and Leydesdorff, 2006). Yet despite the importance of high-growth firms to national and regional economic well-being, many governments develop policy supports focused only on small business. Interestingly, Shane (2009) proposes that encouraging start-ups in general is bad public policy and that policy makers should target the small subset of new businesses with high-growth potential. Nevertheless, focusing policies on high-growth firms assumes public administrators can identify such enterprises (Kolar, 2014, p. 8).

Rather than attempting to 'pick winners', authors such as Henrekson and Johansson (2010) and Botham (2012) argue that policy support to increase the overall volume of start-ups may be an effective way of generating more high-growth firms. As Botham (2012, p. 10) argues, 'high-growth and high-tech start-ups require a good entrepreneurial environment capable of supporting "normal" new starts. Consequently, policies for high-growth and high-tech new starts need to build on policies for increasing the volume of new starts.'

Appropriate policy support can encourage high-growth firms to emerge through stimulating markets, technological and business services and appropriate financial structures (Avnimelech et al., 2007). Following Botham, this may take the form of policies supporting the overall ecosystem rather than policies explicitly targeting high-growth firms. In the Australian context, the Australian Innovation Systems Report (Department of Industry, Innovation and Science, 2017) alludes to the fact that, while high-growth firms make large contributions to the economy, it is difficult to target high-growth firms with policy supports. It thus proposes that 'underlying policy should continue to focus on creating a macroeconomic environment conducive to innovation and growth by improving framework conditions' (Department of Industry, Innovation and Science, 2017, p. 86) such as increasing the skills available to small firms.

For women entrepreneurs, improving the environment for innovation and growth requires attention to the gender responsiveness of policy supports. The Gender-Global Entrepreneurship and Development Index (Gender-GEDI) (Global Entrepreneurship and Development Institute, 2013) conducted a pilot analysis on the conditions that foster high-potential female entrepreneurship, and identified that 'gender-blind business support measures do not support women's enterprise development to the extent that they support men-owned firms' (Global Entrepreneurship and Development Institute, 2013, p. 4). Enabling enterprising women to reach high-growth requires attention to how the business environment influences growth trajectories (Global Entrepreneurship and Development Institute, 2013, p. 5). This chapter therefore advocates for the need for policies to create a responsive 'support ecosystem' to nurture enterprising women's start-ups and support and enable them to move from start-up to high-growth.

Until the launch of The Diana Project in 1999, few studies looked at the growth of women-led businesses (Huq and Tan, 2014). The Diana Project aimed to conceptualise and build explanatory theories on the growth process of women-owned businesses (Brush et al., 2006a, p. 4), exposing a disparity

Table 4.2   Typology of policy areas for supporting high-growth firms

Policy measure	Evidence
A. Framework conditions for innovation and growth	Taxation, including tax landscape for investors; finance (public and private); education (secondary and higher education); publicly funded research
B. Stimulation of innovation demand	Innovation public procurement; pre-commercial procurement; standardisation; product market regulations; IPR management; support to internationalisation
C. Financing innovation and growth	Equity provision; corporate venturing; loans; grants for R&D and innovative activities
D. An ecosystem for innovative firms	Science parks; incubators; clusters; human networks; human resources; mentoring
E. Policies supporting entrepreneurship and high-growth	Awareness raising; skill development; accelerators
F. Business support services	Consultancy; sectoral federations; professional associations; chambers of commerce; clubs

Source: Adapted from: Lilischkis et al. (2013, pp. 51–52)

between men- and women-owned ventures and their access to funding. This chapter aims to add to the debate on the growth of women-led businesses by focusing on the supports available for developing high-growth firms in two Australian regions: metropolitan Melbourne and North West Tasmania. To guide the analysis of regional 'support ecosystems', the study adopted Lilischkis et al.'s (2013) typology of policy areas for supporting high-growth firms (see Table 4.2). Other approaches including Korlaar et al. (2015) and Morris et al. (2015) were reviewed but Lilischkis et al. (2013) was considered the most comprehensive. This typology (Table 4.2) framed the initial methodological approach for identifying and mapping supports.

3.   DATA SOURCES AND METHODOLOGY

Data for the study comes from desktop research supplemented by key informant consultations in each of the two regions: Melbourne and North West Tasmania. First, a desk-based research approach was adopted using Lilischkis et al.'s (2013) typology as a benchmark. The federal and state government websites for Victoria and Tasmania were examined using a Boolean search approach incorporating the policy measures provided by Lilischkis et al.'s (2013) typology. Further internet searches were conducted to develop a database of available supports for women entrepreneurs and prospective entrepreneurs in each region, as well as policies and programmes broadly available at state or federal level. These were categorised to develop a preliminary typology of supports and visualised as a support ecosystem map (see Figure 4.1).

To identify key informants for the research, members of the research team and local partners reached out to their local networks, leveraging existing databases and mailing lists of entrepreneurs and service providers, as well as personal contacts and local organisations that had been identified through the desktop research. The invitation to participate in the research was disseminated to established and emerging women entrepreneurs and business-related service providers and networks in Melbourne and in North West Tasmania, with the aim to maximise outreach in each case. Thus, invitees were encouraged to pass on the information to other local enterprising women or enterprise service providers. In North West Tasmania, the project was also promoted via social media by project partners, while in Melbourne targeted invitations were sent to a project-specific database of support organisations developed through the desktop research.

Key informants were invited to participate in discussion roundtables. In Melbourne, two roundtables were held: one with enterprising women (established and emerging women entrepreneurs based in Melbourne) and one with enterprise service providers. Seven enterprising women and nine enterprise service providers participated as key informants in the Melbourne roundtables. In Tasmania, a roundtable was held with enterprising women (established and emerging women entrepreneurs based in North West Tasmania), co-hosted by a key service provider. Fourteen enterprising women attended the rural North West Tasmania roundtable.[1]

At each of the roundtables, participants were informed about the purpose of the research and consented to participate. Each roundtable had a facilitator and at least three scribes who recorded the table discussions. The facilitator asked the participants to identify what kinds of resources and supports are/are not available for enterprising women in their location, in dialogue with their preliminary support ecosystem map (Figures 4.1 and 4.3). Enterprising women were asked to explore the map for their local region and to answer a series of questions in small groups to refine the map. They were asked to reflect on what supports were available, identify what was missing from the map, and identify if they have used these supports and their experiences with them. A similar approach was adopted with service providers. This participatory mapping process developed a more refined, practice-focused typology of supports, based on the needs and experiences of enterprising women. The next section describes the results of the research.

4.   RESULTS AND DISCUSSION

4.1   Mapping the Support Ecosystem in Melbourne

Melbourne promotes itself as a 'smart city', aims to create a strong start-up culture (City of Melbourne, 2018), and is perhaps the most likely place to look for a healthy support ecosystem for enterprising women in Australia. The findings of the desktop-based review of supports described above identified about three dozen organisations providing a range of support for women entrepreneurs, from multiple sectors: Government, Not for Profit, and Community. This information, not available through any other source, had to be constructed from the ground up. Based on these findings, the research team grouped the database of support organisations into six categories that, together, described the range of types of organisations—from incubators and accelerators, to providers of financial capital. Further desk-based research clarified where organisations belonged to multiple categories; for instance, NGO business development programmes that also provide financial capital. The organisations and categories of support were then mapped into a preliminary visual representation of the support ecosystem (Figure 4.1). While based on a rigorous scan of desktop data, it was necessarily incomplete, as not all forms of support came from organisations with a visible internet site in the local region. Nevertheless, this preliminary map (Figure 4.1) provided a useful starting point for face-to-face discussions with enterprising women and service providers.

To refine the support ecosystem map and enhance rigour and validity, the second stage of the ecosystem mapping was conducted as a participatory process with enterprising women and service providers. The preliminary map was presented to all the participants for review and reflection. Participants were asked to identify forms of support that were missing from the map, and to consider whether the categories of support nominated by the research team resonated with them, or whether other categories would be more useful. The roundtables enabled this preliminary mapping to be significantly expanded and refined. The refined map included over 80 specific organisations—including many social media-based groups and networks—classified into five categories. The categories that resonated with participants were those with specific reference to support function, rather than, for instance, specifying whether they were governmental or non-governmental supports (Figure 4.2).

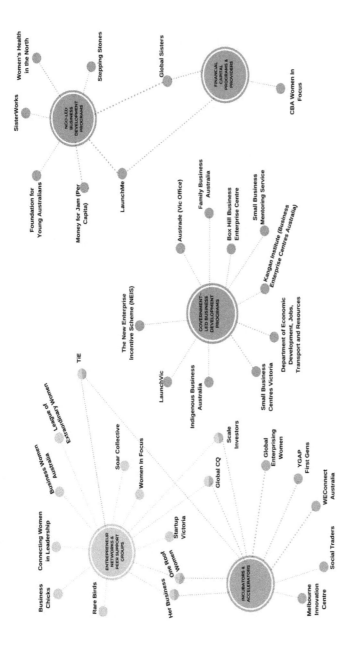

Figure 4.1   Preliminary desktop mapping of supports for enterprising women in Melbourne

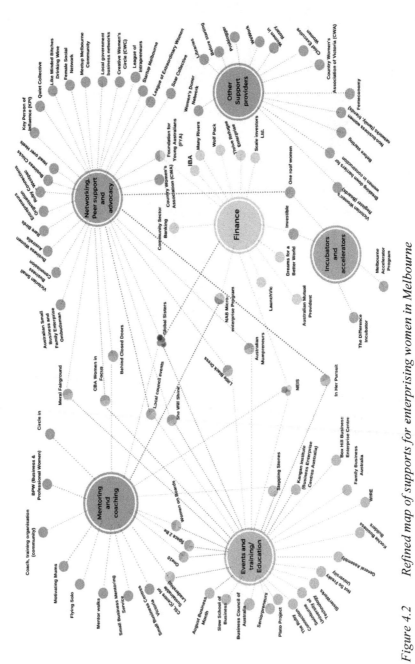

Figure 4.2   Refined map of supports for enterprising women in Melbourne

These were:

1. Finance Providers
2. Peer Support Networks and Advocacy Groups
3. Incubators and Accelerators
4. Education and Training Providers
5. Mentoring and Coaching Providers.

This typology of five categories of support—Finance, Peer Networks and Groups, Incubators and Accelerators, Education and Training, and Mentoring and Coaching—developed through the roundtable process, provided a practical way to talk about the kinds of support that different organisations in the ecosystem were providing—with some organisations providing multiple forms of support. In addition, this process identified a category of 'Other' supports: organisations and individuals that were described as part of the support ecosystem, but often not specific to entrepreneurship: such as professional services (e.g., accountancy firms), community services (e.g., libraries), and informal supports (family, friends). The refined visual representation of the support ecosystem in Melbourne in Figure 4.2 demonstrates that a significant number of organisations were providing supports for enterprising women in one or more of these categories.

The process of constructing a map of the support ecosystem and reflecting upon it with enterprise service providers and women entrepreneurs generated several insights. First, the mapping process revealed the *availability* of many organisations offering different kinds of support to enterprising women in the urban context. Nevertheless, these support resources were not necessarily *accessible*, as entrepreneurs did not always know about them; in one of the roundtables it was explicitly observed 'People don't know where to go' for supports. Well-networked enterprising women who participated in the first roundtable on average had only heard of less than half of the support organisations identified in the desktop mapping. And even support organisations themselves had only heard of a handful of other support organisations.

A second insight from the mapping process was that out of the five categories of supports available to enterprising women in Melbourne, four (Finance, Incubators and Accelerators, Education and Training, and Mentoring and Coaching) were almost exclusively 'gender-blind' or did not acknowledge the specific barriers facing enterprising women. However, there was a notable exception: several informal peer networking groups that had formed through social media (e.g., MeetUp, Facebook) had a specific focus on women as entrepreneurs. These findings suggest that while formal enterprise supports, particularly those offered by government, are largely gender-blind, smaller and less formal peer support networks and groups may be emerging to fill a gap in appropriate supports for enterprising women.

The roundtables drew attention to several gaps in current supports for enterprising women. For instance, one roundtable participant highlighted negative experiences for women in a mainstream business mentoring program, while another observed that participation in activities for tech start-ups in Melbourne required a willingness to go along and eat pizza and drink beer with a roomful of young men. Further, it was telling that the available enterprise supports tended to focus on start-ups and portray enterprise as a strategy for income generation. There seemed to be no effort to identify, recognise or explicitly work with nascent female entrepreneurs with high-growth potential. Further, in mapping the support ecosystem, no supports were identified that specifically targeted established businesses that wanted to scale quickly.

4.2   Mapping the Support Ecosystem in North West Tasmania

North West Tasmania presents a contrasting environment to metropolitan Melbourne: a largely rural island region. The desktop review identified 16 distinct organisations providing support to enterprising women in North West Tasmania. As in Melbourne, these were grouped and then mapped to provide a preliminary visual presentation (Figure 4.3). The categories were a slightly modified variant of the typology developed in Melbourne. As in Melbourne, information on available supports had to be constructed from the ground up, through the desktop review, and then tested and extended through a participatory process with enterprising women and service providers.

Testing this preliminary framework with roundtable participants in North West Tasmania identified ten additional support organisations. The refined support map (Figure 4.4) included 26 organisations or categories of organisations (e.g., 'crowdfunding platforms'), categorised into four types: Finance, Networks and Groups, Training, and Mentoring and Advice. In addition, family and friends were also named as important sources of 'Other' support.

The support map for North West Tasmania describes a mix of local and Tasmanian supports, but an almost complete absence of national-scale supports (except for the Australian Government's New Enterprise Incentive Scheme (NEIS) business start-up program, which is delivered through local providers). Most national organisations and programmes were not picked up in the desktop review as they listed no Tasmanian address, contact, or programme details. A few Tasmania-wide organisations, and national organisations with Tasmanian offices, are included on the support map from the desktop review. Nevertheless, awareness of these organisations among enterprising women in North West Tasmania was low to non-existent.

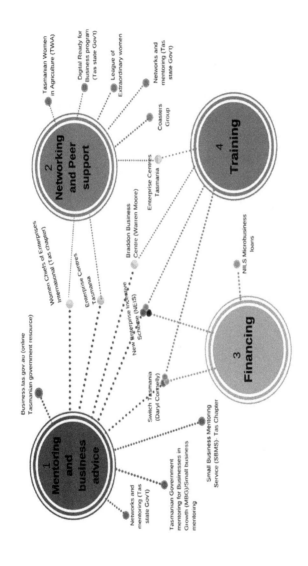

Figure 4.3   Preliminary desktop mapping of supports for enterprising women in North West Tasmania

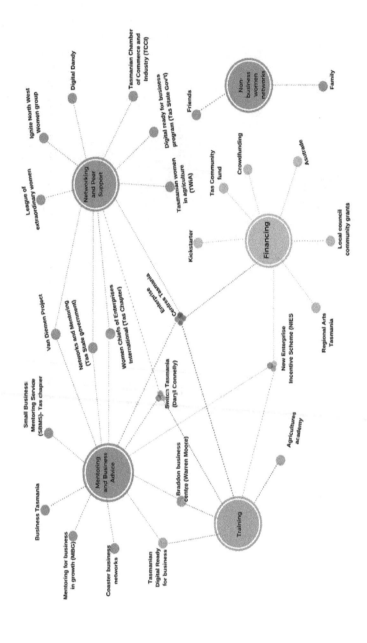

Figure 4.4   Refined map of supports for enterprising women in North West Tasmania

It is an important contextual detail that the Tasmanian offices of many organisations are based in Hobart, the state capital (approximately four hours away by road); thus, many of their activities, while technically available, were not generally accessible to enterprising women on the North West coast. When women in the roundtables were asked what organisations they had heard of, and what supports they had used, these were overwhelmingly locally based organisations and programmes delivered by them, as well as a couple of high-profile online resources (i.e., business.tas.gov.au and Kickstarter).

As in Melbourne, most of the supports available to enterprising women in North West Tasmania were gender-blind: there were no women-specific supports or supports that acknowledged specific barriers facing enterprising women. Nor were there the large number of women's networking groups that were present in Melbourne. At the same time, roundtable participants provided strong endorsement of the usefulness of a few key sources of non-gendered support; particularly, the business mentoring, networking and training support offered by local organisation Switch Tasmania; the Tasmanian Government's digital ready training programme, which had been delivered locally; and the Coasters young professionals network. All were deemed to be accessible and appropriate supports, which several participants had used.

4.3   Comparing Regional Support Ecosystems

Comparing the two support maps, one from a major urban region and the other from a rural region, highlights interesting similarities and differences. Unsurprisingly, there were more support organisations available in Melbourne than in North West Tasmania; more than three times as many. In Melbourne, once roundtable participants had the opportunity to expand the map, there were too many organisations to visually show them all. Nevertheless, despite the abundance of locally available supports in Melbourne, these supports were not necessarily accessible for enterprising women, who were unaware that many of these resources even existed and did not know where they could go to find out about them. Amid a wealth of supports, enterprising women in Melbourne were still experiencing a poverty of support options. The support ecosystem was also poorly coordinated, leading entrepreneurs to rely heavily on person-to-person networks.

In North West Tasmania, by contrast, there were fewer support organisations available and physically accessible to enterprising women; yet women generally knew what those supports were and where to go to access them. Further, when new supports became available—such as a Melbourne-based network that started to run events in the Tasmanian city of Launceston—North West women were quick to find out and take advantage of them where they could, even when this involved several hours' travel to attend events. Finally,

North West Tasmanian enterprising women made the decision to self-organise into a new network as a mechanism for peer support and information exchange. In sharp contrast to Melbourne, enterprising women in North West Tasmania were working in a largely resource-poor environment; nevertheless, they were able to enrich their environment through networking with each other, linking up with key locally based support organisations, and, where possible, tapping into online resources.

One clear gap highlighted by the comparison between urban Melbourne and rural North West Tasmania is in the types of support that were available and accessible in each context. Enterprising women in both rural and urban contexts had access to support organisations across the four broad categories of Mentoring and Advice, Training, Finance, and Peer Networks; though the number and accessibility of these supports varied considerably. However, North West Tasmania had no presence of support organisations in the fifth category: Incubators and Accelerators. This was an area where there was support available for urban enterprising women, but no support available for rural enterprising women.

Further, in North West Tasmania, the different categories of support were highly concentrated within a small number of organisations. Only a few organisations were physically present, and these provided multiple forms of support: most notably Switch Tasmania, a small organisation which single-handedly delivered many of the training, mentoring/advising and networking opportunities available on the North West coast. Indeed, at the time of the project, this organisation had just begun to trial a small incubation hub in response to the absence of this kind of support facility. In Melbourne there were also several organisations that provided multiple forms of support, such as combining networking opportunities and training; but there was not the same sense that the entire support ecosystem depended heavily on the actions of a handful of key organisational players, as was evident in Tasmania.

Across both rural and urban contexts, the mapping of finance supports revealed some interesting insights. 'Finance' itself is a broad category of support encompassing everything from grants and seed funding, to loans of various types and sizes, to equity finance, as well as financial services such as banking and insurance. Interestingly, most of the organisations mapped in the finance category were not traditional banks or investors, but rather targeted social finance organisations and programmes. In Melbourne, there was a strong focus on 'alternative' financial services (community banks, mutuals, etc.) and programmes to support specific social groups (immigrants, youth) while in North West Tasmania, there was a focus on local grants, government programmes and crowdfunding.

In neither context, however, was there a sense that mainstream finance providers were providing visible or important sources of support for enterprising women. While an in-depth exploration of financial supports and women's financial exclusion was beyond the scope of this study, the evident bias towards non-traditional finance providers found across both rural and urban contexts suggests a need to explore potential financial exclusion (Connolly, 2014), i.e., low availability and accessibility of different kinds of financial products for women, particularly products appropriate for enabling high-growth enterprises.

Finally, a key finding from mapping support ecosystems across two very different regional contexts was that supports for enterprising people were not attuned to the needs of enterprising women. With a few exceptions, supports were gender-blind and did not address identified issues limiting the growth of women's enterprises. This did not mean that they were necessarily inappropriate to women's needs—women found some of these supports very useful; but it did mean that there were clear gaps in the support infrastructure for enterprising women in both rural and urban contexts. It is notable that the supports nominated by roundtable participants in both contexts included several non-enterprise-specific supports, for women in leadership or women in particular fields (e.g., agriculture, management), in the absence of supports for enterprising women. Further, the documented growth of peer networks suggests that, in the absence of appropriate institutional supports provided by government, private, or community sectors, enterprising women are creating these supports for themselves.

5.   CONCLUSION AND RECOMMENDATIONS

This chapter sought to answer the question, 'what does the current support ecosystem for enterprising women look like in Australia; how well does it currently work to encourage women's entrepreneurship; and how can it be improved?' Reflecting on the findings of the study in two local regions, it is evident that a support ecosystem is present in both, with some common components as well as localised differences. Yet these support ecosystems are not attuned to the needs of enterprising women. This chapter has identified some means by which they can be improved.

Shortfalls identified through the participatory mapping of support ecosystems can help to explain our observed issues about women-led businesses' disproportionate tendency to start and stay small, and the comparatively small presence of women among high-growth Australian start-ups. Available enterprise supports were identified across five key areas—Mentoring and Advice, Training, Finance, Incubators and Accelerators, and Peer Networks—but there are serious issues with their accessibility and appropriateness for women entrepreneurs.

Both Mentoring/Advice and Training supports, for instance, are broadly available to enterprising women in both urban and rural regions studied. These supports build entrepreneurs' skills through informal or formal learning. In rural North West Tasmania, the presence of a trusted community-based enterprise service provider facilitated access to mentoring and training services: both local programmes and funded programmes from elsewhere. While women in North West Tasmania were happy with these locally embedded services, they still expressed a need for mentoring and training approaches that would enable them to learn through in-depth conversations and exchange with others. They expressed a distinct preference for relational learning, rather than the more common transactional structure of trainers or mentors providing information or advice. In Melbourne, by contrast, while abundant mentoring, coaching, education and training supports are available, there was little information about what they were or how to access them. This problem is likely not particular to women, but women were particularly conscious of their lack of information when seeking out services: not only about what services were available, but also about the appropriateness of services for them; gendered issues such as 'mentors not looking/feeling like me' and 'bad mentors/people preying on women', as well as the cost of training and time pressures, were flagged as barriers. Service providers in Melbourne emphasised the need for some kind of 'one stop shop' to make enterprise supports more accessible to enterprising women. Examining models for 'one stop shops' and their impact would be an interesting area of future study, as would the question of women entrepreneurs' preferred models for accessing training and mentoring.

Finance is another key type of enterprise support, as businesses require capital. Financial inclusion, i.e., access to safe, affordable and appropriate finance, is imperative for women entrepreneurs, as evidence shows that they are less likely to garner investment when pitching to investors (Brooks et al., 2014). Nevertheless, mapping processes in both Melbourne and North West Tasmania demonstrated a narrow range of available financial supports, and perceived distance from mainstream banking and investment institutions. Further, there was a marked absence of woman-specific financial supports. These findings suggest a lack of access to appropriate finance for enterprising women in both urban and rural contexts, in line with previous Diana Project findings. Because women are more likely to lack collateral than men and less likely to have a credit history, women-friendly financial instruments would ideally have lower hurdles for women, based on the strength of their business idea and capability. Further, there could be a need for initiatives, such as gender awareness training, to minimise bias from bank staff at the assessment end. The question of finance accessibility for female entrepreneurs warrants further research in the Australian context.

Enterprise Incubation and Acceleration supports varied markedly across the urban and rural contexts. These supports provide a mix of infrastructure and services to support business start-up and growth. They were abundantly available in urban Melbourne, but not in rural Tasmania. Further, while most of these facilities were gender-blind, there was an important exception in Melbourne—an organisation that had been set up specifically to provide a women-friendly co-working space. While not a women-only space, this organisation specifically focused on supporting women entrepreneurs. It emphasised a strong community environment that actively provided opportunities for relationship building and learning. By contrast, enterprise incubation and acceleration supports were not present in rural North West Tasmania— either for women or for men. This suggests a potentially important gap in the rural enterprise support ecosystem. Future research could explore the impact of these meso-environmental spaces for women entrepreneurs and incipient high-growth firms, and the implications of their absence in local regions, as well as the potential benefits of women-focused incubation and acceleration spaces.

Melbourne also demonstrated an abundance of support in the form of peer networks and other support and advocacy groups, including many peer support networks with an explicit focus on women entrepreneurs. These networks were, however, mostly informal, and many tend to be short-lived, relying on the energy of their founder or founders to be sustainable. Peer networks were much less common but also present in rural North West Tasmania. Future research could examine the role these networks play and explore their impact on women's entrepreneurial trajectories.

Finally, the great majority of supports across both regions were 'gender-blind'. Previous research has identified that 'gender-blind business support measures do not support women's enterprise development to the extent that they support men-owned firms' (Global Entrepreneurship and Development Institute, 2013, p. 4). Of course, both Melbourne and North West Tasmania have produced successful women entrepreneurs with high-growth businesses; but these are still the extraordinary and notable rather than the accepted norm. Our work with enterprising women, while still in its early stages, has begun to interrogate the support ecosystem for enterprising women in different local contexts and explore how strengthening these ecosystems can widen the pipeline for more high-growth women's entrepreneurship.

NOTE

1. Three other roundtables were held in Tasmania and two in Melbourne as part of the larger Enterprising Women programme; the findings of these roundtables are not discussed here.

REFERENCES

Aidis, R. and J. Weeks (2016), 'Mapping the gendered ecosystem: the evolution of measurement tools for comparative high-impact female entrepreneur development', *International Journal of Gender and Entrepreneurship*, 8(4), 330–352.

Aidis, R., J. Weeks and K. Anacker (2015), *The Global Women Entrepreneur Leaders Scorecard 2015: Country-level Five Category Scores*, Report, ACG Inc.

Audretsch, D.B. (2012), 'Determinants of high growth entrepreneurship', OECD, Copenhagen: Danish Business Authority.

Aulet, B. (2008), 'How to build a successful innovation ecosystem: education, network and celebrate', accessed 11 December 2018 at https://www.xconomy.com/national/2008/10/14/how-tobuild-a-successful-innovation-ecosystem-educate-networkand-celebrate/?single_page=true.

Australian Innovation Systems (2017), *Australian Innovation System Report*, accessed 23 July 2018 at https://publications.industry.gov.au/publications/australianinnovationsystemreport2017/index.htm.

Autio, E. (2007), *Global Entrepreneurship Monitor: 2007 Global Report on High-Growth Entrepreneurship*, Babson College, London Business School and Global Entrepreneurship Research Consortium.

Avnimelech, G., D. Schwartz and R. Bar-El (2007), 'Entrepreneurial high-tech cluster development: Israel's experience with venture capital and technological incubators', *European Planning Studies*, 15(9), 1181–1198.

Botham, R. (2012), 'Entrepreneurship and regional development: high-growth, high-tech or simply 21 more new starts?', accessed 27 June 2018 at http://www.rbotham.co.uk/home/reports-and-papers.

Brooks, A., L. Huang, S. Kearney and F. Murray (2014), 'Investors prefer entrepreneurial ventures pitched by attractive men', *PNAS*, 111(12), 4427–4431.

Brush, C. (2014), 'Exploring the concept of an entrepreneurship education ecosystem', in S. Hoskinson and D. Kuratko (eds.), *Innovative Pathways for University Entrepreneurship in the 21st Century: Advances in the Study of Entrepreneurship, Innovation and Growth* (Vol. 24), Bingley: Emerald.

Brush, C., N.M. Carter, E.J. Gatewood, P.G. Greene and M. Hart (2006a), 'The Diana Project: women business owners and equity capital: the myths dispelled', Babson College Center for Entrepreneurship Research Paper No. 2009-11.

Brush, C., N.M. Carter, E.J. Gatewood, P.G. Greene and M. Hart (eds.) (2006b), *Growth-Oriented Women Entrepreneurs and their Business: A Global Research Perspective*, Cheltenham, UK and Northampton, MA, USA: Edward Elgar Publishing.

Brush, C., L.F. Edelman, T. Manolova and F. Welter (2018), 'A gendered look at entrepreneurship ecosystems', *Small Business Economics*, 1–16, Online First.

City of Melbourne (2018), 'Melbourne Innovation Districts', accessed 24 July 2018 at https://www.melbourne.vic.gov.au/about-melbourne/melbourne-profile/smart-city/Pages/melbourne-innovation-districts.aspx.

Clark, M., M. Eaton, D. Meeki, E. Pye and R. Tuhin (2012), 'Australian small business: key statistics and analysis', Department of Industry, Innovation, Science, Research and Tertiary Education, Canberra.

Connolly, C. (2014), 'Measuring financial exclusion in Australia, Centre for Social Impact (CSI)', accessed 30 July 2018 at https://www.nab.com.au/content/dam/

nabrwd/About-Us/corporate-responsibilty/docs/measuring_financial_exclusion_in
_australia_2014_final.pdf.

Conway, T. (2015), 'Closing the gender-funding gap', accessed 3 July 2018 at
https://www.smh.com.au/business/small-business/closing-the-genderfunding-gap
-20150305-13w2u5.html.

Cooke, P. and L. Leydesdorff (2006), 'Regional development in the knowledge-based
economy: the construction of advantage', *Journal of Technology Transfer*, 31, 5–15.

Department of Industry, Innovation and Science (2017), *A Profile of Australian Women
in Business*, Australia: Office for Women.

Dias, D. (2016), 'Tasmanian startup ecosystem reaches a "tipping point" as state government invests in innovation', accessed 13 July 2018 at https://www.smartcompany
.com.au/startupsmart/advice/startupsmart-growth/startupsmart-innovation/
tasmanian-government-breaks-startup-tipping-point-with-half-a-million-in
-innovation-hubs/.

Drexler, M. and M. Eltogby (2013), *Entrepreneurial Ecosystems around the Globe and
Early-Stage Company Growth Dynamics*, Geneva: World Economic Forum.

Farrell, N. (2016), 'Tasmania's startup scene', accessed 10 July 2018 at http://www
.pollenizer.com/2016/06/21/tasmanian-startup-scene/.

Feld, B. (2012), *Startup Communities: Building an Entrepreneurial Ecosystem in your
City*, Hoboken, NJ: John Wiley & Sons.

Fetters, M., P.G. Greene and M.P. Rice (eds.) (2010), *The Development of
University-Based Entrepreneurship Ecosystems: Global Practices*, Cheltenham, UK
and Northampton, MA, USA: Edward Elgar Publishing.

Global Entrepreneurship and Development Institute (2013), *The Global
Entrepreneurship and Development Index (GEDI): A 17-Country Pilot Analysis
of the Conditions that Foster High-Potential Female Entrepreneurship*, accessed
12 July 2018 at http://i.dell.com/sites/doccontent/corporate/secure/en/Documents/
Gender_GEDI_Executive_Report.pdf.

Global Entrepreneurship Monitor (GEM) (2016/2017), *Global Entrepreneurship
Monitor 2016/2017: Report on Women's Entrepreneurship*. Wellesley: GERA
Research Association.

Hazell, N. (2017), 'Women make up less than one in five global startup founders: that's
a massive missed opportunity', accessed 10 July 2018 at https://www.smartcompany
.com.au/startupsmart/news-analysis/women-make-less-1-5-global-startup-founders
-thats-massive-missed-opportunity/.

Hendrickson, L., S. Bucifcal, A. Balaguer and D. Hansell (2015), *The Employment
Dynamics of Australian Entrepreneurship*, Office of the Chief Scientist, Department
of Industry and Science, Australian Government.

Henrekson, M. and D. Johansson (2010), 'Firm growth, institutions and structural
transformation', IFN Working Paper No. 820, accessed 13 July 2018 at http://www
.ifn.se/Wfiles/wp/wp820.pdf.

Huq, A. and C. Tan (2014), 'Women in Australian fast growth SMEs: how do they
approach growth as a deliberate choice?', paper presented at the ICSB Conference,
Dublin, 14 June.

Isenberg, D.J. (2010), 'How to start an entrepreneurial revolution: to ignite venture
creation and growth, governments need to create an ecosystem that sustains entrepreneurs. Here's what really works', *Harvard Business Review* (June), 41–50.

Kantis, H.D. and J.S. Federico (2012), 'Entrepreneurial ecosystems in Latin America:
the role of policies', Argentina: Entrepreneurial Development Programme, Institute
of Industry, Universidad Nacional de General Sarmiento.

Kimmorley, S. (2018), '11 charts show how Melbourne's startup sector compares to other major cities around the world', accessed 26 July 2018 at https://www.businessinsider.com.au/11-charts-showing-how-melbournes-startup-sector-compares-to-other-major-cities-around-the-world-2018-5.

Kinner, C. (2015), *Crossroads 2015: An Action Plan to Develop a Vibrant Tech Startup Ecosystem in Australia*, StartupAus, Australia.

Kolar, J. (2014), *Policies to Support High Growth Innovative Enterprises: Final Report from the SESSION II of the 2014 ERAC Mutual Learning Seminar on Research and Innovation Policies*, Brussels: European Commission.

Korlaar, L., M. Janssen, F. Barjak, R. Meyer and S. Lilischkis (2015), *Policies in Support of High-Growth Innovative Enterprises, Part 2: Policy Measures to Improve the Conditions for the Growth of Innovative Enterprises*, Luxembourg: European Commission, Publications of Office of the European Commission.

LaunchVic (2017), 'Victorian startup ecosystem mapping report', accessed 6 August 2019 at https://launchvic.org/files/Victorian-Startup-Ecosystem-Mapping-Report-2018.pdf.

Li, M., S.J. Goetz, M. Partridge and D.A. Fleming (2016), 'Location determinants of high-growth firms', *Entrepreneurship and Regional Development*, 28(1–2), 97–125.

Lilischkis, S., L. Korlaar, F. Barjak and R. Meyer (2013), 'Policies in support of high-growth innovative enterprises', accessed 10 July 2018 at http://www.eban.org/wpcontent/uploads/2013/12/HGEI-Policies_Policy-Brief-l_FinaLvl.3.pdf.

Mason, C. and R. Brown (2014), 'Entrepreneurial ecosystems and growth oriented entrepreneurship', in *Final Report to OECD*, Paris 30(1), 77–102.

Mazzarol, T. (2015), 'Entrepreneurial ecosystems and the role of regulation and infrastructure', accessed 6 August 2019 at http://theconversation.com/entrepreneurialecosystemsandtheroleofregulationandinfrastructure37030.

Morris, M.H., X. Neumeyer and D.F. Kuratko (2015), 'A portfolio perspective on entrepreneurship and economic development', *Small Business Economics*, 45(4), 713–728.

OECD (2008), *Measuring Entrepreneurship: A Digest of Indicators*, accessed 28 June 2018 at http://www.insme.org/files/3861/view.

Roper, S. (2016), 'Policy measures to support high-growth SMEs in the Western Balkans', OECD, accessed 10 July 2018 at https://www.oecd.org/global-relations/43469926.pdf.

Shane, S. (2009), 'Why encouraging more people to become entrepreneurs is bad public policy', *Small Business Economics*, 33(2), 141–149.

Stam, E. (2015), 'Entrepreneurial ecosystems and regional policy: a sympathetic critique', *European Planning Studies*, 23(9), 1759–1769.

Stam, E. and B. Spigel (2016), *Entrepreneurship Ecosystems*, The Netherlands: Tjalling C. Koopmans Research Institute.

Startup Genome (2018), *Melbourne Startup Ecosystem Report: Leading Australia into a New Economic Future*, accessed 10 December 2018 at https://startupgenome.com/.

Steffens, P.R., P. Davidsson and A. Omarova (2017), 'GEM Australia – 2016/17 Australian National Report', ACE Research Briefing Paper, 012, Australian Centre for Entrepreneurship Research, Brisbane, Queensland.

Steffens, P. and D. Hechavarría (2015), *Global Entrepreneurship Monitor: GEM Australia – 2014 National Report*, Australian Centre for Entrepreneurship Research, QUT Business School.

Steffens, P. and D. Hechavarría (2015), *Global Entrepreneurship Monitor: GEM Australia – 2014 National Report*, Australian Centre for Entrepreneurship Research, QUT Business School.

Steffens, P. and A. Omarova (2017), *Global Entrepreneurship Monitor: GEM Australia – 2016/17 National Report*, Australian Centre for Entrepreneurship Research, QUT Business School.

Tasmanian Government (2017a), 'Tasmania's key facts', accessed 13 July 2018 at https://www.cg.tas.gov.au/home/investment_attraction/why_invest_in_tasmania/tasmanias_key_facts.

Tasmanian Government (2017b), 'Department of State growth business statistics snapshot – June 2017', accessed 24 July 2018 at https://www.business.tas.gov.au/_data/assets/pdf_file/0006/168630/Small_Business_Statistics_Update_March_2018_3.pdf.

Vega, Y. (2012), *National Research on Women Business Owners and Female Entrepreneurs*, Australian Women Chamber of Commerce and Industry, Australia.

White, S.B. and P.D. Reynolds (1996), 'Government programs and high-growth new firms', *Frontiers of Entrepreneurship*, Wellesley, MA, Babson College.

World Economic Forum (2011), *Global Entrepreneurship and the Successful Growth Strategies of Early-Stage Companies*, accessed 1 July 2018 at http://www3.weforum.org/docs/WEF_Entrepreneurship_Report_2011.pdf.

World Economic Forum (2013), *Entrepreneurial Ecosystems around the Globe and Company Growth Dynamics*, Report Summary for the Annual Meeting of the New Champions 2013.

5. STEM education and women entrepreneurs in technology enterprises: explorations from Australia

Dilek Cetindamar, Elayn James, Thorsten Lammers, Alicia Pearce and Elizabeth Sullivan

1.   INTRODUCTION

Even though the entrepreneurship literature is overloaded with studies emphasising innovation-driven entrepreneurship, gender issues in these types of entrepreneurial ventures are essentially neglected (Brush et al., 2004; Ozkazanc-Pan and Muntean, 2018; Ranga and Etzkowitz, 2010). Considering technology entrepreneurship as gender neutral, the literature lacks observations of the relationship between gender and entrepreneurial activities in high-growth, high-technology, and knowledge-intensive business sectors (Dy et al., 2018). A number of recent studies have started to examine the positive relationship between gender differences in science, technology, engineering, and mathematics (STEM) education and entrepreneurship (Blume-Kohout, 2014). In particular, the findings of one study (Dilli and Westerhuis, 2018) clearly show that the high gender gap in science education enrolments reduces women's entrepreneurial activity in knowledge-intensive business sectors.

The study by Dilli and Westerhuis (2018) points out that, on average, the probability of finding female entrepreneurs in highly knowledge-intensive business sectors is 25 per cent higher in countries that achieve gender equality in science education compared to countries that do not. However, this relationship is not automatic as the analysis of individual countries included in the study (i.e., 19 European Union (EU) countries and the USA) shows different trends (Dilli and Westerhuis, 2018).

Educational background generally reflects an aspect of the exploration of the individual characteristics of entrepreneurs (Cetindamar et al., 2012).

However, educational organisations are embedded in institutions that collaboratively influence not only the educational access of individuals but also their occupational decisions after graduation (Bergmann et al., 2018). That is why any study considering women as entrepreneurs in technology-based areas needs to also seek to understand institutional factors, such as being excluded from certain technological fields and positions (Cetindamar and Beyhan, 2019; Ding et al., 2007; Faltholm et al., 2010). In other words, empirical studies about women's entrepreneurship need to develop knowledge of different institutional environments. One such empirical study, the Global Entrepreneurship Monitor (GEM) (2012) report, shows that the ratio of companies owned by women to companies owned by men varies a great deal from country to country: the lowest being 2 per cent, in Suriname and Japan, and the highest being 41 per cent, in Nigeria and Zambia. Another study (Thebaud, 2015) confirms the differences across 24 industrialised countries, pointing out institutions in the form of work–family as the main reason for these differences.

That is why the purpose of this chapter is to draw attention to the relationship between STEM education and women's entrepreneurship in technology enterprises by using an institutional perspective. To do so, we conduct a case study in Australia, as an example of a particular institutional environment. Even though our study is a preliminary research based on secondary resources, we still hope to explore some key factors that might explain why increasing the number of women entrepreneurs in high-tech ventures is not an automatic outcome of higher involvement of women students in STEM fields.

The chapter has five sections. After this short introduction, in the second section we will demonstrate the strong link between STEM education and women's entrepreneurship in high-technology sectors. The third section then explains the methodology used for this chapter, followed by the fourth section, presenting an Australian case study. In that section, we will explain developments in Australia as they relate to gender equality, STEM education and employment, as well as female entrepreneurship in high-technology sectors. It will also introduce a recent programme, called Science in Australia Gender Equity (SAGE), aimed at improving the gender gap in STEM education. In addition, we conduct an analysis of a specific educational institution that is a member of SAGE, namely the University of Technology, Sydney (UTS). The goal is to illustrate a specific implementation of the SAGE programme in a real-world context. The fifth and final section discusses the findings and insights gained from the analysis of the Australian example, and concludes with suggestions for further studies.

2.   UNVEILING THE RELATIONSHIP BETWEEN STEM EDUCATION AND WOMEN ENTREPRENEURS IN TECHNOLOGY ENTERPRISES

Female technology entrepreneurship remains outside the scope of entrepreneurship studies (Marlow and Dy, 2018), perhaps because women generally have proportionally less involvement (as a population) in science and technology-related education and, therefore, in STEM jobs (Orser et al., 2012). However, the scarcity of data concerning technology entrepreneurship by women makes it extremely challenging to pinpoint the problems that prevent women from participating in, or founding, science and technology-related businesses (Ozkazanc-Pan and Muntean, 2018). This is not to say that there are no STEM women entrepreneurs, simply that women in technology-based areas seem to struggle against institutional factors, such as being excluded from certain technological fields, particularly from positions associated with design and innovation, or access to social networks (Faltholm et al., 2010; Murray and Graham, 2007). This then affects the entrepreneurship pipeline.

This chapter focuses on female entrepreneurs in technology fields and attempts to tackle the limitations of the existing literature by focusing attention on the relationship between STEM education and women entrepreneurship in technology sectors.

Although women's engagement with higher education is increasing, the gender gap across certain disciplines and seniority levels is still central to academia. For a long time, enrolment of female students in tertiary education was the problem. However, policies focusing on closing the gender gap in tertiary education and encouraging women to access higher education have yielded positive outcomes. An OECD (2012) report reveals that the number of female students in tertiary education exceeded that of male students in most of the countries except Germany, Korea, Japan and Turkey (Sugimoto et al., 2015). Eurostat statistics show that in 2015, the percentage of female and male population (aged between 30 and 34) who have successfully completed tertiary education was 43.4 per cent and 34 per cent respectively in the EU28 countries (Eurostat, 2016). Women are embracing higher education—but not necessarily in STEM.

Therefore, although women's access to tertiary education has been increasing, due to gender stereotypes, women prefer to be educated outside STEM fields (Dilli and Westerhuis, 2018). The causes for the under-representation of women in these fields can be multi-factorial: a desire for work–life balance, the self-efficacy and lower self-confidence of women in mathematical or scientific fields, and the lack of role models and parental encouragement

(Cech et al., 2011; Sax and Bryant, 2006), plus a number of other reasons. EU statistics show that the number of higher educated female graduates in mathematics, science and technology fields per thousand persons aged 20–29 in 28 EU countries is 11.2, while that number is 22.9 for males (Eurostat, 2016). Compounding this situation, a recent investigation (Dilli and Westerhuis, 2018) shows how the enrolments of women into STEM have been unilaterally dropping across countries since 1970.

Gender inequality is not just rooted in women's limited access to—or uptake of—tertiary education in science and technology-related fields. Even after accessing tertiary education and pursuing an academic career or equivalent professional career, most women face formal and informal hurdles/barriers that restrict their achievements during their working lives. Studies reveal that female scientists produce fewer scholarly outputs, for example, which is problematic, as scholarly output is linked to academic advancement. Moreover, academic works with women as the first author receive fewer citations than those with male-first authors; and, unfortunately, this is valid across various disciplines and countries (Lariviere et al., 2013). Merit-based evaluation and promotion systems in academia, which rely on these markers as measures of competence, success or impact, therefore lead to fewer positions offered to female scientists and fewer opportunities for senior and executive positions. The antecedents of this productivity problem, however, are mostly ignored and male and female scientists are treated as having equal opportunities. Lariviere et al. (2013) point to women's networks as the cause of low productivity and low influence. While male scholars have better chances of accessing international networks, female scholars are mainly confined to national or local networks. Therefore, they suffer from a lack of adequate resources and cannot exploit the benefits of internationally collaborative networks to the same extent as their male counterparts do (Abreu and Grinevich, 2013; Ozkazanc-Pan and Muntean, 2018). West et al. (2013) argue that while the gender gap in the number of publications is closing, there is no significant change in how women are allocated more prestigious author positions in publications and in the number of solo-female-authored publications. Since hiring or promotions in academia are largely based on the number of publications by an individual, and their influence, women's careers and chances of rising to senior positions are directly influenced by these factors.

In fact, as studies indicate (Acker, 2006; Bird, 2011), gendered cultures within universities play a crucial role in shaping academic identities and careers. A general factor linked to this is the strong 'masculine' culture of traditional science workplaces. When the majority of the people working in science departments and laboratories are men, women can feel unwelcome, marginalised and intimidated by the atmosphere of such places. Women constitute only between 5 and 15 per cent of technology entrepreneurs within

Europe, and register a fraction of the patents for innovative products and processes (Wynarczyk and Marlow, 2010).

A leading question is, how are those types of hierarchical environments more masculine-supportive? Masculine culture is materialised in power relations, the underlying structures and governance mechanisms (Karataş-Özkan and Chell, 2015). A study (Rosa and Dawson, 2006) about female founders of United Kingdom (UK) university spinout companies in 20 leading universities shows that the proportion of female founders is 12 per cent. This is not surprising since, according to the 1999 data, 11.6 per cent of professors in UK higher education were female, and women represented only 3.1 per cent in engineering and technology faculties. When a woman is much less likely to become a scientist, she is, therefore, also less likely to become a science entrepreneur. That is why women are especially under-represented in the categories of science, innovation and entrepreneurship (Kyro and Hyrsky, 2008).

There is a need for new mechanisms to change attitudes towards, and perceptions of, women, and positively shift environmental and institutional factors. Ding et al. (2007) and Murray and Graham (2007) suggest that the gender gap among younger generations is closing. One reason is the equal mentoring by commercially active and, most probably, male advisers. One hypothesis is that female scientists who receive mentoring about technology commercialisation in the early stages of their career would probably attempt to access and build larger industry networks. Not having larger industry networks is a significant factor that prevents women from participating in entrepreneurial activities (Abreu and Grinevich, 2013; Ding and Choi, 2011; Faltholm et al., 2010; Murray and Graham, 2007). In order to mitigate this problem, women scientists use technology transfer offices (TTOs) as a mechanism that enables them to access industry (Colyvas et al., 2012; Goel et al., 2015). Apparently, development and improvement of such intermediary mechanisms can play an important role in female technology entrepreneurship (Orser et al., 2012). We expect that improved representation at senior levels will challenge the dominant masculine culture and both directly and indirectly increase women's representation in organisations.

3.   METHODOLOGY

Due to the nature of the research goals and the lack of empirical studies in this field, we are using a single case study method (Yin, 2009) for this chapter. By using the Australian case study, we aim to present information about STEM education and women entrepreneurs in high-tech fields for a particular type of country. We focus on the secondary data provided by public and private organisations. Polkowska (2013) uses statistical information provided by Eurostat to explain the barriers that women face in commercialisation in science. Koster

(2008) uses secondary data from various resources to investigate the linkages between economic development and entrepreneurship in India. In case study analysis, using multiple resources is important (Yin, 2009).

In order to seek out existing academic studies about Australia, we conducted a systematic literature review by using the ISI Web of Science (WoS) Core Collection database to find all the literature on the topic that could be of interest. When using the 'topic' field to search the database, ISI-WoS returns all articles with the search terms in their title, keywords, or abstracts. Scholars in management science consider this database to be the most comprehensive and use it frequently in systematic reviews, as discussed in detail by the study of Hausberg and Korreck (2018). We made a search by using the search terms 'women entrepreneur*' and 'Australia' for the period of 2000–2018 in November 2018. We combined the search terms with the constraint that it has to appear in one of the following WoS categories: management, business, economics, and women studies. By this restriction, we ended up with a set of 16 articles. The topics of these papers range from franchise issues to immigrant women entrepreneurs. None of them analyse the topic of women entrepreneurs in Australian technology ventures and we did not come across any coherent and comprehensive view of women's entrepreneurship in the Australian high-technology industry except the Dell (2017) study that is limited to the analysis of the Sydney entrepreneurial ecosystem.

We tried to utilise all relevant data available from secondary sources regarding STEM education and women technology entrepreneurs in Australia. Data came from a wide variety of national and international sources such as the Workplace Gender Equality Agency (2018) and Global Entrepreneurship Monitor (GEM, 2017a, 2017b). We present macro data on Australian women's labour participation, pay gap, female and male industries, STEM education and technology entrepreneurship, in order to provide the country's context. Then, the study presents the SAGE programme and its pilot application at UTS to give an idea of a specific institutional intervention in Australia that could help to create a bridge between STEM education and female entrepreneurship in STEM fields.

4.   INVESTIGATING AUSTRALIAN PRACTICES AND INSTITUTIONAL FACTORS

4.1   General Gender Issues

Australia is one of the world's advanced economies. However, it has low performance in gender equity comparative to its economic performance, both measured by World Economic Forum (WEF) indices. According to the Global Gender Gap Index reported at WEF 2017, Australia ranked 35th out of 144 countries (WEF, 2017). The Global Gender Gap Index examines the gap between men and women in four fundamental categories (sub-indexes): Economic Participation and Opportunity, Educational Attainment, Health and Survival, and Political Empowerment. Among these sub-categories, Australia ranked first in educational attainment, 42nd in economic participation and opportunity, 48th in political empowerment and 104th in the health and survival category. There are two concerns related to gender performance of Australia: (1) compared to its rank of 12th place in 2006 out of 115 countries, it seems the Australian position on gender equity has significantly declined, and (2) its gender equity is disproportionately below its economic success, considering that the Australian economy is 21st out of 144 countries in 2017.

4.1.1   Participation

Most Australian women are in paid employment, but their participation still lags behind that of men, with approximately 60 per cent participation compared with 71 per cent by men. In fact, Figure 5.1 shows that only about 35 per cent of women are in full-time paid employment, and, of employed women, part-time positions make up the largest proportion. What this means is that women continue to have reduced access to the leadership pipeline and higher paying roles, as only an estimated 6.3 per cent of management roles are part-time. There are also multiple repercussions for equity and prosperity over a lifetime. Average full-time weekly earnings for women are $1409, compared with men at $1662.70 (Australian Human Rights Commission (AHRC), 2018; Workplace Gender Equality Agency (WGEA), 2018), though in some industries the wage gap is significantly higher. In financial services, for example, the disparity is approximately 34 per cent (WGEA, 2018). The cumulative effect of these experiences is that Australian women retire on just more than half of the superannuation savings (58 per cent) of men (Chief Executive Women (CEW), 2017). A compounding factor is that women are the society's primary caregivers: 70 per cent of unpaid primary carers for children are women and 58 per cent of the primary carers for the elderly, and people with a disability or long-term health condition, are women (AHRC, 2018). They also live longer than men do.

Discrimination against Australian working mothers is also prevalent, with 50 per cent of women reporting workplace discrimination because of their pregnancy, parental leave or return to work after the birth of a child (AHRC, 2018). Sexual harassment, physical or sexual violence and violence from a partner are also part of the personal landscape of Australian women, with half experiencing sexual harassment and one in three women over the age of 15 experiencing physical or sexual violence (AHRC, 2018).

However, this current landscape of discrimination is at odds with Australia being acknowledged as one of the world leaders in the 2006 Gender Gap

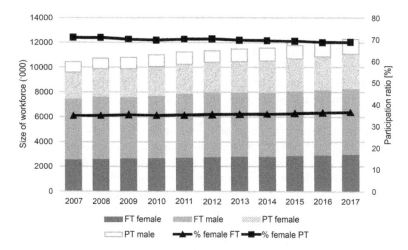

Source: Derived from ABS, 2018, Table 1. Labour force status by Sex, Australia – Trend, Seasonally adjusted and Original Publication 62021 http://www.abs.gov.au/AUSSTATS/abs@ .nsf/DetailsPage/6202.0Jun%202018?OpenDocument.

Figure 5.1   *Gender-specific development of full-time and part-time workforce participation in Australia*

Report at the WEF (Barns and Preston, 2010). A closer look at the analysis of that time seems to reveal it as being due to the increased participation rates reported in the area of part-time employment, low paid or precarious work (Barns and Preston, 2010), a questionable consideration. In short, although arguably ahead of many countries at that time, having now slipped to a rank of 35 (AHRC, 2018), progress for women and girls is challenged as a practical reality in recent history in Australia and is, in fact, going backwards.

There is also a query about the way participation rates, and other WEF Gender Gap Index categories are measured; they may not be appropriately applied and 'fail to capture the nuances and complexities of women's everyday lives' (Barns and Preston, 2010, p. 83). This implies that improved parity from social mobility, advancement and economic perspectives remains aspirational, and women continue to be locked out of more senior, potentially better paying, roles, and access to economic and financial security. In addition, the role of measurement comes into the spotlight, to help more usefully track progress and disadvantage. Encouragingly, in 2013 the Australian Council of Governments (COAG) launched its first national report on gender.

Some things, though, are changing. More women are now graduating from Australian universities than men (100 women for 80 men) (CEW, 2017), so there is an opportunity for improved employment access and participation in the future, especially if other barriers can be addressed.

4.1.2   The gender pay gap

Though women now outnumber male university graduates, female graduate salaries are 3.6 per cent lower than males (CEW, 2017), which is an improvement on recent years, where male starting salaries were about 9.6 per cent higher (CEW, 2016). This earning disparity then increases over time, reaching a peak disparity between the ages of 45 and 54 (WGEA, 2018), at which time men earn an average of 20 per cent more than women do. Referred to colloquially as the peak earnings period, the implications for the future economic security of women is, by then, significantly compromised.

According to the WGEA report of February 2018, there remains a pay gap of approximately 22.4 per cent for non-public sector organisations with 100 or more employees, so men working full-time earn nearly $26,527 a year more than women working full-time. On average, though, it sits at about 15 per cent, across public and private sectors. In some industries, however, the disparity is much greater. The pay gap is widest in the financial services and insurance sector (34.7 per cent), followed by the real estate (30 per cent) and construction (29 per cent) sectors, and lowest in the public sector. The fairest industries for male/female pay are public administration and safety (8.2 per cent gap), and accommodation and food services (6.3 per cent); followed by education and training (12.3 per cent), then healthcare and social assistance (13.3 per cent). The financial services and insurance sectors are also one of the bigger employment sectors for women—who make up approximately 55 per cent of the workforce— and yet these sectors have the largest overall pay disparity.

When analysed for STEM-based employers, in the top six industries to employ STEM graduates, as seen in Figure 5.2, there is a spread of disparity, from high wage gap to lower-end gap. Professional, scientific and technical services, for example, have a gap of 26 per cent compared with 15 per cent in manufacturing. This means that women entering STEM workplaces are likely to continue to have differing work experiences than their male counterparts.

4.1.3   Female and male industries and STEM

Figure 5.2 shows the biggest employers of women in Australia are: healthcare and social assistance (80 per cent female workforce), education and training (63 per cent), retail (58 per cent), financial and insurance (55 per cent), accommodation and food services (hospitality) (52 per cent), and arts and recreation (50 per cent). However, these industries do not offer the highest paying jobs at executive levels with the exception of finance and retail. Although the public administration sector has one of the lowest wage gaps, it is also one of the lowest employers of women, with a 79 per cent male workforce. Other

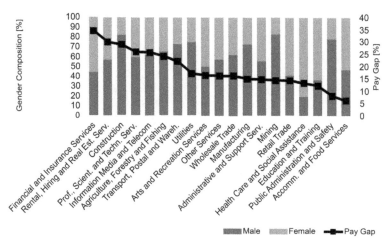

Source: Derived from WGEA, 2018 – Workplace Gender Equality Agency and Chief Scientist, 2016 – Australia's STEM workforce.

Figure 5.2   *Gender composition and pay gaps in Australian industries, 2017*

industry sectors that have predominantly male workforces are mining (84 per cent), construction (83 per cent), utilities (76 per cent), transport (74 per cent), and manufacturing (74 per cent). In the top six industries that are significant employers of STEM graduates, women can expect an average pay disparity of about 18 per cent, with a range from 8 to 34 per cent.

Another area where industries vary widely is in relation to leadership attainment. Seemingly, in the STEM sectors that employ a proportionally higher number of women, there is a higher level of female seniority attainment as shown in Figure 5.3. In the healthcare and education sectors, for example, the head of the business or CEO is female 37.5 per cent and 35 per cent of the time, respectively. That said, given that the workforce is 80 per cent and 63 per cent female this is still a significant decline in representation (a disparity of 44 per cent for healthcare), although 'as good as it gets', in terms of female executive leadership in the Australian context (37.5 per cent). The highest disparate representation between workforce gender and CEO is the financial services sector, with a 50 per cent gap.

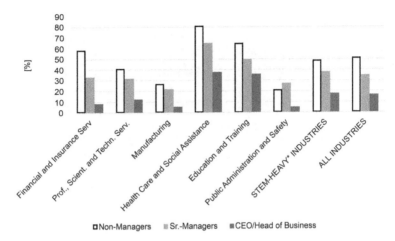

Note: Average of STEM-heavy industries to the left (which include 65% of all STEM graduates).

Source: Derived from WGEA, 2018 – Workplace Gender Equality Agency and Chief Scientist, 2016 – Australia's STEM workforce report.

Figure 5.3   *Female share of workforce across STEM-heavy industries and seniority levels in 2017*

4.2   STEM Education

Australia is a relatively 'late adopter' (Blackley and Howell, 2015) to the emphasis on STEM education. However, the movement has been rapidly gaining pace since 2013 following the publication of a number of influential papers arguing that STEM education will be vital to the future environmental, health, food, water, energy and economic needs of the country. The Australian state and territory governments signed the National STEM School Education Strategy 2016–2026 in December 2015, marking a significant step forward for the national STEM agenda.

That said, the number of women doing undergraduate studies in STEM fields in Australia has declined slightly over the past ten years, from approximately 38 per cent to 35 per cent of total student intake (see Figure 5.4). However, of those women that do study STEM, a slightly higher number are now pursuing postgraduate qualifications, up from 27 per cent in 2006 to 33 per cent in 2016.

There is also the question of whether the students are local or international, as a major and growing industry for Australia is that of tertiary education. It is unknown what proportion of the female STEM students are international,

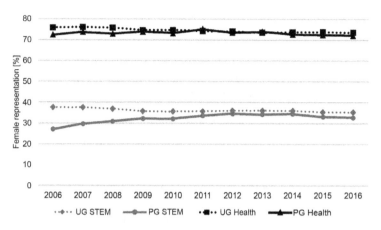

Notes: UG = Undergraduate; PG = Postgraduate; STEM contains the fields of education 'natural and physical sciences', 'information technology', 'engineering and related technologies', 'architecture and building', and 'agriculture environmental and related studies' as defined by the Department of Education and Training.

Source: Derived from uCube, 2018 – Department of Education and Training – Higher Education and Training Statistics http://highereducationstatistics.education.gov.au/Default.aspx.

Figure 5.4   Development of female representation in tertiary education completions in STEM and medicine fields

so the actual picture of the state of STEM education for residents of Australia and Australia's future STEM capabilities may not be represented by these statistics: further investigation of this issue is warranted. Although a number of international students will seek to remain in Australia after graduation, potentially for the medium to longer term, most return to their countries of origin, taking with them their STEM qualifications and future potential. In health studies, women continue to be the dominant population, making up approximately 74 per cent of the undergraduate students and 72 per cent of the postgraduate students (see Figure 5.4).

Consideration of the pathway beyond postgraduate study includes the possibility of the pursuit of an academic career. Though most postgraduates go on to private sector or public service careers, some will consider their involvement in academia. Of those that do, there is a distinct drop-off in academic seniority between Level A/B (Assistant Lecturer in the Australian higher education system) and Level E (corresponding to Professor) ranks for women. The question arises as to why women's academic careers falter beyond Level A/B. Men's careers, in contrast to most women's, accelerate beyond A/B, with disproportionately fewer women attaining senior academic roles. Factors affecting women's academic career trajectories include among others: equity in gaining ongoing secure employment; the availability of supportive, flexible workplaces during family formation (that also encourage men to have a role in family life); and the availability of re-entry programmes to support workforce re-engagement for primary caregivers. Social factors, such as networks and isolation, may also play a part. Again, this aspect of the topic warrants further investigation.

4.3   Technology Entrepreneurship and Entrepreneurship

Given that technology access and literacy impacts a person's ability to generate income, economic stability, or even wealth, it bodes well that a relatively high percentage of women in Sydney—the business and, arguably, technology capital of Australia—have access to the internet and own a smartphone, both respectively 89 per cent (Dell, 2017). Australia remains behind many comparable countries with regard to access to high speed, fibre-based internet, though the rollout of the National Broadband Network, a government programme, is helping to improve this situation.

However, despite high access to technology, women are under-represented in Australian start-ups. In recent years, the start-up scene in Australia has gained significant momentum, particularly in Sydney, an emerging entrepreneurship centre, ranked 23rd in the Technology pillar of the Dell WE Cities 2017 report. Yet women (Dell, 2017) lead only one in four start-ups. Further, only 10–18 per cent of venture-backed companies have a female founder (Dell, 2017). Access to capital is seen as a limiting factor in the success of most new businesses, especially those involving patents or spinouts from a university context (Allen et al., 2007; Rasmussen and Wright, 2015) and it appears to be a limiting factor for female entrepreneurs also (StartupMuster, 2018).

In a review of female participation in total early-stage entrepreneurial activity across G20 countries (see Figure 5.5), where data were available, Australia ranks in the bottom 50 per cent for female participation (the percentage of females who are in the process of starting a business), at 39 per cent, with a rank of 11 out of 17. The top five countries with the highest female participation rates are Indonesia (55 per cent), Brazil (51 per cent), Russia (45 per cent), Argentina (45 per cent) and Saudi Arabia (42 per cent). The United States just makes it into the top ten countries with the highest female participation rates, with a rank of 10 (41.5 per cent), but is the only country in the top ten with an innovation-driven categorisation. In Australia, many commentators would be surprised, even shocked, to discover that Australia ranks behind Saudi Arabia, and China, in terms of female participation in entrepreneurship, though obviously country-based distinctions do play a role, and it is important to understand the contextual and cultural nuances. France and Germany, for example, have very low general participation in entrepreneurship, male or female, possibly due to the high level of social stability. In Australia, and other countries, participation in entrepreneurship can be a sign of potential disadvantage—necessity-based entrepreneurialism—rather than a progressive agenda.

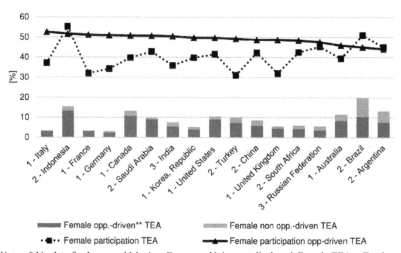

Notes: * No data for Japan and Mexico; European Union not displayed. Female TEA = Total Early-stage Entrepreneurial Activity – Percentage of the adult female population between the ages of 18 and 64 years who are in the process of starting a business (a nascent entrepreneur) or owner-manager of a new business which is less than 42 months old. Country categories according to World Economic Forum classification of economic development: 3: factor-driven; 2: efficiency-driven; 1: innovation-driven. **Opportunity-driven as opposed to necessity-driven.

Source: Derived from GEM, 2017 – Global Entrepreneurship Monitor 2016/17 https://www .gemconsortium.org/report/49812.

Figure 5.5   Female entrepreneurship participation in G20 countries

For female participation in opportunity-driven entrepreneurial activity (the percentage of women as opposed to men who are in the process of starting a business out of opportunity, as opposed to out of necessity), Australia ranks third-last of all countries (behind Brazil and Argentina). It seems, as the study of Thebaud (2015) finds in the study of 24 countries, women in Australia may tend to become business owners as Plan B, due to the prioritisation given to family over work and that is why their start-ups might be less growth-oriented ventures. However, this topic requires further research.

The majority of women do not benefit from progressive corporate policies on gender equity, where they exist. This is because just 36 per cent of women are in full-time employment (as shown above in Figure 5.1) and small businesses are the largest employer of Australians. Rather, women are falling through the cracks, and struggling to create a life for themselves that delivers the financial security they, and their dependants—their children, elderly relatives, disabled family members—need. Given that 81 per cent (ABS, 2018) of single-parent families are female, and only 34 per cent of single-parent families with a child under five have an employed adult, the social impact of this is enormous. This may explain why the necessity-driven participation of women in entrepreneurial activities in Australia is surprisingly high.

Other factors may relate to the entrepreneurial environment (Brush et al., 2017). The mainstream start-up movement, for example, is not gender neutral (Marlow and McAdam, 2015): there is an inherent masculine bias. The dominant narrative of entrepreneurship is male, and reflective of the embedded societal bias (Marlow and Dy, 2018). 'Entrepreneur' is not a gender-neutral term, nor is 'the internet' or 'digital technologies' (Dy et al., 2017), though they are falsely perceived as levellers or equal playing fields. Ideally, the world of entrepreneurs is meritocratic—and yet, the gendered nature of that environment has implications for access to the resources required for entrepreneurial success, such as engagement with third parties, mentoring, access to role models and support networks (Clarysse et al., 2011; Karataş-Özkan and Chell, 2015; Orser et al., 2012). These types of barriers inhibit the realisation of potential for female founders, and discourage entrepreneurialism in the first instance. In addition, personal factors, such as confidence and self-belief, without a supportive peer network, as well as exposure to entrepreneurialism in their early career, play an influential role in women's entrepreneurial activity (Brush et al., 2017).

Given that nearly 42 per cent of Level A academics (corresponding to research assistantship positions in Australia) are female (see Figure 5.6), a statistic many businesses would envy in terms of gender balance, the possibility of boosting female entrepreneurship from inside universities, before they depart or become discouraged, is one route to consider. However, despite efforts by the Australian Technology Network of Universities to boost the number of businesses they give birth to, academic entrepreneurship remains low. Even members of the SAGE programme have not been able to shift the dial yet.

The universities that do seem to be relatively successful in creating start-up companies as extensions of student work are the Australian Group of Eight (G8) universities: the older, most prestigious universities with the highest general and research reputations. The reasons why are not clear, but could be hypothesised as relating to access to capital and networks, typically required

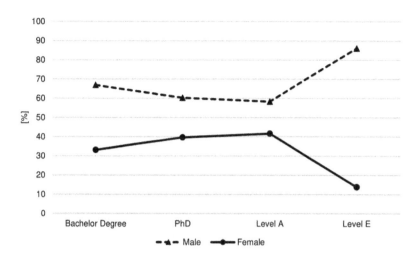

Source: Derived from SAGE, 2018 – http://www.sciencegenderequity.org.au/gender-equity-in-stem/.

Figure 5.6   *Gender representation by student enrolments and academic level in STEM, Australia 2014*

by any start-up, inside or outside academia, to get off the ground. Culture or environment may also be a factor. As shown in Figure 5.7, although UTS is slightly above average compared with all universities, and average compared with other technology universities, the G8 universities have consistently beaten all other categorisations in the number of start-ups created over the last few years.

4.4 SAGE Programme

A recent sector-wide approach in Australia, the SAGE Athena SWAN pilot, acknowledges that outdated workplace conditions and culture may be affecting the participation of women in STEM and medicine (M) research careers. The pilot is based upon the Athena SWAN accreditation framework from the United Kingdom that has been in place since 2005. While this pilot is in its infancy, with the first of three cohorts lodging applications for initial accreditation in early 2018 and the others in 2019, developments at one participant, the University of Technology Sydney (UTS), show that the pilot is already affecting university and faculty approaches to managing diversity.

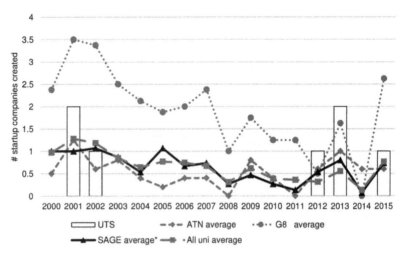

Note: Comprising university members of SAGE cohort 1 (SAGE, 2018).

Sources: Derived from SAGE, 2018 – http://www.sciencegenderequity.org.au/cohort-1
-members/ and NSRC, 2018 – https://www.industry.gov.au/data-and-publications/national
-survey-of-research-commercialisation-nsrc.

Figure 5.7   Number of start-up companies created from universities

SAGE is a joint forum of the Australian Academy of Science and the Australian Academy of Technology and Engineering, developed specifically in response to issues of gender imbalance in representation within the Academy, and in STEM and medicine more generally. SAGE states that one of the drivers of this change was an event in 2013 where the year's cohort of fellows elected to the Academy of Science was 100 per cent male (SAGE, 2018).

In 2014, a forum and workshop was convened to consider measures to address unequal outcomes for women in the academy election process and STEM more generally. Discussion at the forum focused on higher education participation and workforce presence, and noted that less than one in five professorial positions were then held by women in science, even though there is gender parity at the postdoctoral level. Figure 5.4 melds two data sets—student completion figures and cross-sector university workforce figures provided to the Commonwealth Department of Education—to attempt a representation of gender presence at each level of academic attainment. It shows that while women make up 40 per cent of doctoral completions and 42 per cent of entry-level academic workers, attrition of women occurs throughout this pipeline to create a highly significant under-representation of women at senior positions, dropping to around 10 per cent at Level E positions as given in Figure 5.6.

While the impact on entrepreneurship was not specifically considered, one of the key workshop discussions related to ways that rigid academic structures impacted mobility across sectors, particularly where stints in industry affected publication rates and, therefore, the potential for academic career progression. Figure 5.7 bears this analysis out, showing that the number of start-up companies created from universities had decreased sector-wide over the years 2000–2015, despite consistently higher rates of conversion from the G8 universities. Workshop participants felt that disciplinary silos and silos between industry and higher education reduce the opportunity for collaboration and career pathways that mix industry and academic research expertise, to the detriment of all sectors. The workshop concluded that women disproportionately felt the impact of this lack of mobility, since their opportunities were likely to be greater if there was greater mobility after career interruptions.

Reviewing the data, workshop participants concluded that gender equity in the sciences was a long-term project in Australia. To achieve a long-term elimination of gender imbalance in the sciences, a short-term indicator of success would be achieving widespread support in the sector for action to combat gender inequity. The outcome of this forum was to license to Australia the Athena SWAN pilot from the ECU with this aim.

Athena SWAN can be characterised as a continuous improvement programme for gender good practice. A staged programme, conducted in the medium and long term, requires the organisation, and its constituent faculties, schools or departments, to attain accreditation under the Athena SWAN Bronze, Silver and Gold Award scheme. Qualification for progression requires incrementally more leadership internally and in the sector, investment and evidence of progress in redressing gender inequality, with the organisation as a whole unable to progress past the bronze level award without individual accreditation of the majority of its constituent areas. In the United Kingdom, participation in the programme was linked to eligibility to apply for some of the National Institute for Health Research funding, with a silver award required for shortlisting for Biomedical Research Centre funding.

In the first instance, 32 Australian national research and higher education bodies signed up to the ten principles of the Athena SWAN Charter and contributed subscription fees to participate in a sector-wide pilot in two cohorts. Later, this was expanded to a third cohort of eight additional institutions.

4.5   UTS

UTS, a sector leader in equity and diversity already, had a strong reputation for innovative and progressive approaches to gender equity, holding the

Workplace Gender Equality Agency's Employer of Choice award since its inception; and through the Research Equity Initiative that was implemented from the Office of the Deputy Vice Chancellor Research in 2012. This suite of programmes provided targeted research support that women and primary carers could access to maintain research activity, outputs, and conference attendance during times of intensive carer responsibilities and on returning from parental and carers leave. The Athena SWAN programme was arguably an extension of this sector-leader approach. As such, UTS applied to participate in the SAGE pilot in 2015, nominating successfully for the first cohort and commencing the pilot in late 2015, and was awarded an Athena SWAN Bronze Award with the first cohort of applicants in December 2018.

There was widespread executive support and championing of the pilot from the Vice Chancellor and senior university and faculty leadership. UTS adopted the ten charter principles and actively engaged in the process from the outset, with proactive engagement from STEM faculties. UTS included three faculties and two schools in STEM, the faculties of Science, Engineering and Information Technology, and Health, and the Graduate School of Health and the School of Architecture. UTS does not have a medical school but included the health faculty (comprising nursing, midwifery, sports and exercise science and public health) and graduate school of health (comprising psychology, pharmacy, orthoptics and physiotherapy) under the 'M' in STEM(M). UTS, as a member of the first cohort, followed a highly proscriptive pilot programme with sequential training, working towards submission of the first bronze award applications in March 2018. This included appointing a senior Academic Lead of the pilot (Assistant Deputy Vice Chancellor Research), who chaired and established the UTS Self-Assessment Team (SAT) to oversee the award application and development of a four-year action plan to address gender inequity. The SAT was a university-wide committee with a gendered and diverse membership of academic levels. At a faculty or school level, equity and diversity committees were established to engage staff in the workplace around the investigation of gender equity in STEM(M). The SAT drove a programme of collation and gendered analysis of disparate and varying fit-for-purpose electronic and paper-based human resources, recruitment, training, promotion, equity and diversity; and research metrics data to develop a snapshot of the current state of gender equity in its STEM(M) disciplines. Any gaps in the data were augmented by qualitative interviews and focus groups of academics and professional staff in STEM(M) to contextualise gender experiences in research in STEM(M). A gendered lens was taken to existing policies and practices with the qualitative research identifying barriers to effective policy implementation at an operational level in the faculties. Other data were sourced from routine sector surveys the university participated in, and combined with the quantitative and qualitative data aforementioned, to provide a comprehensive picture of the institutional structures, systems, and culture which contribute to gender inequity at UTS. In response to this, a four-year action plan was developed and signed off by the university executive to address gender inequity in its STEM(M) disciplines and more widely across the university from 2018–2022.

A major outcome to date of UTS's participation on the Athena SWAN pilot has been the compiling of evidence, by organisational level, showing differing pictures of gender inequity, and these have been successfully disseminated at all levels of the university. This had led to executive action and faculty and school ownership and engagement; a systematic reframing of gender equity to business-as-usual; and commitment to policy review and resourcing of the four-year action plan to progress gender equity at UTS.

Table 5.1 presents faculty profiles and areas identified for inclusive improvement, including UTS staff concerns such as the recruitment of women, particularly in areas where there are few women; promotion of women; increased conversion of postdoctoral fellowships to continuing roles; more effective staff induction programmes; and workforce and organisational culture.

Similarly, the initiatives taken by each faculty at UTS show a wide variety, as given in Table 5.2. The major initiative seems to be giving intentional focus on the recruitment of women to senior leadership positions, including direct appointments.

UTS engaged with the SAGE programme to start to better understand how structural bias was affecting women and what was influencing access to opportunities. With a clearer view of how it functions as an institution a number of interventions, evolutions and processes can be put in place. Of the 40 higher education organisations within Australia who have now engaged with the SAGE programme, UTS is one of the major supporters of women in STEM and entrepreneurship generally. Top management at UTS has rolled out a programme of interventions to enhance the opportunities for women at UTS. The experience of UTS clearly shows the importance of institutions in shaping organisational interventions through the generation of a gender-inclusive environment for both STEM education and the workplace.

4.6   The Women in STEM Decadal Plan

Addressing workforce and pipeline issues affecting women's participation in STEM research and business activity is an area of emerging national policy development in Australia, with possible positive impacts for STEM entrepreneurship activity. The Women in STEM Decadal Plan, launched in April 2019, has been developed by the Australian Academy of Science and the Australian Academy of Technology and Engineering at the request of the Australian Government (Decadal Plan, 2019). These bodies are also the sponsor bodies of the Athena SWAN pilot.

Table 5.1   *Faculty profiles and areas identified for inclusive improvement as at 31 March 2017*

Faculty	Number of schools	Overall gender balance	Gender distribution	Areas identified by staff and committees for focus
Engineering and Information Technology	5 Increased to 6 over life of pilot	Majority male	Women more concentrated at junior levels Segmented by discipline, related to gender profile of candidate pool Increase in proportion of women at senior levels over life of the pilot	Recruitment of women, particularly in areas where there are few women Promotion of women Increased conversion of postdoctoral fellowships to continuing roles More effective staff induction programmes
Science	2	Majority male	Women more concentrated at junior levels Segmented by discipline, with life sciences more balanced than mathematical and physical sciences	Recruitment Workforce development Workforce and organisational culture
Health	1 (5 internal disciplines)	Majority female	Men more concentrated at more senior levels Segmented by discipline	Recruitment and appointment of women Retention and professional support Workplace culture
Graduate School of Health	1 (6 internal disciplines)	Majority female	Men more concentrated at senior levels	Recruitment Development and promotion Workplace culture
Architecture	1	Gender balanced*	Women more concentrated at junior levels	Workplace culture

Note: Within 45–55% range.

Source: Town meeting held on 12 December 2017, Sydney, Australia.

Table 5.2   *Specific equity measures by faculty*

Faculty and Focus	Initiatives
Engineering and Information Technology	Unconscious bias training for executive and unit heads
	Intentional focus on recruitment of women to senior leadership positions, including direct appointments
	Staff mentoring programme established
	Formalised induction programme
	Core meeting hours guideline
	Parental leave support—engagement of a postdoctoral fellow to continue research and engagement activities while an academic is on parental leave
Science	Recommendations to use direct appointments to amend gender balance
	Focusing recruitment language to attract and support female candidates
	Pilot evaluation of specific recruitment rounds to identify potential bias or process changes
	Review of discipline profiles to include equity concerns
	Access to specific professional development opportunities for identified female staff
	Letters of commendation from the Dean recommending particular community-building activities
	Dean's awards for community contributions—positive recognition of community-building activities undertaken by women in disproportionate measure
	Core meeting hours guidelines
	Events showcasing and celebrating women in STEMM
Graduate School of Health	Ensure gender balance on recruitment panels
	Develop a framework of cultural sensitivity across platforms to aid retention and recruitment
	Core meeting hours guidelines
	Gender-balanced representation on all committees
	Establishment of a mechanism to review workload guidelines
	Workshops and events focusing on discipline-based cultural inclusion
Faculty of Health	Review recruitment processes for unconscious bias
	Review workload protocol with an 'equity and diversity lens'
	Create standing item for equity and diversity at discipline and centre team meetings
	Review other faculty initiatives with a view to adaptation and adoption

Source: Town meeting held on 12 December 2017, Sydney, Australia.

The purpose of the Decadal Plan is to provide a ten-year roadmap to build sustained higher levels of engagement with STEM education and careers among women and girls, focusing on participation and retention from school through to the workforce, including outcomes related to:

- long-term improvements in gender equity
- improved quality in STEM skills and expertise in Australia

- increased access for women and girls to participate in STEM
- expanded career and study opportunities for women
- benefits to business from increased access to STEM skills.

In 2018, the Decadal Plan office released a discussion paper and conducted extensive industry and sector consultations around these matters. The discussion paper raised issues around STEM career paths, workforce culture and pipelines, and the value of diversity to business outcomes, and recognised the difficulty faced by many women in setting up small businesses both within and outside STEM streams. Questions for consultation focused on addressing barriers to STEM careers and educational engagement, and asked stakeholders to outline areas where effort would be best placed in a strategic approach to improving life cycle participation. Submissions to the process were not made public. The launch of the Plan signals the conclusion of a significant programme of work to map stakeholder and community responses to the challenge of addressing these issues.

5.   CONCLUDING REMARKS

After highlighting the deficiency in the literature of studies on women's technology entrepreneurship, this chapter argues that entrepreneurship theory should take into account the role of organisational/institutional factors in order to overcome existing gender-blind frameworks available in the extant literature. To illustrate how an institutional lens could improve our understanding of gender issues in entrepreneurship, this chapter examines the link between STEM education and female technology entrepreneurship. In line with the findings of a few recent works (Dilli and Westerhuis, 2018), our study shows that even though STEM education could possibly lead to careers in entrepreneurship in tech ventures, this progression is not an automatic link. Many institutional factors are in play determining the outcome. For example, the Australian case study shows that having successful programmes in STEM education has to be complemented with clear programmes related to entrepreneurship initiatives.

In addition, this chapter contributes to empirical works in the entrepreneurship literature. It presents a macro-level analysis of Australia as a case study, to understand how institutional factors in education, such as programmes targeting the education of women in STEM fields, could increase the likelihood of women becoming entrepreneurs in technology ventures. The chapter highlights a few key lessons from the analysis of the Australian case and proposes a number of policy suggestions that can be relevant to many countries searching for ways of improving their female technology entrepreneurs.

5.1   Lessons from Australia

Australia is not as progressive as may be assumed internationally when it comes to gender equality, and, in fact, has slipped backwards in recent years. Upon closer analysis, a perception of success closing the gender gap may be unpicked—participation rates include part-time work, low income and precarious work. Equal pay remains elusive, with pay gaps widening over lifetimes, and despite more women graduating from universities than men, the pipeline into management, senior manager, executive and board-level roles drops away by mid-career. Pay peaks around age 45 and then slides, while men's pay continues to grow until their mid-50s. Infamously, women ultimately retire on about half of that of men, but live an additional five or six years. Only about 25 per cent of Australian Stock Exchange-listed Top 300 companies' board members are women (Australian Institute of Company Directors, July 2018), and women remain under-represented in political office, with one of the leading parties, in particular, currently in the midst of a gender crisis, following a leadership coup in August 2018.

Viewed as a vital capability for the workforce of the future, careers in STEM could offer women an opportunity for closing the economic gap and improving social mobility. The STEM education agenda has gained significant momentum in the last couple of years in Australia with significant results to reduce the gender gap. Both boys and girls are now more exposed to STEM throughout their education—from early childhood, through to primary and high school. Educational institutions have a key role to play, since their interventions can help to preserve the female STEM pipeline not just through the educational process, but also beyond, once these women are in the workforce. The Australian exercise of the SAGE programme has such an intervention logic and it has been in practice since 2015. Since this programme is a new one, its full impact will be realised in the coming years. However, as a whole, SAGE is a well-regarded initiative that offers constructive insight for an international audience to understand how organisations in Australia are attempting to address gender inequality starting with STEM education. In line with recent studies (Bergmann et al., 2018), we believe that supportive organisational environments will, in turn, improve gendered cultures within universities thereby improving opportunities for women, and play a crucial role in shaping academic identities and careers for women in STEM fields, including entrepreneurial careers.

As Dilli and Westerhuis (2018) have pointed out, STEM education is the first step in the right direction for establishing careers in technology entrepreneurships for women. Australia seems to have a good starting point through programmes such as SAGE in supporting STEM education and opportunities, but it seems to fail in taking the next step for women's entrepreneurship in technology fields. Given that nearly 42 per cent of Level A academics in Australia are women, the possibility of boosting female entrepreneurship from inside universities, before they depart or become discouraged, is one route to consider for a positive long-term impact on a pipeline of female technology entrepreneurs. Thus, Australia should start considering complementary programmes that could strengthen the link between education and entrepreneurship in STEM fields. It might be through either SAGE initiatives or new independent programmes.

Australia set a great example by producing organisational policies such as SAGE and the Decadal Plan that show the commitment and stakeholder involvement in producing a long-term policy agenda for STEM education and careers among Australian women and girls. Based on our observations from these policies that are strong institutional interventions, we would like to offer a few policy suggestions that might improve the relationship between STEM education and women entrepreneurship in high-technology fields:

- A clear focus on technology entrepreneurship is absent from the national policy discussion on STEM education and careers. This is a fertile field for research calling for a focused partnership approach between the Australian Government and the entrepreneurship sector, building on the Women in STEM Decadal Plan.
- It would be beneficial to take a life cycle approach in the education system to build positive cultural attitudes encouraging women and girls to enter STEM fields. Such integrated education initiatives contribute to awareness of STEM careers too and exposure to female role models in STEM plays a major part in developing girls' positive self-identity in STEM that can further help women to see STEM as an inclusive and viable career pathway.
- It is necessary to give access to scholarships and fellowships for women in STEM as a targeted policy measure to promote gender equality and achieve quotas to encourage women's participation in STEM education and careers.
- Organisations could develop support through intermediary mechanisms. For example, women scientists need to access industry, and technology transfer offices can play an important role in female technology entrepreneurship.
- Female scientists who receive mentoring and training about technology commercialisation in the early stages of their career would probably attempt to access and build larger industry networks and consider becoming entrepreneurs. There is a need to supply mentoring and training for entrepreneurship.
- Programmes need to systematically address structural and organisational gender bias in STEM in the tertiary education sector through monitoring

of institutional policy, processes and outcomes by gender. For example, Athena SWAN follows policies specific to recruitment and career progression by gender; and monitors access to nationally competitive research funding by gender of investigators with the aim of uncovering informal and formal barriers to gender equity and inclusion.

- Cultural changes in the workplace are necessary for education as well as career building. As shown in the Athena SWAN pilot and other targeted sectoral workplace culture programmes, support for proactive changes to cultures of bias reduces gender disparity. An important consideration of the Athena SWAN programme into the next cycle will be the intersectional relationship between cultural background and gendered progression, and in an Australian context, strategies to ensure a positive model of Indigenous STEM workforce engagement are a priority.
- Organisations must consider increasing women representation at senior levels. Having women scientists at senior levels will challenge the dominant masculine culture and both directly and indirectly increase women representation in organisations. This is also true for entrepreneurial ventures.

5.2   Limitations

This study is not without its flaws but we consider it a preliminary work to scratch the surface and catch the attention of researchers in the examination of how institutions influence STEM education and their long-lasting impact on women technology entrepreneurs in Australia and beyond. There are four key limitations. First, our analysis derives mainly from macro-level data in Australia and there are some limitations. For example, data about female high-technology entrepreneurship are almost non-existent. Second, considering that SAGE started in 2015, its full impact is yet to come and outcomes are currently immature. Third, the study covers only Australia as a case study. Having one country with a unique cultural setting constrains the generalisability of our findings. It would be beneficial to have more studies from other countries in order to enrich the observation of the dynamics at play. Fourth, this study has not taken into consideration individual or cultural-level factors that could also influence the number of women choosing to become entrepreneurs in high-technology ventures. Additionally, there might also be significant organisational factors women interact with in a number of ways. This could be a fruitful research topic for future studies.

5.3   Suggestions for Future Research

In line with the findings of Dilli and Westerhuis (2018), educational institutions have critical roles in supporting not only education but also the career choices of students in the long term, and their inclinations towards becoming entrepreneurs. Given the variety of institutional differences across countries, it would be valuable to pursue cross-cultural studies to identify different programmes and policies designed to overcome institutional barriers for women. In particular, it seems the Australian study shows a centralised and proactive effort in diffusing gender equity in Australian universities, through SAGE. There is a significant improvement opportunity with respect to the education of women in STEM fields.

However, the improvement is not yet satisfactory in employment participation in certain sectors with STEM degrees and still low levels of participation in high-technology ventures, and it is unfortunately failing to result in senior female positions across sectors. Therefore, even though a higher ratio of women in STEM education could positively influence the likelihood of women becoming technology and science entrepreneurs, future studies could more deeply investigate the question of what kind of institutional policies and programmes could facilitate the smooth progression of women graduates from higher education into careers in STEM fields, in particular, becoming entrepreneurs. As the study of Bergmann et al. (2018) shows, researchers need to find out ways of changing institutional environments to foster and accommodate female entrepreneurs. In academia, progress might be reflected in having a higher ratio of women in STEM employment and securing senior positions for women.

Additionally, further studies might consider combining individual, organisational, and societal factors in a comprehensive framework and start to observe their complex interactions as mentioned above. That is why a micro-level analysis of women technology entrepreneurs in-depth, through surveys and interviews, would be desirable for a thorough investigation that could help to generate pervasive conclusions. Only then could academic research start to deliver a more-informed line of inquiry, to establish whether organisational factors might overcome societal and/or individual limitations on women in STEM or vice versa.

We hope this chapter draws the attention of colleagues interested in these topics and their future exploration.

REFERENCES

Abreu, M. and V. Grinevich (2013), 'The nature of academic entrepreneurship in the UK: widening the focus on entrepreneurial activities', *Research Policy*, 42(2), 408–422.

ABS (Australian Bureau of Statistics) (2018), 'Labour force status', accessed 10 August 2018 at http://www.abs.gov.au/AUSSTATS/abs@.nsf/DetailsPage/6202.0Jun%202018?OpenDocument.

Acker, J. (2006), 'Inequality regimes: gender, class and race in organizations', *Gender & Society*, 20(4), 441–464.

Allen, S.D., A.N. Link and D.T. Rosenbaum (2007), 'Entrepreneurship and human capital: evidence of patenting activity from the academic sector', *Entrepreneurship Theory and Practice*, 32(6), 937–951.

Australian Human Rights Commission (2018), 'Gender equality: face the facts', accessed 15 August 2018 at https://www.humanrights.gov.au/sites/default/files/2018_Face_the_Facts_Gender_Equality.pdf.

Australian Institute of Company Directors (2018), 'Board diversity statistics', ASX Top 300, March, accessed 12 August 2018 at https://aicd.companydirectors.com.au/advocacy/board-diversity/statistics.

Barns, A. and A. Preston (2010), 'Is Australia really a world leader in closing the gender gap?', *Feminist Economics*, 16(4), 81–103.

Bergmann, H., M. Geissler, C. Hundt and B. Grave (2018), 'The climate for entrepreneurship at higher education institutions', *Research Policy*, 47(4), 700–716.

Bird, S.R. (2011), 'Unsettling universities' incongruous, gendered bureaucratic structures: a case-study approach', *Gender, Work & Organization*, 18(2), 202–230.

Blackley, S. and J. Howell (2015), 'A STEM narrative: 15 years in the making', *Australian Journal of Teacher Education*, 40(7), 102–112.

Blume-Kohout, M. (2014), 'Understanding the gender gap in STEM fields entrepreneurship', SSRN scholarly paper, Rochester: Social Science Research Network, accessed 11 July 2018 at https://papers.ssrn.com/abstract=2506835.

Brush, C., A. Ali, D. Kelley and P. Greene (2017), 'The influence of human capital factors and context on women's entrepreneurship: which matters more?', *Journal of Business Venturing Insights*, 18, 105–113.

Brush, C.G., N.M. Carter, E.J. Gatewood, P.G. Greene and M.M. Hart (2004), *Clearing the Hurdles: Women Building High-Growth Businesses*, Upper Saddle River, NJ: Financial Times/Prentice Hall.

Cech, E., B. Rubineau, S. Silbey and C. Seron (2011), 'Professional role confidence and gendered persistence in engineering', *American Sociological Review*, 76(5), 641–666.

Cetindamar, D. and B. Beyhan (2019), 'Unveiling women entrepreneurship in technology ventures: gendered organization and gendered society interactions', in F.P. Appio, F. Therin and H. Yoon (eds.), *Handbook of Research on Techno-Entrepreneurial Ecosystems*, 3rd edition, Cheltenham, UK and Northampton, MA, USA: Edward Elgar Publishing.

Cetindamar, D., V. Gupta, E. Karadeniz and N. Egrican (2012), 'What the numbers tell: the impact of human, family, and financial capital on women and men's entry into entrepreneurship in Turkey', *Entrepreneurship and Regional Development*, 24(1/2), 29–51.

Chief Executive Women (2016), 'A long way to the top', accessed 1 July 2018 at https://cew.org.au/wp-content/uploads/2016/07/CEW%20A%20long%20way %20to%20the%20top.pdf.

Chief Executive Women (2017), 'A long way to the top – updated March 2017', accessed 1 July 2018 at https://cew.org.au/wp-content/uploads/2017/03/A-long-way -to-the-top_Updated-MARCH-17.pdf.

Clarysse, B., V. Tartari and A. Salter (2011), 'The impact of entrepreneurial capacity, experience and organizational support on academic entrepreneurship', *Research Policy*, 40(8), 1084–1093.

Colyvas, J.A., K. Snellman, B. Bercovitz and M. Feldman (2012), 'Disentangling effort and performance: a renewed look at gender differences in commercializing medical school research', *Journal of Technology Transfer*, 37(4), 478–489.

Decadal Plan (2019), 'Women in STEM Decadal Plan', accessed 28 March 2019 at https://aas.eventsair.com/women-in-stem/scope.

Dell (2017), 'WE Cities 2017', IHS Markit, accessed 3 July 2018 at https://www.dell .com/learn/si/en/sicorp1/press-releases/2017-07-17-dell-ranks-top-50-global-cities -for-women-entrepreneurs.

Dilli, S. and G. Westerhuis (2018), 'How institutions and gender differences in edu- cation shape entrepreneurial activity: a cross-national perspective', *Small Business Economics*, 52(2), 371–392.

Ding, W. and E. Choi (2011), 'Divergent paths to commercial science: a comparison of scientists' founding and advising activities', *Research Policy*, 40(1), 69–80.

Ding, W.W., F. Murray and T.E. Stuart (2007), 'Gender differences in patenting in the academic life sciences', *Science*, 313, 665–667.

Dy, A.M., S. Marlow and L. Martin (2017), 'A web of opportunity or the same old story? Women digital entrepreneurs and intersectionality theory', *Human Relations*, 70(3), 286–311.

Dy, A.M., L. Martin and S. Marlow (2018), 'Emancipation through digital entrepre- neurship? A critical realist analysis', *Organization*, 25(5), 585–608.

Eurostat (2016), 'European Statistics', accessed 10 July 2018 at http://ec.europa.eu/ eurostat/statistics-explained/index.php/Tertiary_education_statistics.

Faltholm, Y., L. Abrahamsson and E. Kallhammer (2010), 'Academic entrepreneur- ship: gendered discourses and ghettos', *Journal of Technology Management & Innovation*, 5(1), 51–63.

GEM (2012), *GEM 2012 Women's Report*, London: GEM (prepared by D.J. Kelley, C.G. Brush, P.G. Greene, Y. Litovsky and Global Entrepreneurship Research Association), accessed 31 May 2018 at http://www.babson.edu/Academics/ centers/blank-center/global-research/gem/Documents/GEM%202012%20Womens %20Report.pdf.

GEM (2017a), *GEM Australia 2016/17 Report*, accessed 3 May 2018 at https://www .gemconsortium.org/report/50035.

GEM (2017b), *Global Entrepreneurship Monitor 2016/17*, accessed 3 May 2018 at https://www.gemconsortium.org/report/49812.

Goel, R.K., D. Goktepe-Hulten and R. Ram (2015), 'Academics' entrepreneurship pro- pensities and gender differences', *Journal of Technology Transfer*, 40(1), 161–177.

Hausberg, J.P. and S. Korreck (2018), 'Business incubators and accelerators: a co-citation analysis-based, systematic literature review', *Journal of Technology Transfer*, accessed 20 November 2018 at https://doi.org/10.1007/s10961-018-9651 -y.

Karataş-Özkan, M. and E. Chell (2015), 'Gender inequalities in academic innovation and enterprise: a Bourdieuian analysis', *British Journal of Management*, 26(1), 109–125.

Koster, S. (2008), 'Entrepreneurship and economic development in a developing country: a case study of India', *Journal of Entrepreneurship*, 17(2), 117–137.

Kyro, P. and K. Hyrsky (2008), 'Woman entrepreneurship programme breaks government's gender neutrality in Finland', *International Journal of Entrepreneurship & Innovation Management*, 8(6), 607–623.

Lariviere, V., C. Ni, Y. Gingras, B. Cronin and C.R. Sugimoto (2013), 'Global gender disparities in science', *Nature*, 504, 211–213.

Marlow, S. and M. Dy (2018), 'Annual review article: is it time to rethink the gender agenda in entrepreneurship research?', *International Small Business Journal: Researching Entrepreneurship*, 36(1), 3–22.

Marlow, S. and M. McAdam (2015), 'Incubation or induction? Gendered identity work in the context of technology business incubation', *Journal of Entrepreneurship Theory and Practice*, 39(4), 791–816.

Murray, F. and L. Graham (2007), 'Buying science and selling science: gender differences in the market for commercial science', *Industrial and Corporate Change*, 16(4), 657–689.

NSRC (2018), *National Survey of Research Commercialization*, Australian Government Department of Industry, Innovation and Science, accessed 22 May 2018 at https://www.industry.gov.au/data-and-publications/national-survey-of-research -commercialisation-nsrc.

OECD (2012), *Education at a Glance 2012*, Paris: OECD.

Orser, B., A. Riding and J. Stanley (2012), 'Perceived career challenges and response strategies of women in the advanced technology sector', *Entrepreneurship and Regional Development*, 24(1/2), 73–93.

Ozkazanc-Pan, B. and S.C. Muntean (2018), 'Networking towards (in)equality: women entrepreneurs in technology', *Gender, Work & Organization*, 25(4), 379–400.

Polkowska, D. (2013), 'Women scientists in the leaking pipeline: barriers to the commercialisation of scientific knowledge by women', *Journal of Technology Management & Innovation*, 8(2), 156–165.

Ranga, M. and H. Etzkowitz (2010), 'Athena in the world of techne: the gender dimension of technology, innovation and entrepreneurship', *Journal of Technology Management and Innovation*, 5(1), 1–12.

Rasmussen, E. and M. Wright (2015), 'How can universities facilitate academic spin-offs? An entrepreneurial competency perspective', *Journal of Technology Transfer*, 40(5), 782–799.

Rosa, P. and A. Dawson (2006), 'Gender and the commercialization of university science: academic founders of spinout companies', *Entrepreneurship and Regional Development*, 18(4), 341–366.

SAGE (2018), *Gender Equity in STEM*, accessed 22 May 2018 at http://www .sciencegenderequity.org.au/gender-equity-in-stem/.

Sax, L.J. and A.N. Bryant (2006), 'The impact of college on sex-atypical career choices of women and men', *Journal of Vocational Behavior*, 68(1), 52–63.

StartupMuster (2018), *Startup Muster 2017 Report*, accessed 25 October 2018 at https://www.startupmuster.com/reports.

Sugimoto, C.R., C. Ni and V. Lariviere (2015), 'On the relationship between gender disparities in scholarly communication and country-level development indicators', *Science and Public Policy*, 42(6), 789–810.

Thebaud, S. (2015), 'Business as plan B: institutional foundations of gender inequality in entrepreneurship across 24 industrialized countries', *Administrative Science Quarterly*, 60(4), 671–711.

uCube (2018), 'Higher education and training statistics', Department of Education and Training, accessed 20 July 2018 at http://highereducationstatistics.education.gov.au/Default.aspx.

West, J.D., J. Jacquet, M.M. King, S.J. Correll and C.T. Bergstrom (2013), 'The role of gender in scholarly authorship', *PlosONE*, 8(7), e66212, accessed 14 May 2018 at http://dx.doi.org/10.1371/journal.pone.0066212.

Workplace Gender Equality Agency (2018), 'Australia's gender pay gap statistics', accessed 20 May 2018 at https://www.wgea.gov.au/sites/default/files/gender-pay-gap-statistics.pdf.

World Economic Forum (2017), *Global Gender Gap Index*, Geneva: WEF.

Wynarczyk, P. and S. Marlow (eds.) (2010), *Innovating Women*, Bingley: Emerald.

Yin, R. (2009), *Case Study Research: Design and Methods*, 4th edition, Newbury Park, CA: Sage Publications.

6. Exploring gender differences in entrepreneurship: how the regulatory environment mitigates differences in early-stage growth aspirations

Christopher J. Boudreaux and Boris Nikolaev

1.   INTRODUCTION

Why are there gender differences in the performance of new ventures? Some argue that women have less start-up capital, human capital, and work experience than their male counterparts (Alsos et al., 2006; Cheraghi and Schøtt, 2015; Fairlie and Robb, 2009; Fischer et al., 1993). Others say that women have different priorities than men, i.e., 'social feminist theory' (Fischer et al., 1993) or often choose entrepreneurship for reasons such as flexibility or to circumvent the 'glass ceiling' in traditional employment settings (Fairlie and Robb, 2009; Kephart and Schumacher, 2005; Shane, 2008). Recent advances, however, have shed light on these gender disparities, and argue that once gender selection characteristics have been sufficiently considered, e.g., firm size, sector, and risk preferences, there is no difference between genders when it comes to entrepreneurial performance (Orser et al., 2006; Robb and Watson, 2012).

Despite these advances, gender differences in entrepreneurial activity still remain (Hechavarría et al., 2018), and societal influences continue to deter the entrepreneurial growth aspirations of women (Estrin and Mickiewicz, 2011). More work needs to be done to explain the persistence of gender differences in growth aspirations. The purpose of this study is to examine the factors that mitigate gender differences in the growth aspirations of early-stage entrepreneurs, which help to predict later actual growth (Autio, 2007). We believe this is important. Discovering contexts under which the gender differences of entrepreneurs' growth aspirations are minimized provides policy solutions toward removing the barriers women face in high-growth entrepreneurship. We propose that one factor—the regulatory environment—is a vital component that needs to be considered when examining why gender differences in entrepreneurs' early-stage growth aspirations continue to persist.

There are several reasons to expect the regulatory environment to affect gender differences in the growth aspirations of early-stage entrepreneurs. Financial regulations affect the availability of capital, and good financial regulations ease liquidity constraints, which might disproportionately harm female entrepreneurs. Business regulations affect the ease of doing business, which might also have important gender effects, such as the role of social capital and how it disproportionately helps male entrepreneurs. Lastly, labor regulations might also play an important role, if one considers how rampant sexual violence has affected women in the workplace. Importantly, we hypothesize that gender differences in the early-stage growth aspirations of entrepreneurs are less pronounced as the quality of the regulatory environment improves.

Using data from 43 countries available in the Global Entrepreneurship Monitor (GEM) and regulatory data from the Economic Freedom of the World Index (Gwartney et al., 2017), we find that female entrepreneurs have lower growth aspirations than their male counterparts. Once one considers the quality of the regulatory environment—especially credit market regulations—we find that gender differences are reduced. More specifically, our results indicate that improving the quality of the credit market is associated with a smaller gender difference in early-stage growth aspirations.

These findings are important for several reasons. First, our findings highlight the existence of significant gender differences in early-stage growth aspirations. While our results do reveal that women entrepreneurs have lower growth aspirations than men, our findings suggest these differences can be mitigated. Because we find smaller differences in early-stage growth aspirations between genders as the credit market regulatory environment improves, we are hopeful that our findings will increase the attention paid to how regulations affect gender. Second, and relatedly, these findings have important policy implications. If one desires to remove gender differences and offer an equal playing field, then our study suggests that revisiting the credit market is a good place to start.

2.   THEORY AND HYPOTHESES

2.1   Feminist Theory

Before we proceed with our theory, it is important to clarify what is meant by 'feminist theory'. As explained in Watson (2002, p. 91), there are two types of feminist theory:

> *Liberal feminist theory* (Fischer et al. 1993) suggests that small and medium enterprises (SMEs) run by women will exhibit poorer performance because women are overtly discriminated against (by lenders, for example) or because of other systematic factors that deprive women of important resources (for example, business education and experience). By way of contrast, *social feminist theory* (Fischer et al. 1993) suggests that men and women are inherently different by nature. These differences do not imply that women will be less effective in business than men, but only that they may adopt different approaches, which may or may not be as effective as the approaches adopted by men.

In this study, we argue that regulatory barriers might play an important role in shaping how gender differences emerge in early-stage entrepreneurship, which is based on *liberal feminist theory* (Fischer et al., 1993). Certainly, there might be some merit to examining socio-cultural approaches consistent with *social feminist theory*, but we believe this is less relevant in our context.

Feminist theory[1] recognizes that there are inherent cultural and gender biases toward women. Aristotle stated that 'women were weak, cautious, domesticated, and nurturing while men occupy the opposite stance thus, making them naturally superior' (Marlow and Patton, 2005, p. 720). Further, men have been equated with 'the male, public citizen who is deemed rational, abstract, impartial, independent, active, and strong whereas women, linked with the private sphere of the home, are characterized as noncitizens as they are assumed to be emotional, irrational, dependent, passive, and focused upon domestic concerns' (Lister, 2003, p. 71).

These socio-cultural biases are problematic if one considers how society often devalues female credibility. Occupational segregation and domestic/caring responsibilities are prevalent for women (Maushart, 2008), and these 'splits' (Hall, 1997) often act as impediments for women to acquire credibility and raise capital (Marlow, 2002). Hence, in the context of early-stage entrepreneurship, feminist theory suggests that women face substantial hurdles in the venture creation process. The liberal feminist solution[2] is to remove the financial, administrative, and labor market barriers that disproportionately affect women entrepreneurs, and consequently, 'level the playing field' (Cockburn, 1991; Marlow and Patton, 2005). Accordingly, we tie liberal feminist theory to institutional theory to relate how these regulatory barriers might disproportionately affect women entrepreneurs.

2.2   Institutional Theory

Institutions are 'the humanly devised constraints that shape human interaction' (North, 1990, p. 3). Institutions 'consist of both informal constraints (sanctions, taboos, customs, traditions, codes of conduct), and formal rules (constitutions, laws, property rights)' (North, 1991, p. 97). Informal constraints refer to the norms of social customs and are often referred to as 'culture' whereas formal rules are created by the government and represent the laws we must abide by. Mirroring this framework, institutions have also been described under the heading of regulative, normative, and cultural-cognitive (Scott, 2008). Regulative denotes regulations, laws, and legislation that affect behavior. Normative refers to the social norms and cultural-cognitive refers to the deeply embedded beliefs that affect behavior.

Williamson (2000) illustrates these formal rules and informal sanctions using a conceptual framework in a four-level hierarchy, which has been recently applied to the institutional context of entrepreneurial action (Bylund and McCaffrey, 2017; Estrin et al., 2013; Misangyi et al., 2008; Pacheco et al., 2010). This framework begins at the top (level one) with the informal constraints (i.e., customs, traditions, and norms). These institutions are entrenched in society and emerge spontaneously over a long period of time (100 to 1000 years). Formal institutions (level two) represent the institutional environment that defines the 'rules of the game' (North, 1991, p. 98), which take less time to change (10 to 100 years). Formal institutions are the rules that define action, which often define property rights and regulatory actions. These are the rules that entrepreneurs must abide by. Governance (level three) represents the play of the game or how governance structures align with transactions. Governance structures take even less time to change (1 to 10 years). Lastly, individual action (level four) depicts the choices individuals make, which include resource allocation and employment choices (e.g., entrepreneurship). The choices entrepreneurs make depend critically on the higher three levels of hierarchy (Bylund and McCaffrey, 2017; Williamson, 2000).

Institutions are considered vital for entrepreneurship (Acemoglu et al., 2005; Baumol, 1990; Williamson, 2000), and evidence suggests that high-quality pro-market institutions encourage productive entrepreneurship and innovation (Bjørnskov and Foss, 2008, 2016; Boudreaux, 2014, 2017; Boudreaux et al., 2019; McMullen et al., 2008; Nyström, 2008; Sobel, 2008). Depending on the context, institutions can either encourage innovation and the market process (i.e., productive), encourage redistributive effects (i.e., unproductive), or encourage rent seeking and the creation of entry barriers (i.e., destructive) to reduce contestability (Baumol, 1990; Sobel, 2008). This occurs because the institutional context affects the *allocation* of the supply of entrepreneurs toward different sectors (Boudreaux et al., 2017; Gohmann et al., 2008; Murphy et al., 1991). When the returns to productive entrepreneurship exceed the returns to lobbying, entrepreneurs find it more profitable to engage in productive entrepreneurship and vice versa. In support of these findings, recent sensitivity analyses conclude that economic institutions (level two) are the strongest antecedents of opportunity-motivated entrepreneurship across countries (Nikolaev et al., 2018), which supports a general consensus that government size, the tax burden, and the welfare state are robustly negatively correlated with entrepreneurial activity (Bjørnskov and Foss, 2008; Boudreaux et al., 2017; Lihn and Bjørnskov, 2017; Nyström, 2008). We now turn to an analysis of how these level two economic institutions (i.e., regulative) affect the early-stage growth aspirations of different genders.

2.3   Hypotheses Development

2.3.1   Financial regulations
A substantial literature indicates that financial capital[3] is an important antecedent of entrepreneurship (Acs and Szerb, 2007; Fairlie and Krashinsky, 2012). By alleviating liquidity constraints,[4] financial capital helps assist nascent firm survival (Blanchflower and Oswald, 1998; Evans and Jovanovic, 1989; Holtz-Eakin et al., 1994; Lindh and Ohlsson, 1996)—especially during firms' formative years (Bates, 1990). However, there is reason to believe that one's gender plays an important role in the credit rationing decision, and this might consequently explain some of the variation in entrepreneurial activity between genders.

Liberal feminist theory (Fischer et al., 1993) argues that women face discrimination in financial lending. Because women face socio-cultural biases (Chell and Baines, 1998; Minniti and Nardone, 2007), women are perceived to be less credible than men (Marlow and Patton, 2005). For instance, findings from The Diana Project indicate that women face gender myths, which hinder their ability to raise venture capital (Brush et al., 2008). Studies suggest that men have better access to capital than women—especially external equity capital (Orser et al., 2006)—and women must pay higher interest rates, on average, when they do gain access to the loans (Muravyev et al., 2009). This has important implications for entrepreneurship.

We expect it is more difficult for women to grow their ventures in low-quality financial regulatory environments, which significantly hampers their expectations for future growth. In this environment entrepreneurs must rely on their own sources of capital and funding because it is more difficult to navigate the difficult financial regulations. This is especially true for women, who face

discrimination in lending (Muravyev et al., 2009). Burdensome financial regulations deter entry and existing job growth by increasing the administrative
burden (Djankov et al., 2002). This is important because venture capital has
been shown to increase entrepreneurship (Kortum and Lerner, 2001).

In contrast, it should become easier for women to grow their ventures in
high-quality financial regulatory environments, which has a positive effect on
growth aspirations. An environment that has high-quality financial regulations
has lower interest rates and better access to capital and other external sources
of funding, such as collateral (Simoes et al., 2016). Therefore, increasing the
quality of financial regulations should make it easier for women to receive
financial capital. Consequently, this should help alleviate gender differences
in lending, which should provide a more even playing field for women, since
women now find it easier to access capital. Finally, if women find it easier
to access capital in high-quality financial regulatory environments, then men
will no longer have an advantage over women, all else held equal. For these
reasons, we propose our first hypothesis:

*Hypothesis 1: Higher-quality credit market regulations reduce gender differ-
ences in early-stage growth aspirations.*

2.3.2   Business regulations

High entry barriers reduce new venture entry (Dean and Meyer, 1996), and
one such entry barrier—business regulations—has been shown to deter new
venture start-up rates (De Soto, 2000; Djankov et al., 2002) and growth rates of
new ventures. These business regulations increase the costs of doing business
including licensing restrictions, administrative requirements, bureaucracy
costs, tax compliance, and even the costs associated with bribes and favorit-
ism (Djankov et al., 2002; Gwartney et al., 2017). Business regulations deter
entry by increasing the costs of new venture formation (Ho and Wong, 2007),
however, there are reasons to believe that business regulations might affect
entrepreneurs' early-stage growth aspirations differently for men and women.

Liberal feminist theory (Fischer et al., 1993) argues that women face discrimination that is imbued in socio-cultural biases. These biases, in turn, deter
entry and existing firm growth through high regulatory costs and have different
effects on women than men. We expect that it is more difficult for women to
form productive entrepreneurial ventures in low-quality administrative regulatory environments that have higher costs of doing business. Consequently,
we expect women entrepreneurs to have lower early-stage growth aspirations
than men. For instance, studies show that highly regulated economies are sus-
ceptible to corruption (Holcombe and Boudreaux, 2015). If bribes are a cost of
doing business that is often required to get the business established (De Soto,
2000), then it is reasonable to believe that these highly regulated environments

might disproportionately harm women because women bribe less than men (Swamy et al., 2001).

It should be easier, however, for women to grow their ventures in an environment that decreases the costs of doing business. As a result, we expect that women entrepreneurs will increase their growth aspirations as the quality of the business environment improves. In contrast to the low-quality environments, there is less corruption (Mauro, 1995; Mo, 2001), and because women bribe less than men (Swamy et al., 2001), women are less affected by these burdensome administrative and regulatory costs. Work experience and human capital accumulation also alleviate gender differences in entrepreneurship (Cheraghi and Schøtt, 2015) and lower costs of doing business (Djankov et al., 2002). This might make it easier to accumulate work experience and human capital through on-the-job training. We expect these environments to help mitigate gender differences in early-stage growth aspirations. Thus, the high-quality business regulatory environment should even the playing field, which is important because it can help reduce discrimination, which has been argued to attribute to gender disparities in areas such as lending and consumption (Fairlie and Robb, 2009). Based on these findings we propose that:

Hypothesis 2: Higher-quality business regulations reduce gender differences in early-stage growth aspirations.

2.3.3   Labor market regulations

Liberal feminist theory (Fischer et al., 1993) argues that women face discrimination in society. While we have suggested this discrimination affects financial and business regulations, it is also possible that the discrimination works through labor regulations, such as hiring and firing regulations, the costs of worker dismissals, and collective bargaining issues.

An important literature on labor market regulations and entrepreneurial intensity explains how restrictive labor market regulations reduce entrepreneurship rates across countries (Acs and Szerb, 2007; Van Stel et al., 2007). Consider, for example, how more flexible labor regulations might influence entrepreneurial activity:

> On the side of employees, the safety of their paid job is less which may make them more likely to decide to start their own business (push effect). On the side of the entrepreneurs, they have more flexibility in running their business which makes business ownership more attractive (pull effect). (Van Stel et al., 2007, p. 182)

Moreover, there are reasons to believe that these labor market regulations might have important gender effects on the early-stage growth aspirations of entrepreneurs.

We expect that labor market regulations disproportionately affect early-stage growth aspirations of women entrepreneurs in low-quality labor regulatory environments. In these environments, labor regulations are rigid, and it is difficult to fire workers, which reduces the incentive for entrepreneurs to seek self-employment or entrepreneurship. This is especially true for women who face gender biases such as occupational segregation (Lerner et al., 1997) and gender-based occupational stereotypes (Eccles, 1994; Eccles et al., 1993). If women face biases in entrepreneurship, and labor markets are more rigid, then low-quality labor regulatory environments provide fewer incentives for women to quit traditional employment in the hopes of starting a new venture.

In contrast, women's early-stage growth aspirations are less deterred relative to men in high-quality labor regulatory environments because these environments promote job flexibility. When the labor market is more flexible, entrepreneurs can run their business in more attractive ways. They have more freedom to hire and fire workers and are not penalized for this flexibility (Gwartney et al., 2017). This is consistent with findings that economic freedom correlated with higher women's rights (Fike, 2017). As labor market freedom increases, women entrepreneurs might have better outlooks and expectations for the future. Similarly, more job flexibility is associated with higher rates of new firm entry (Van Stel et al., 2007), which might equal the playing field between genders. Thus, we propose that:

Hypothesis 3: Higher-quality labor market regulations reduce gender differences in early-stage growth aspirations.

3.   DATA AND ANALYSIS

3.1   Dependent Variable

Our dependent variable of interest in this study is taken from the Global Entrepreneurship Monitor (GEM) (Reynolds et al., 2005). Growth aspirations is taken from the GEM variable, TEAYYJG5. This variable asks whether the respondent expects to employ more than five employees in the next five years, and covers entrepreneurs during the early stages of start-up activity. We use this variable to create our measure of growth aspirations, which takes a value of 1 if an individual is involved in early-stage entrepreneurial activity and expects to employ more than five employees in the next five years. It takes a value of 0 otherwise.

3.2   Predictor Variables

We use regulatory data from the Economic Freedom of the World Index (Gwartney et al., 2017) to construct our regulatory measure. Regulation is the fifth area component of the Economic Freedom of the World Index (EFW), and it is comprised of three sub-components including (a) credit market regulations, (b) labor market regulations, and (c) business regulations. We examine each of these area five sub-components. Credit market regulations are calculated as the average of three measures including (i) ownership of banks, (ii) private sector credit, and (iii) interest rate controls. EFW uses data primarily from the World Bank to compile these capital market measures. Countries with higher proportions of private ownerships of banks, private sector credit, and interest rates that are determined by market forces score higher on the freedom index. Labor market regulations are calculated as the average of six measures including (i) hiring regulations and minimum wage, (ii) hiring and firing regulations, (iii) centralized collective bargaining, (iv) hours regulations, (v) mandated cost of worker dismissal, and (vi) conscription. EFW uses data primarily from the World Bank Doing Business Report and the World Economic Forum Global Competitiveness Report to compile these labor market measures. Countries with more flexible labor regulations, lower costs of firing, and less conscription score higher on the freedom index. Business regulations are calculated as the average of six measures including (i) administrative requirements, (ii) bureaucracy costs, (iii) starting a business, (iv) extra payments/bribes/favoritism, (v) licensing restrictions, and (vi) cost of tax compliance. EFW uses data primarily from the World Bank Doing Business Report and the World Economic Forum Global Competitiveness Report to compile these business regulation measures. Data on bureaucracy costs, however, are compiled from the regulatory burden risk ratings from the IHS Markit. Capital market regulations, labor regulations, and business regulations are all measured on a scale from 0 to 10, where 10 indicates more free and 0 indicates less free.

We also include a measure for the entrepreneur's gender. This variable is dummy coded 1 if the entrepreneur is female and 0 if male. Gender data are taken from the Global Entrepreneurship Monitor (Reynolds et al., 2005).

3.3   Control Variables

In addition to our predictor variables of regulation and gender, we also include other individual-level variables that have been shown to correlate with entrepreneurship. Age and Age (squared) are continuous variables that denote the age of the entrepreneur and its quadratic, respectively. We include an entrepreneur's age and its quadratic to be consistent with prior studies on the aging entrepreneur (Kautonen et al., 2017; Lévesque and Minniti, 2006) as well as others that control for curvilinear effects (Wennberg et al., 2013). High school education is measured as whether an individual has at least graduated from high school or its equivalent (secondary education) or not. It is calculated from the GEMEDUC harmonized education variable where it takes a value of 1 if an individual has a high school education and 0 otherwise. Household income is taken from the variable, GEMHHINC, which is measured in income terciles. Household income high is coded 1 if an individual's household income is in the highest income tercile and 0 if it is in the middle or lowest tercile. Household income middle is coded 1 if an individual's household income is in the middle income tercile and 0 if it is in the highest or lowest tercile. We omit the lowest income tercile, which serves as the baseline income category. Entrepreneurial ties is a proxy for an entrepreneur's social capital. Entrepreneurial ties is coded 1 if an individual knows someone who has created a business in the past two years and 0 otherwise. Entrepreneurial self-efficacy is coded 1 if the individual entrepreneur believes he or she has the knowledge, skills, and experience required to start a new business and 0 otherwise. Opportunity recognition is coded 1 if the entrepreneur envisions good business opportunities in the next six months and 0 otherwise. Fear of failure is coded 1 if the entrepreneur responds that fear of failure is likely to prevent him or her from starting a business and 0 otherwise. Recent research supports their importance in predicting and modifying entrepreneurial activity (Boudreaux and Nikolaev, 2018; De Clercq et al., 2013). These variables are all taken from the Global Entrepreneurship Monitor dataset for the years 2002 to 2012 (Reynolds et al., 2005). We also include a country-level measure of gender equality because gender equality is associated with gender differences in self-employment (Klyver et al., 2013). This measure is taken from the World Economic Forum for the years 2002 to 2010. This variable is measured on a continuous scale from 0 to 1 where 1 indicates complete equality and 0 indicates complete inequality.

Lastly, we also include control variables at the country-level that are expected to influence entrepreneurial behavior. Log GDP is the natural logarithm of a country's gross domestic product per capita. Log pop is the natural logarithm of a country's total population. These variables are taken from the World Bank's country indicator's database for the years 2002 to 2012. Log GDP is used to control for the 'natural rate' of entrepreneurship in economic development (Wennekers et al., 2005). Summary statistics and a correlation matrix are presented in Table 6.1.

Table 6.1   Mean, standard deviation, and correlation matrix

Variable	Mean	SD		1	2	3	4	5	6	7	8	9	10	11	12	13	14	15
Expects more than 5 jobs in 5 years	0.27	0.45	1	1														
Age	39	11	2	−0.03*	1													
Female	0.38	0.48	3	−0.12*	0.03*	1												
Regulations																		
Credit market	8.91	1.22	4	0.03*	0.08*	0.01*	1											
Labor market	6.23	1.58	5	0.05*	0.06*	0.03*	0.24*	1										
Business	6.31	0.95	6	0.07*	0.08*	0.01*	0.47*	0.33*	1									
Household income terciles																		
High income	0.73	0.44	7	0.06*	−0.04*	−0.05*	−0.003	−0.06*	0.06*	1								
Middle income	0.33	0.47	8	−0.04*	−0.03*	−0.001	−0.000	−0.03*	0.01*	0.51*	1							
High school	0.75	0.43	9	0.08*	−0.12*	−0.004	0.03*	0.17*	0.08*	0.08*	−0.004*	1						
Entrepreneurial self-efficacy	0.86	0.35	10	0.05*	−0.01*	−0.16*	−0.01*	0.004*	−0.03*	0.07*	−0.02*	0.09*	1					

Variable	Mean	SD		1	2	3	4	5	6	7	8	9	10	11	12	13	14	15
Opportunity recognition	0.54	0.50	11	0.06*	-0.07*	-0.07*	0.02*	0.03*	0.04*	0.03*	-0.02*	0.06*	0.18*	1				
Fear of failure	0.25	0.43	12	-0.06*	-0.03*	0.07*	-0.01*	-0.08*	-0.04*	-0.03*	0.02*	-0.03*	-0.13*	-0.07*	1			
Entrepreneurial ties	0.64	0.48	13	0.10*	-0.14*	-0.11*	-0.04*	-0.06*	-0.001	0.06*	-0.01*	0.08*	0.24*	0.21*	-0.04*	1		
GDP pc [a]	30.8	17.8	14	0.01*	0.05*	-0.000	0.17*	-0.19*	0.08*	-0.02*	0.001	0.10*	-0.02*	-0.01*	0.06*	-0.01*	1	
Population [b]	152	328	15	-0.04*	0.01*	0.001	-0.31*	0.01*	-0.39*	-0.05*	-0.02*	0.01*	-0.05*	-0.05*	-0.004*	-0.05*	-0.25*	1

Notes:
[a] = denoted in thousands.
[b] = denoted in millions.
* $p < 0.05$.

4.   RESULTS

Our data include observations at both the individual-level and country-level. With multi-level data, standard estimation techniques (e.g., OLS) in the presence of clustered data increase the possibility of Type 1 errors. Standard techniques also underestimate the standard errors due to their non-normal distribution (Hofmann et al., 2000). To account for the multi-level nature of our data and because our dependent variable is dichotomous, we estimate all models using a logistic regression with country-specific random effects (i.e., random intercept model)[5] and year effects. The country-specific effects allow us to consider the nested nature of our data and the year effects allow us to control for the changing general conditions (e.g., the Great Recession in 2007–2009).

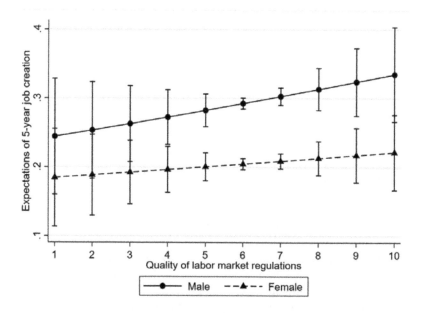

Figure 6.1   *Interaction between labor market regulations and gender on five-year job-growth aspirations*

We begin our analysis with an examination of how the regulatory environment affects gender differences in entrepreneurs' early-stage growth aspirations. These results are presented in Table 6.2. More specifically, model 1 is our baseline model that includes a gender dummy, the three measures of the regu-

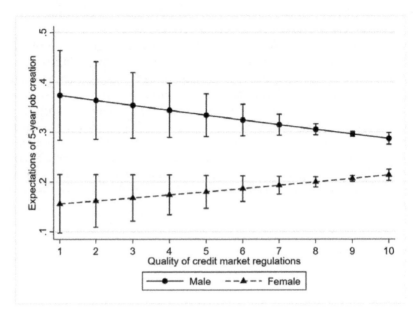

Figure 6.2   Interaction between credit market regulations and gender on five-year job-growth aspirations

latory environment, and a vector of control variables. Models 2–4 augment this model to include the interaction terms between each of the regulatory variables and the gender dummy.

The results from Table 6.2 indicate that there are significant gender differences in early-stage growth aspirations. Across all models, we find a negative and statistically significant effect of being female on early-stage growth aspirations, which is consistent with claims that gender differences persist in entrepreneurial activity (Fairlie and Robb, 2009; Hechavarría et al., 2018). More importantly, the findings from model 2 suggest that the quality of the credit market regulatory environment plays an important role in explaining the persistence of gender differences in early-stage growth aspirations. That is, while women entrepreneurs have lower early-stage growth aspirations, improving the quality of the credit market reduces these gender differences. This can be observed in the credit market but not in the labor market or for business regulations. These findings support hypothesis 1 but fail to support hypotheses 2 and 3. Based on these results, we conclude that gender differences in early-stage growth aspirations are largest when there are burdensome credit market regulations, and gender differences in early-stage growth aspirations are smaller when there are higher-quality credit market regulations.

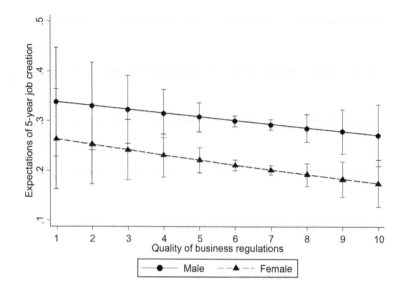

Figure 6.3   Interaction between business regulations and gender on five-year job-growth aspirations

Because interaction effects are notoriously difficult to interpret in non-linear models such as logit (Ai and Norton, 2003), we plot the moderating effects in Figures 6.1, 6.2, and 6.3. The findings from these interaction effects support the empirical analysis in Table 6.2. Consistent with the findings in Table 6.2, we find that credit market regulations moderate the relationship between gender and early-stage growth aspirations. That is, while women entrepreneurs have lower early-stage growth aspirations than men, improving the quality of the credit market reduces these gender differences. We find no evidence that the quality of the business regulations or the labor market regulations moderate the relationship between gender and early-stage growth aspirations.

5.   DISCUSSION, LIMITATIONS, AND CONCLUDING REMARKS

5.1   Discussion

Based on insights from institutional theory (North, 1990; Scott, 2008; Williamson, 2000) and feminist theory (Fischer et al., 1993), we investigated how the quality of the regulatory environment moderates gender differences in

Table 6.2　　Effects of gender and regulations on future job expectations

Dependent variable – Expect more than five jobs in five years

Variables	(1)		(2)		(3)		(4)		(5)	
Age	-0.022**	(0.01)	-0.021**	(0.01)	-0.022**	(0.01)	-0.022**	(0.01)	-0.021**	(0.01)
Age2	0.0002*	(0.00)	0.0002*	(0.00)	0.0002*	(0.00)	0.0002*	(0.00)	0.0002*	(0.00)
Female (F)	-0.490***	(0.03)	-1.491***	(0.23)	-0.365***	(0.12)	-0.467*	(0.21)	-1.21***	(0.25)
Household income[a]										
High income tercile	0.625***	(0.04)	0.624***	(0.04)	0.625***	(0.04)	0.625***	(0.04)	0.625***	(0.04)
Middle income tercile	-0.420***	(0.03)	-0.419***	(0.03)	-0.420***	(0.03)	-0.420***	(0.03)	-0.420***	(0.03)
High school	0.266***	(0.04)	0.266***	(0.04)	0.267***	(0.04)	0.267***	(0.04)	0.267***	(0.04)
Entrepreneurial self-efficacy	0.239***	(0.04)	0.236***	(0.04)	0.239***	(0.04)	0.239***	(0.04)	0.234***	(0.04)
Opportunity recognition	0.185***	(0.03)	0.186***	(0.03)	0.185***	(0.03)	0.185***	(0.03)	0.186***	(0.03)
Fear of failure	-0.186***	(0.03)	-0.186***	(0.03)	-0.186***	(0.03)	-0.186***	(0.03)	-0.186***	(0.03)
Entrepreneurial ties	0.315***	(0.03)	0.314***	(0.03)	0.316***	(0.03)	0.315***	(0.03)	0.314***	(0.03)
GDP (log) PPP	0.002	(0.12)	-0.001	(0.12)	0.001	(0.12)	0.002	(0.12)	-0.006	(0.12)
Population (log)	2.397	(1.27)	2.454	(1.27)	2.397	(1.27)	2.398	(1.27)	2.49	(1.28)
Regulations										
Credit market	-0.006	(0.03)	-0.04	(0.03)	-0.006	(0.03)	-0.006	(0.03)	-0.053	(0.03)
Labor market	0.031	(0.06)	0.033	(0.06)	0.036	(0.06)	0.031	(0.06)	0.042	(0.06)
Business	-0.087	(0.06)	-0.081	(0.06)	-0.087	(0.06)	-0.086	(0.06)	-0.057	(0.06)
Moderating effects										
F x Credit market regulations			0.112***	(0.03)					0.161***	(0.03)

Dependent variable – Expect more than five jobs in five years					
Variables	(1)	(2)	(3)	(4)	(5)
F x Labor market regulations			-0.02 (0.02)		-0.041 (0.02)
F x Business regulations				-0.004 (0.03)	-0.074 (0.04)
Number of observations	29,194	29,194	29,194	29,194	29,194
Number of groups (countries)	43	43	43	43	43
AIC	32245	32227	32246	32247	32220
Log-likelihood	-16061	-16051	-16060	-16061	-16045
LR test	—	***	***		***

Notes:
[a] = the omitted household income category is the low income tercile (bottom third of the income distribution).
*** $p < 0.001$; ** $p < 0.01$; * $p < 0.05$.

the growth aspirations of early-stage entrepreneurs. Building on findings that identify gender discrimination in lending and credit markets (Marlow, 2002) as well as the ways entry barriers (Djankov et al., 2002) and labor mobility (Van Stel et al., 2007) might affect women and men differently, we hypothesized that gender differences in early-stage entrepreneurship will be largest in the worst regulatory environments. Importantly, we hypothesized that gender differences in the growth aspirations of early-stage entrepreneurs will be mitigated as the quality of the regulatory environment improves.

Overall, we found support for some but not all of our hypotheses. Our results indicate that the relationship between gender and early-stage growth aspirations depends on the quality of the credit market regulatory environment. While we find that women entrepreneurs have lower early-stage growth aspirations compared to men, these gender differences are attenuated as the quality of credit market regulations improves. We did not find any evidence to suggest that improving the quality of business regulations and labor market regulations helps to mitigate gender differences in early-stage growth aspirations.

These findings have important implications. If policy makers desire to reduce gender differences in entrepreneurship, our evidence suggests that policies designed to enhance the quality of regulations—particularly regulations in the credit market—are a good place to start. Improving the functioning of credit rationing is associated with smaller gender differences in the aspirations of early-stage entrepreneurs, which are important preconditions of future growth (Autio, 2007).

The finding that low-quality credit markets have the largest gender differences in early-stage entrepreneurship suggests that some degree of discrimination is occurring in these countries, and while we have focused on early-stage growth aspirations in this chapter, we also found similar evidence for early-stage opportunity-motivated entrepreneurship.[6] Our results are also important because they highlight that not all regulations have the same effect on attenuating these gender differences in early-stage entrepreneurship. As a result, improving the quality of labor market regulations or easing the costs of doing business are unlikely to have an effect on these gender differences. Thus, credit regulations have different effects on early-stage growth aspirations than business and labor market regulations. One potential explanation for this difference is that several studies have uncovered discrimination in lending (Marlow and Patton, 2005; Muravyev et al., 2009). Conversely, while labor and business regulations might impose barriers to entrepreneurial entry, studies typically do not suggest discrimination as an additional entry barrier (Djankov et al., 2002).

One practical implication, therefore, is for policy makers to look to improve the quality and functioning of credit markets, which should ultimately help to reduce the gender gap in entrepreneurship. Practical ways to improve this functioning include improving the extent of private sector credit (relative to public sector), improving the reliance of bank deposits in the private sector, and reducing the control of interest rates by a country's government or central bank. Our research indicates that these broad activities, which comprise a country's quality of credit market regulations, can substantially help to reduce the gender gap in high-growth entrepreneurship.

5.2   Limitations

Inevitably, our study does face some limitations. Our findings are not unanimous for all three regulatory measures. While our findings largely suggest that gender differences in early-stage growth aspirations are most pronounced in low-quality credit market regulatory environments and become less pronounced as the quality of the regulations improves, we do not find any evidence to suggest that business regulations or labor market regulations moderate the relationship between gender and early-stage growth aspirations. Therefore, future work should emphasize why different regulations have heterogeneous effects on the gender differences in early-stage growth aspirations.

Moreover, our findings should not be taken as causal evidence that improving the quality of credit market rationing will lead to smaller gender differences in early-stage entrepreneurial aspirations, nor should our evidence imply that discrimination is unequivocally occurring in these credit markets. More specific and direct policy changes are needed to assess these causal relationships and to uncover the degree of discrimination in lending.

NOTES

1. This section draws heavily from Marlow and Patton (2005).
2. It is important to mention that social feminist theory is critical of such a solution. Social feminist theory argues that these biases are endemic in society and culture, and as such, removing regulatory barriers will not improve the inherent biases that affect women (Marlow and Patton, 2005).
3. Financial capital is measured as household income, which is strongly correlated with wealth (Bricker et al., 2016; Saez and Zucman, 2016).
4. Hurst and Lusardi (2004) argue that liquidity constraints are not really present as the majority of the relationship between assets and entrepreneurial entry is found only for those with wealth beyond the 95th percentile in the wealth distribution. However, Fairlie and Krashinsky (2012) bifurcate samples into opportunity and necessity entrepreneurs and find that, when this selection bias is considered, liquidity constraints are found to be present.
5. We tested for an alternative model of random slopes but found it did not significantly improve model fit.
6. Results available upon request.

REFERENCES

Acemoglu, D., S. Johnson and J.A. Robinson (2005), 'Institutions as a fundamental cause of long-run growth', in P. Aghion and S.N. Durlauf (eds.), *Handbook of Economic Growth*, vol. 1, Part A, Amsterdam: Elsevier.

Acs, Z. and L. Szerb (2007), 'Entrepreneurship, economic growth and public policy', *Small Business Economics*, 28(2–3), 109–122.

Ai, C. and E.C. Norton (2003), 'Interaction terms in logit and probit models', *Economics Letters*, 80(1), 123–129.

Alsos, G.A., E.J. Isaksen and E. Ljunggren (2006), 'New venture financing and subsequent business growth in men- and women-led businesses', *Entrepreneurship Theory and Practice*, 30(5), 667–686.

Autio, E. (2007), *Global Report on High-Growth Entrepreneurship*, Babson College, London Business School, and Global Entrpreneurship Research Consortium (GERA).

Bates, T. (1990), 'Entrepreneur human capital inputs and small business longevity', *Review of Economics and Statistics*, 72(4), 551–559.

Baumol, W.J. (1990), 'Entrepreneurship: productive, unproductive, and destructive', *Journal of Political Economy*, 98(5/1), 893–921.

Bjørnskov, C. and N.J. Foss (2008), 'Economic freedom and entrepreneurial activity: some cross-country evidence', *Public Choice*, 3(134), 307–328.

Bjørnskov, C. and N.J. Foss (2016), 'Institutions, entrepreneurship, and economic growth: what do we know and what do we still need to know?', *The Academy of Management Perspectives*, 30(3), 292–315.

Blanchflower, D.G. and A.J. Oswald (1998), 'What makes an entrepreneur?', *Journal of Labor Economics*, 16(1), 26–60.

Boudreaux, C.J. (2014), 'Jumping off of the Great Gatsby curve: how institutions facilitate entrepreneurship and intergenerational mobility', *Journal of Institutional Economics*, 10(2), 231–255.

Boudreaux, C.J. (2017), 'Institutional quality and innovation: some cross-country evidence', *Journal of Entrepreneurship and Public Policy*, 6(1), 26–40.

Boudreaux, C.J. and B. Nikolaev (2018), 'Capital is not enough: opportunity entrepreneurship and formal institutions', *Small Business Economics*, 1–30, Online First.

Boudreaux, C.J., B. Nikolaev and P. Klein (2017), 'Entrepreneurial traits, institutions, and the motivation to engage in entrepreneurship', *Academy of Management Proceedings*, 2017(1), 16427.

Boudreaux, C.J., B. Nikolaev and P. Klein (2019), 'Socio-cognitive traits and entrepreneurship: the moderating role of economic institutions', *Journal of Business Venturing*, 34(1), 178–196.

Bricker, J., A. Henriques, J. Krimmel and J. Sabelhaus (2016), 'Measuring income and wealth at the top using administrative and survey data', *Brookings Papers on Economic Activity*, 2016(1), 261–331.

Brush, C., N.M. Carter, E. Gatewood, P. Greene and M. Hart (2008), *The Diana Project: Women Business Owners and Equity Capital: The Myths Dispelled*, SSRN Scholarly Paper ID 1262312, Rochester, NY: Social Science Research Network, September 5, accessed December 10, 2017 at https://papers.ssrn.com/abstract=1262312.

Bylund, P.L. and M. McCaffrey (2017), 'A theory of entrepreneurship and institutional uncertainty', *Journal of Business Venturing*, 32(5), 461–475.

Chell, E. and S. Baines (1998), 'Does gender affect business "performance"? A study of microbusinesses in business services in the UK', *Entrepreneurship & Regional Development*, 10(2), 117–135.

Cheraghi, M. and T. Schøtt (2015), 'Education and training benefiting a career as entrepreneur: gender gaps and gendered competencies and benefits', *International Journal of Gender and Entrepreneurship*, 7(3), 321–343.

Cockburn, C. (1991), *In the Way of Women: Men's Resistance to Sex Equality in Organizations*, Basingstoke: Macmillan.

De Clercq, D., D. Lim and C. Oh (2013), 'Individual-level resources and new business activity: the contingent role of institutional context', *Entrepreneurship Theory and Practice*, 37(2), 303–330.

De Soto, H. (2000), *The Mystery of Capital: Why Capitalism Triumphs in the West and Fails Everywhere Else*, New York: Basic Books.

Dean, T.J. and G.D. Meyer (1996), 'Industry environments and new venture formations in U.S. manufacturing: a conceptual and empirical analysis of demand determinants', *Journal of Business Venturing*, 11(2), 107–132.

Djankov, S., R. La Porta, F. Lopez-de-Silanes and A. Shleifer (2002), 'The regulation of entry', *Quarterly Journal of Economics*, 117(1), 1–37.

Eccles, J.S. (1994), 'Understanding women's educational and occupational choices: applying the Eccles et al. model of achievement-related choices', *Psychology of Women Quarterly*, 18(4), 585–609.

Eccles, J., A. Wigfield, R.D. Harold and P. Blumenfeld (1993), 'Age and gender differences in children's self- and task perceptions during elementary school', *Child Development*, 64(3), 830–847.

Estrin, S., J. Korosteleva and T. Mickiewicz (2013), 'Which institutions encourage entrepreneurial growth aspirations?', *Journal of Business Venturing*, 28(4), 564–580.

Estrin, S. and T. Mickiewicz (2011), 'Institutions and female entrepreneurship', *Small Business Economics*, 37(4), 397–415.

Evans, D.S. and B. Jovanovic (1989), 'An estimated model of entrepreneurial choice under liquidity constraints', *Journal of Political Economy*, 97(4), 808–827.

Fairlie, R.W. and H.A. Krashinsky (2012), 'Liquidity constraints, household wealth, and entrepreneurship revisited', *Review of Income and Wealth*, 58(2), 279–306.

Fairlie, R.W. and A.M. Robb (2009), 'Gender differences in business performance: evidence from the Characteristics of Business Owners survey', *Small Business Economics*, 33(4), 375–395.

Fike, R. (2017), 'Adjusting for gender disparity in economic freedom and why it matters', in J. Gwartney, R. Lawson and J. Hall, *Economic Freedom of the World Annual Report*, Vancouver: The Fraser Institute.

Fischer, E.M., A.R. Reuber and L.S. Dyke (1993), 'A theoretical overview and extension of research on sex, gender, and entrepreneurship', *Journal of Business Venturing*, 8(2), 151–168.

Gohmann, S.F., B.K. Hobbs and M. McCrickard (2008), 'Economic freedom and service industry growth in the United States', *Entrepreneurship Theory and Practice*, 32(5), 855–874.

Gwartney, J., R. Lawson and J. Hall (2017), *Economic Freedom of the World 2017 Annual Report*, Vancouver: The Fraser Institute.

Hall, S. (1997), *Representation: Cultural Representations and Signifying Practices*, vol. 2, London: Sage Publications.

Hechavarría, D.M., S.A. Terjesen, P. Stenholm, M. Brännback and S. Lång (2018), 'More than words: do gendered linguistic structures widen the gender gap in entrepreneurial activity?', *Entrepreneurship Theory and Practice*, 42(5), 797–817.

Ho, Y.-P. and P.-K. Wong (2007), 'Financing, regulatory costs and entrepreneurial propensity', *Small Business Economics*, 28(2–3), 187–204.

Hofmann, D.A., M.A. Griffin and M.B. Gavin (2000), 'The application of hierarchical linear modeling to organizational research', in K.J. Klein and S.W.J. Kozlowski (eds.), *Multilevel Theory, Research, and Methods in Organizations: Foundations, Extensions, and New Directions*, San Francisco, CA: Jossey-Bass.

Holcombe, R.G. and C.J. Boudreaux (2015), 'Regulation and corruption', *Public Choice*, 164(1–2), 75–85.

Holtz-Eakin, D., D. Joulfaian and H. Rosen (1994), 'Entrepreneurial decisions and liquidity constraints', *RAND Journal of Economics*, 25, 334–347.

Hurst, E. and A. Lusardi (2004), 'Liquidity constraints, household wealth, and entrepreneurship', *Journal of Political Economy*, 112(2), 319–347.

Kautonen, T., E. Kibler and M. Minniti (2017), 'Late-career entrepreneurship, income and quality of life', *Journal of Business Venturing*, 32(3), 318–333.

Kephart, P. and L. Schumacher (2005), 'Has the "glass ceiling" cracked? An exploration of women entrepreneurship', *Journal of Leadership & Organizational Studies*, 12(1), 2–15.

Klyver, K., S.L. Nielsen and M.R. Evald (2013), 'Women's self-employment: an act of institutional (dis)integration? A multilevel, cross-country study', *Journal of Business Venturing*, 28(4), 474–488.

Kortum, S. and J. Lerner (2001), 'Does venture capital spur innovation?', in G.D. Libecap (ed.), *Entrepreneurial Inputs and Outcomes: New Studies of Entrepreneurship in the United States*, Bingley: Emerald Group.

Lerner, M., C. Brush and R. Hisrich (1997), 'Israeli women entrepreneurs: an examination of factors affecting performance', *Journal of Business Venturing*, 12(4), 315–339.

Lévesque, M. and M. Minniti (2006), 'The effect of aging on entrepreneurial behavior', *Journal of Business Venturing*, 21(2), 177–194.

Lihn, J. and C. Bjørnskov (2017), 'Economic freedom and veto players jointly affect entrepreneurship', *Journal of Entrepreneurship and Public Policy*, 6(3), 340–358.

Lindh, T. and H. Ohlsson (1996), 'Self-employment and windfall gains: evidence from the Swedish lottery', *Economic Journal*, 106(439), 1515–1526.

Lister, R. (2003), *Citizenship: Feminist Perspectives*, New York: New York University Press.

Marlow, S. (2002), 'Women and self-employment: a part of or apart from theoretical construct?', *The International Journal of Entrepreneurship and Innovation*, 3(2), 83–91.

Marlow, S. and D. Patton (2005), 'All credit to men? Entrepreneurship, finance, and gender', *Entrepreneurship Theory and Practice*, 29(6), 717–735.

Mauro, P. (1995), 'Corruption and growth', *Quarterly Journal of Economics*, 110(3), 681–712.

Maushart, S. (2008), *Wifework: What Marriage Really Means for Women*, New York: Bloomsbury.

McMullen, J.S., D.R. Bagby and L.E. Palich (2008), 'Economic freedom and the motivation to engage in entrepreneurial action', *Entrepreneurship Theory and Practice*, 32(5), 875–895.

Minniti, M. and C. Nardone (2007), 'Being in someone else's shoes: the role of gender in nascent entrepreneurship', *Small Business Economics*, 28(2–3), 223–238.

Misangyi, V.F., G.R. Weaver and H. Elms (2008), 'Ending corruption: the interplay among institutional logics, resources, and institutional entrepreneurs', *Academy of Management Review*, 33(3), 750–770.

Mo, P.H. (2001), 'Corruption and economic growth', *Journal of Comparative Economics*, 29(1), 66–79.

Muravyev, A., O. Talavera and D. Schäfer (2009), 'Entrepreneurs' gender and financial constraints: evidence from international data', *Journal of Comparative Economics*, 37(2), 270–286.

Murphy, K.M., A. Shleifer and R.W. Vishny (1991), 'The allocation of talent: implications for growth', *Quarterly Journal of Economics*, 106(2), 503–530.

Nikolaev, B., C.J. Boudreaux and L.E. Palich (2018), 'Cross-country determinants of early stage necessity and opportunity-motivated entrepreneurship: accounting for model uncertainty', *Journal of Small Business Management*, 56(1), 243–280.

North, D.C. (1990), *Institutions, Institutional Change and Economic Performance*, Cambridge: Cambridge University Press.

North, D.C. (1991), 'Institutions', *Journal of Economic Perspectives*, 5(1), 97–112.

Nyström, K. (2008), 'The institutions of economic freedom and entrepreneurship: evidence from panel data', *Public Choice*, 136(3–4), 269–282.

Orser, B.J., A.L. Riding and K. Manley (2006), 'Women entrepreneurs and financial capital', *Entrepreneurship Theory and Practice*, 30(5), 643–665.

Pacheco, D.F., J.G. York, T.J. Dean and S.D. Sarasvathy (2010), 'The coevolution of institutional entrepreneurship: a tale of two theories', *Journal of Management*, 36(4), 974–1010.

Reynolds, P., N. Bosma, E. Autio, S. Hunt, N.D. Bono, I. Servais, P. Lopez-Garcia and N. Chin (2005), 'Global Entrepreneurship Monitor: data collection design and implementation 1998–2003', *Small Business Economics*, 24(3), 205–231.

Robb, A.M. and J. Watson (2012), 'Gender differences in firm performance: evidence from new ventures in the United States', *Journal of Business Venturing*, 27(5), 544–558.

Saez, E. and G. Zucman (2016), 'Wealth inequality in the United States since 1913: evidence from capitalized income tax data', *Quarterly Journal of Economics*, 131(2), 519–578.

Scott, W.R. (2008), *Institutions and Organizations: Ideas and Interests*, London: Sage Publications.

Shane, S. (2008), *The Illusions of Entrepreneurship: The Costly Myths That Entrepreneurs, Investors, and Policy Makers Live By*, New Haven, CT: Yale University Press.

Simoes, N., N. Crespo and S.B. Moreira (2016), 'Individual determinants of self-employment entry: what do we really know?', *Journal of Economic Surveys*, 30(4), 783–806.

Sobel, R.S. (2008), 'Testing Baumol: institutional quality and the productivity of entrepreneurship', *Journal of Business Venturing*, 23(6), 641–655.

Swamy, A., S. Knack, Y. Lee and O. Azfar (2001), 'Gender and corruption', *Journal of Development Economics*, 64(1), 25–55.

Van Stel, A., D.J. Storey and A.R. Thurik (2007), 'The effect of business regulations on nascent and young business entrepreneurship', *Small Business Economics*, 28(2–3), 171–186.

Watson, J. (2002), 'Comparing the performance of male- and female-controlled businesses: relating outputs to inputs', *Entrepreneurship Theory and Practice*, 26(3), 91–101.

Wennberg, K., S. Pathak and E. Autio (2013), 'How culture moulds the effects of self-efficacy and fear of failure on entrepreneurship', *Entrepreneurship & Regional Development*, 25(9–10), 756–780.

Wennekers, S., A. van Wennekers, R. Thurik and P. Reynolds (2005), 'Nascent entrepreneurship and the level of economic development', *Small Business Economics*, 24(3), 293–309.

Williamson, O.E. (2000), 'The new institutional economics: taking stock, looking ahead', *Journal of Economic Literature*, 38(3), 595–613.

7. Gender gap in perceived financing opportunities for high-growth enterprises

Blaž Frešer, Karin Širec and Polona Tominc

1. INTRODUCTION

Even though the term *enterprise growth* was present earlier in the scientific research area, research on high-growth enterprises (HGEs) dates back only to the late 1970s, when David Birch started what was, for that time, quite a controversial argument about the importance of HGEs for the economy, employment and well-being (Landström, 2010). Research in the field of HGEs (Birch, 1979; Delmar et al., 2003; Henrekson and Johansson, 2010) clearly suggests that the capability of an economy to grow is significantly dependent on the capability of that economy to create HGEs.

As previous research suggests, enterprise growth is neither a self-evident phenomenon nor a matter of chance (Močnik and Širec, 2016, p. 300). In line with the Penrosean theory of growth (Penrose, 1959), it is widely agreed that growth occurs when—in addition to motivation and opportunity—a proper strategy and corresponding resources are also in place (Gilbert et al., 2006). Thus, if an enterprise wants to achieve high growth rates, access to financial resources is extremely important, since the enterprise will likely need to acquire additional financial resources to support enterprise development and growth (Beck and Demirguc-Kunt, 2006). Financial resources, as well as their access, are thus among the most important elements of the enterprise development and growth process (IFC, 2011) and one of the key challenges of the modern entrepreneurial process (Grichnik et al., 2014), as insufficient or inadequate financial resources can lead to a lack of proper functioning and could reduce the enterprises' ability to grow (Beck and Demirguc-Kunt, 2006). Previous research on HGEs has shown that these enterprises are usually younger (Delmar et al., 2003, pp. 208–209) and more prone to risk-taking (Davidsson and Delmar, 2006) and to higher innovation levels (Shane, 2009), as compared to other non-growing enterprises. Therefore, financing of HGEs

133

will considerably differ from financing of non-growing enterprises, not only in terms of different types of financial resources needed, but also in terms of their amount (Tajnikar, 2006, p. 180).

There is also substantial evidence of the importance of women entrepreneurs in the economic development of a country, with regard to their contribution to job creation and economic growth (Tominc and Rebernik, 2006). Prior studies have suggested that men can obtain, on average, more generous external financing than women (Alsos et al., 2006). For example, Brush et al. (2004b) have indicated that men-owned firms have better access than women-owned firms to formal and informal venture capital investments; consequently, the former's enterprises will grow more rapidly, supporting Delmar and Holmquist's (2004) findings that growth rates of women-controlled HGEs are usually lower than growth rates of men-controlled HGEs.

As previous research suggests, entrepreneurial orientation (EO), human capital and social capital (including networking) can have an important influence on acquiring financial resources (Carter et al., 2007, p. 434; Freel, 2007; Lukkarinen et al., 2016; OECD, 2018; Shepherd, 1999). Even though women in developed economies formally have the same opportunities as men to pursue ideas that can lead to fast-growing businesses, a substantial proportion of previous research reports a lack of entrepreneurship skills among women (OECD, 2015, p. 86) and finds that women in the European Union typically have relatively smaller professional networks compared to their male counterparts (OECD, 2015, p. 91). These might represent constraints for women when acquiring financial resources needed for growth of their enterprises, explaining why women are more likely than men to be discouraged borrowers, i.e., people who do not apply for financial resources because they believe these financial resources will not be appropriate, or that they will not be successful in their acquisition process (OECD, 2016). To minimize this gender gap, some good practices for women's entrepreneurship policies and programmes have been introduced. However, much still needs to be improved, resulting in a call for continued public policy action (OECD, 2016, p. 16).

Regarding the EO and HGEs' capital (our focal interest) as factors that influence the perceived accessibility of financial resources, traditional policy recommendations are rather limited. Therefore, the purpose of our research is to address these important issues and give some insight into relevant aspects of gender-specific policy recommendations by finding an answer to the key research questions: 'Do EO, human capital and networking capability of HGEs impact the perceived accessibility of financial resources? Are there any gender differences in this regard?' To answer these questions, our research aims to identify to what extent differences in the influence of EO and HGEs' capital (limited to human capital and networking capability, as part of social capital) on the perceived accessibility of various forms of financing exist among women- and men-controlled HGEs. Thus, the conceptual research model combines EO, HGEs' capital (human capital, networking capability) and perceived accessibility to different financial resources. The research model was used to test the gender gap between men- and women-controlled HGEs based on a sample of 125 Slovenian HGEs.

This chapter provides three main contributions. First, the chapter seeks to obtain clear insights into the relationship between EO, HGEs' capital and perceived accessibility to different financial resources. The originality lies in the research model which comprehensively analyses all the most relevant types of financial resources, using the random sample of HGEs. Second, it seeks to explain differences between men- and women-controlled HGEs in the perception of financial resource accessibility. The third main contribution is in the development of some policy recommendations aiming to support the financing of women-controlled HGEs. The research is thus important from the academic/scientific viewpoint as well as for the programmes, policies and practices related to high-growth women's entrepreneurship.

2.   LITERATURE REVIEW, HYPOTHESES DEVELOPMENT AND RESEARCH MODEL

2.1   Entrepreneurial Orientation (EO) and Financial Resources

The phenomenon of an EO as a driving force behind the organizational pursuit of entrepreneurial activities has become a central focus of entrepreneurship research in recent decades, even though many variations in the definition of EO exist (Covin and Wales, 2012). They are mostly, at least at the baseline, related to Miller's (1983) definition of an entrepreneurial firm (Hughes and Morgan, 2007, p. 652). Miller defined the entrepreneurial firm as an enterprise 'that engages in product-market innovation, undertakes somewhat risky ventures, and is first to come up with "proactive" innovations, beating competitors to the punch' (Miller, 1983, p. 771). The prominence of the concept of EO thus lies within the assumption that EO represents a continuous variable (or set of variables) upon which all enterprises can be positioned or plotted somewhere along a conceptual continuum of entrepreneurship capability (Covin and Wales, 2012, p. 677). To achieve this, from the perspective of the enterprise, EO includes at least innovativeness, risk-taking, and proactiveness (Miller, 1983) and was later extended with other factors, like competitive aggressiveness and autonomy (Hughes and Morgan, 2007). Innovativeness can drastically increase an enterprise's financial requirements, as financial resources are needed to support large innovative projects (OECD, 2018, p. 6). Additionally, the funding requirements of HGEs in innovation-driven economies are substantially higher (approximately six to ten times higher) than those of HGEs in efficiency- and factor-driven economies (Daniels et al., 2016, p. 7). However, previous research emphasizes the possibility that highly innovation-intensive enterprises can have more difficulties in securing funds, as innovativeness is associated with a lower level of loan application success (Freel, 2007). On the other hand, innovativeness can enhance access to other financial resource types, such as venture capitalist investors (Engel and Keilbach, 2007) and business angels (Bilau and Sarkar, 2016), as innovativeness increases the possibility for higher future growth and profits (Cho and Pucik, 2005). Risk-taking propensity is an aspect that measures willingness to engage in risky activities (Shane, 2003, p. 103). Different financial resources are associated with different risk levels; thus, when making financial decisions, owner/manager risk aversion is found to be important (Lewellen, 2006). Excessive risk-taking can decrease accessibility to some financial resources, especially financial resources from banks (Cowling et al., 2012), or enhance accessibility to other financial resources like venture capital investors (Sahlman, 1990). They provide funds to enterprises willing to take risks, which creates the potential for future growth and the possibility to achieve superior profits. Proactiveness and competitive aggressiveness refer to how enterprises relate to market opportunities by taking the initiative in the marketplace, as well as how they react to competitive trends and demands that already exist in the industries and markets (Lumpkin and Dess, 2001, p. 429). Prior studies have shown that venture capital investors prefer pioneers over followers (Shepherd, 1999, p. 627), so proactiveness and competitive aggressiveness also play an important role when choosing and accessing different forms of financial resources.

Based on the theory presented above, hypothesis H1 was formed:

H1: The EO of HGE has an impact on the perceived accessibility of financial resources.

2.2   HGEs' Capital and Financial Resources

Enterprise capital can be divided into five elementary dimensions (Goodwin, 2003): financial capital (as internal and external accumulated financial resources), natural capital (available natural resources and accompanying climate regulations), produced capital (physical stocks, material objects and ecosystems created by humans), human capital (knowledge, skills, experiences, etc.) and social capital (including networks). When analysing HGEs' capital, our research is limited to human capital and networking capability (as part of enterprise social capital). Human capital is defined as the 'knowledge, skills, competencies and attributes embodied in individuals that facilitate the creation of personal, social and economic well-being' (OECD, 2007, p. 29). Networking capability is 'the ability of an enterprise to exploit its existing ties (both strong and weak) and explore new ties (both strong and weak) with external entities to achieve resource (re)configurations and strategic competitive advantage' (Mu and Di Benedetto, 2012, p. 5).

Prior studies have shown that different investors (providers of financial resources) pay great attention to these elements of human capital in the process of making investment decisions. This applies to venture capital investors (Shepherd, 1999), business angel investors (Clark, 2008), microfinance investors (Allison et al., 2013) and decisions made by banks, where the experiences of the applicant play an important role (Carter et al., 2007, p. 434). For new enterprises, Talaia et al. (2016) have also shown a significant relationship between the ability to acquire financial resources and the level of top managers' education. Prior studies have also shown that social capital with networking can significantly reduce the cost of capital, especially the cost of bank loans (Uzzi, 1999, p. 498), and can influence the investment decisions of venture capitalists (Batjargal and Liu, 2004), the investment decisions of microfinance investors (Aggarwal et al., 2015), or crowdfunding campaign success (Lukkarinen et al., 2016). The structure of top managers' social networks will also influence the information they will receive about potential markets, employees, ways to organize, and possible sources of financing (Shane, 2003, p. 49). Networks will also influence the quality and quantity of information received, as well as the speed with which it is received (Shane, 2003, p. 49). Available information will be important when making financial decisions, and its inaccessibility makes the financial resources acquisition process more difficult (Ogoi, 2016, pp. 70–71).

Based on the above presented theory, hypothesis H2 was formed:

H2: HGEs' human capital and networking capability have an impact on the perceived accessibility of financial resources.

2.3   Gender Gap: Men- vs. Women-Controlled HGEs

Past research has revealed that women and men top managers differ in terms of strategies and perceptions of enterprise funding (Carter and Rosa, 1998). Difference can be attributed to the type of enterprise, management style and financial management experiences of managers (Verheul and Thurik, 2001), or other EO factors. Past studies on gender differences between EO factors, especially innovativeness and risk-taking, are vague, as women- and men-controlled enterprises have been found to have similar levels of risk-taking propensities as well as innovation levels (Sonfield et al., 2001); however, at the same time, Runyan et al. (2006, pp. 470–471) have also detected some statistically significant gender differences for the above-mentioned EO factors. Regarding risk-taking, researchers (Charness and Gneezy, 2012) have also shown that women make smaller investments in risky assets than men do, and thus women appear to be financially more risk averse. Verheul and Thurik (2001) emphasized that gender may have a direct and/or indirect effect on financial resources accessibility. An indirect effect may be associated with different factors of EO, while additional differences are likely to be a consequence of industry differentiation (e.g., predomination of women-controlled enterprises in the services sector) and lower growth aspirations of women in comparison with their male counterparts (OECD, 2015). A direct effect, called 'a gender-discriminatory effect' can emerge when women and men with the same enterprise characteristics differ with respect to their access opportunities to acquire financial resources to finance their enterprises (Verheul and Thurik, 2001, p. 332).

Based on the above presented theory, hypothesis H3 was formed:

H3: The impact of EO on the perceived accessibility of financial resources differs for men- and women-controlled HGEs.

Men- and women-controlled HGEs can also differ with regard to their human capital and networking capability. Men and women possess unique stocks of human capital (DeTienne and Chandler, 2007). In addition, men and women have different networks (Watson, 2011, p. 537). Nevertheless, women were found to possess larger social networks (Ajrouch et al., 2005); however, their professional networks, which are especially important for HGEs (Barringer et al., 2005), are typically smaller compared to their male counterparts' (OECD, 2015, p. 86). Social capital (a broader concept than networks) was found to be statistically different for men and women in some cases (Runyan et al., 2006, p. 469), indicating the possibility that an indirect effect on perceived financial resource accessibility exists. As women are more likely to be financially constrained (OECD, 2015, p. 90), a direct effect also can emerge. A possible cause of such direct effect is that women rely more heavily on internal than on external financial resources (Adema et al., 2014, p. 16), indicating the possibility that women have different ambitions than men (Verheul and Thurik, 2001). Additionally, the direct effect can be attributed to lower confidence of women in their entrepreneurial capabilities, as they face a relative lack in growth motivation (OECD, 2015, p. 87). Moreover, it is also possible that women may simply be subject to investors' discriminatory behaviour (Verheul and Thurik, 2001, p. 337).

Based on the above presented theory, hypothesis H4 was formed:

H4: The impact of HGE human capital and network capability on the perceived accessibility of financial resources differs for men- and women-controlled HGEs.

Based on the above literature review, we have formed the conceptual research model presented in Figure 7.1.

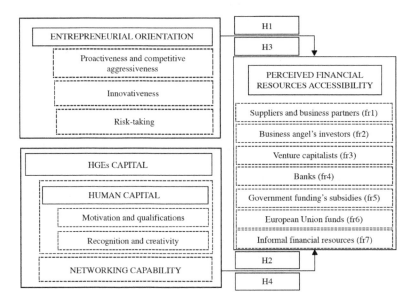

Figure 7.1   Conceptual research model

3.   DATA SOURCES AND METHODOLOGY

3.1   Sample Description

The population of the HGEs is defined by the Agency of the Republic of Slovenia for Public Legal Records and Related Services (AJPES) and consists of 8194 enterprises that have been listed as HGEs at least once between 2011 and 2016, thus fulfilling several predetermined criteria.[1] A total of 2788 HGEs were randomly selected for CATIs (computer-assisted telephone interviews) and CAWIs (computer-assisted web interviews), resulting in a random sample of n = 125 Slovenian HGEs (CATI n = 86; CAWI n = 39). Since only the owners (who are at the same time top managers of the companies) as well as top managers/non-owners of the HGEs were eligible to participate in the survey, a low response rate was expected. The survey was conducted in May 2018. The structure of the sample regarding HGEs' size is in line with the size structure of all Slovenian HGEs in the year 2016 (AJPES, 2017). In the sample, there are 59 (47.2 per cent) men-controlled HGEs and 66 (52.8 per cent) women-controlled HGEs. More than half of all respondents are also (co)owners of the HGEs. On average, HGEs included in the sample employ 24.38 employees and have raised, on average, EUR 4.4 million of capital. In both categories, men-controlled HGEs dominate (average capital amount: 8 504 839 EUR; average number of employees: 36.72), meaning that the size of women-controlled HGEs is smaller on average in terms of both capital requirements (average capital amount: 676 397 EUR) and the number of employees employed (average number of employees: 13.34), which is also in line with previous research (Coleman and Robb, 2014, p. 12).

3.2   Variables

The EO measurement scale was extracted from Hughes and Morgan (2007). The same measurement scale was also suggested by Covin and Wales (2012, p. 695) as one of the best possible choices for measuring EO. For the purpose of this research, the 'Autonomy' items were excluded, since they are related particularly to the autonomy and independence of employees at lower hier-archical levels, performing work tasks in the workplace. By establishing autonomy, top managers demonstrate to their employees that they have faith in their abilities. Autonomy is thus an important driver of employees' flexibility, but it still appears to have no influence whatsoever on business performance (Hughes and Morgan, 2007).

Human capital (HC) was measured with the 13 items of Vidotto Farasson et al.'s (2017) measurement scale. For defining networking capabilities, the 11-item measurement scale developed by Mu and Di Benedetto (2012) was used. All items were measured using a Likert scale, where respondents indicated the level of agreement with statements (1 – completely disagree to 7 – completely agree).

For perceived financial resources accessibility (dependent variables), Brown's (1996) measurement scale was adopted. A 7-point Likert scale was used, and respondents indicated their agreement with statements related to their ability to successfully raise financial resources from different providers. In our research, there were seven financial resource providers included:

- Financial resources from suppliers and business partners (*fr1*);
- Business angel investors (*fr2*);
- Venture capitalists (*fr3*);
- Banks (*fr4*);
- Government funding subsidies (*fr5*);
- European Union funds (*fr6*); and
- Informal financial resources, such as family and friends (*fr7*).

3.3   Methodology

The methodological approach includes factor analysis to form constructs (multidimensional variables) of a research model. Bartlett's test of sphericity was used to determine whether there was a high enough degree of significant correlation between the variables (items) included (Janssens et al., 2008, p. 255). The Kaiser-Meyer-Olkin measure of sampling adequacy was used as well (acceptable if above 0.50), indicating whether distinct and reliable factors can be produced (Yong and Pearce, 2013, p. 88). Communalities show the share of variance of each variable (item) that is explained by a given number of factors (Janssens et al., 2008, p. 257); a cut-off value of 0.50 was used. This is adequate for sample sizes between 100 and 200 provided responses, with relatively few factors, with only a small number of items each (Field, 2009, p. 647). The same cut-off value was also used when determining factor loadings. Factor loadings must be at least 0.50 for sample sizes higher than 100 in order to assign an item to a certain factor (Janssens et al., 2008, p. 260). A reliability analysis was performed using Cronbach's Alpha (Field, 2009, p. 675), with a threshold value of 0.60 (Janssens et al., 2008, p. 275). In a second step, regression analysis was used to test the hypotheses. For testing H1 and H2, a regression analysis for the entire sample was performed. In the multiple regression model ij, the perceived accessibility of the i-th individual financial resource, $i = 1, 2, ..., 7$, was analysed as the dependent variable, regarding the j-th group of independent variables, $j = 1, 2$ (group of factors of EO and HGEs capital). With H3 and H4 the gender gap was analysed. Multiple regression models for the gender-based subsamples were performed, and the differences between the regression coefficients were tested. The 0.10 significance level was considered.

4.   RESULTS

4.1   Factor Analysis Results

Results of the factor analysis are presented in Table 7.1. Three EO factors have been identified: proactiveness and competitive aggressiveness (EO_1: 5 items), innovativeness (EO_2: 3 items), and risk-taking (EO_3: 3 items). Results are in line with Hughes and Morgan's (2007) measurement scale for the factors innovativeness and risk-taking and with Miller/Covin and Slevin's definition of EO where proactiveness and competitive aggressiveness is combined in a single factor (Covin and Wales, 2012). Item Q9 of EO (*We initiate actions to which other organizations respond*) was excluded due to a communality lower than 0.5.

Regarding human capital, two factors have been identified: motivation and qualifications (HC_1: 4 items) and recognition and creativity (HC_2: 4 items). Some of the items of human capital were excluded: *Q20* (*The organization supports employees in upgrading their skills and qualifications where necessary*) and *Q25* (*The organization is assured that it is getting the most from its employees*) were eliminated due to factor loadings (< 0.5); in addition, *Q19* (*When an employee leaves the enterprise we have a training programme for a successor*) was eliminated based on Inter-Total statistics analysis, to increase Cronbach's Alpha. Finally, items *Q14* (*Our employees have leadership skills*) and *Q24* (*Our employees are satisfied with the organization*) were excluded based on communalities (< 0.5).

With factor analysis, one factor for networking capability (NC: 9 items) was formed. Two of the items were excluded: *Q27* (*We search globally to find proper network partners*), based on Item-Total Statistic analysis to increase Cronbach's Alpha, and *Q26* (*We search locally to identify appropriate network partners*), based on communality (< 0.5).

4.2   Regression Analysis Results

Results of the regression analysis for testing H1 and H2 are presented in Table 7.2. Results for testing H3 and H4 are presented in Tables 7.2 and 7.3.

4.2.1   Hypothesis H1

Results indicate that EO factors have some influence on perceived financial resource accessibility for financial resources from suppliers and business partners (*fr1*), venture capitalists (*fr3*), banks (*fr4*), government funding subsidies (*fr5*), and European Union funds (*fr6*). Correlation coefficients (R) are quite low (from .273 to .331), indicating weak to moderate relationships between EO factors and perceived financial resource accessibility. The determination coefficient (Adjusted R square) indicates that, as expected, several other factors influence the perceived accessibility to financial resources, but for the above-mentioned financial resources the regression models are significant. Among the three factors of EO, risk-taking seems to play the most important role in shaping perceived financial resource accessibility. Regression coefficients for risk-taking range between .380 (for *fr3*—financial resources from venture capitalists) and .601 (for *fr4*—financial resources from banks) and are statistically significant at $p \leq 0.01$. Other than for risk-taking, statistically significant positive regression coefficients are also observed for proactiveness and competitive aggressiveness (for *fr1*—financial resources from suppliers and business partners, at $p \leq 0.05$, and for *fr3*—financial resources from venture capitalists, at $p \leq 0.10$).

Table 7.1a   *Factor analysis results for entrepreneurial orientation*

	ITEM	Communalities	FACTORS		
			EO_1	EO_2	EO_3
Entrepreneurial Orientation (EO)	Q1 The term 'risk taker' is considered a positive attribute for people in our business.	0.627			0.735
	Q2 People in our business are encouraged to take calculated risks with new ideas.	0.629			0.749
	Q3 Our business emphasizes both exploration and experimentation for opportunities.	0.648			0.672
	Q4 We actively introduce improvements and innovations in our business.	0.643		0.795	
	Q5 Our business is creative in its methods of operation.	0.632		0.754	
	Q6 Our business seeks out new ways to do things.	0.583		0.674	
	Q7 We always try to take the initiative in every situation (e.g., against competitors, in projects when working with others).	0.503	0.537		
	Q8 We excel at identifying opportunities.	0.569	0.512		
	Q10 Our business is intensely competitive.	0.643	0.763		
	Q11 In general, our business takes a bold or aggressive approach when competing.	0.725	0.826		
	Q12 We try to undo and out-manoeuvre the competition as best as we can.	0.706	0.840		
	% of Variance explained		39.78	13.93	9.11
	Cumulative variance explained			62.82	
	Cronbach's Alpha		0.821	0.714	0.637
	Bartlett's Test ($p < 0.05$)			483.15	
	KMO			0.815	

Table 7.1b　Factor analysis results for HGEs capital

	ITEM	Communalities	FACTORS HC_1	HC_2	NC
HGEs capital	Q13 Our employees constantly do their best.	0.683	0.801		
	Q16 Employees generally perform tasks with a lot of energy.	0.767	0.760		
	Q17 Employees learn from each other.	0.624	0.737		
	Q18 Our employees' competence is at a suitable level.	0.569	0.753		
	Q15 Our organization's employees evaluate their actions.	0.549		0.700	
	Q21 Our enterprise's employees are considered intelligent (gifted).	0.657		0.656	
	Q22 Our employees are widely considered the best in the whole sector.	0.692		0.723	
	Q23 Our organization consistently generates new ideas.	0.681		0.825	
	Q28 We search widely to look for right partners.	0.515			0.718
	Q29 If something is going wrong in relations with partners, we try hard to figure out why.	0.806			0.898
	Q30 If the relationship with a partner is successful, we try to understand what makes it work well.	0.813			0.902
	Q31 We constantly assess and analyse our relationships with partners so that we know what adjustments to make.	0.692			0.832
	Q32 Dynamically integrating networking activities into business operational process is part of our enterprise's strategy.	0.753			0.868
	Q33 We can find partners to count on in time when the need arises.	0.809			0.899
	Q34 We can be quite accessible to our partners in a timely fashion.	0.784			0.885
	Q35 We can get the needed assistance from our partners in an accurate and timely manner.	0.710			0.843
	Q36 Our partners can refer us to a third party who could help if the partners cannot provide direct help.	0.696			0.834
	% of Variance explained		51.77	13.52	73.09
	Cumulative variance explained			65.29	73.09
	Cronbach's Alpha		0.820	0.760	0.952
	Bartlett's Test (p < 0.05)			423.70	1192.24
	KMO			0.862	0.903

Due to the above results, hypothesis H1 stating that the EO of HGEs has an impact on the perceived accessibility of financial resources can be partially accepted.

4.2.2   Hypothesis H2

Results indicate (Table 7.2, women- and men- controlled HGEs) that HGEs' capital has some influence on perceived financial resource accessibility for financial resources from suppliers and business partners (*fr1*) and from European Union funds (*fr6*). Determination coefficients (Adjusted R square) indicate that, as expected, several other factors influence the perceived accessibility of financial resources, but for the above-mentioned financial resources the regression models are significant. Results suggest that the networking capability factor of the HGEs' capital has the most important (statistically significant and positive) role in shaping perceived financial resource accessibility. Regression coefficients for networking capability range between .495 (for *fr1*—financial resources from suppliers and business partners) and .599 (for *fr6*—European Union funds) and are statistically significant at $p \leq 0.01$.

According to these results, hypothesis H2 stating that HGE human capital and networking capability have an impact on the perceived accessibility of financial resources can only be partially accepted as well.

4.2.3   Hypothesis H3

In Table 7.2, separate regression models for perceived accessibility of i-th financial resource (i=1, 2, ..., 7) based on gender subsamples are presented. For models based on the men-controlled HGEs subsample, among the three factors of EO, in addition to risk-taking, proactiveness and competitive aggressiveness seems to have quite an important role in shaping the perceived accessibility of *fr5* (government funding's subsidies), as the regression coefficient is .519 at p ≤ 0.10, but a negative role in shaping the perceived accessibility of *fr7* (informal financial resources, such as from family and friends), as the regression coefficient is –.565 (at p ≤ 0.10). For models based on the women-controlled HGEs subsample, proactiveness and competitive aggressiveness has a significant and positive role in shaping perceived accessibility only with regard to *fr1* (financial resources from suppliers and business partners). Results also show that the *risk-taking* factor of EO seems to be the most important factor in both men- and women-controlled HGEs. Results suggest that perceptions regarding the accessibility of different financial resources differ between genders. Only for *fr7* (informal financial resources, such as from family and friends), the influence of EO is common for both men- and women-controlled HGEs. While the regression coefficient for innovativeness for the men-controlled HGE subsample is positive and statistically significant, for the women-controlled HGE subsample the regression coefficient is negative, meaning innovativeness plays a negative role in shaping the perceived accessibility of these financial resources.

The significance of differences in regression coefficients (IDRE, 2018) for men and women-controlled HGEs was tested (H3). The dummy *gender* variable (1–women, 0–men) and new variables, defined as the product of the gender variable and each of the three EO factors, were formed and named: *EO_1women*, *EO_2women*, and *EO_3women*. These terms test the null hypotheses that the regression coefficients for men- and women-controlled enterprises are equal. Three groups of regression models were analysed, as presented in the first part of Table 7.3. The results indicate that the regression coefficient that refers to the impact of innovativeness (EO_2women) on the accessibility of financial resource *fr7* (informal financial resources) in women-controlled HGEs significantly differs from that in men-controlled HGEs. From Table 7.2 it can be seen that this financial resource is also the only one in which a statistically significant impact of innovativeness was recorded for both men- and women-controlled HGEs. To summarize, there are some significant differences between men- and women-controlled HGEs regarding the impact of factors of EO on the perceived accessibility of financial resources. Men and women respondents expressed different opinions about the perceived financial resource accessibility. Moreover, the results in Table 7.3 also indicate that the regression coefficients for the impact of innovativeness on perceived informal financial resource accessibility statistically significantly differ between men- and women-controlled HGEs.

Due to the above-described results, hypothesis H3, which states that the impact of EO on the perceived accessibility of financial resources differs for men- and women-controlled HGEs, can be partially accepted.

4.2.4   Hypothesis H4

In Table 7.2, separate regression models for the perceived accessibility to i-th financial resource (i = 1, 2, ..., 7) based on gender subsamples for the impact of HGEs human capital and networking capability are presented. For models based on the men-controlled HGEs subsample, results indicate that only two models are statistically significant, namely *fr1* (financial resources from suppliers and business partners) and *fr4* (financial resources from banks). From the three factors of HGEs' capital, networking capability seems to play the most important role in shaping the perceived accessibility of these financial resources. The regression coefficients are .900 for *fr1* (financial resources from suppliers and business partners; $p \leq 0.01$) and .498 for *fr4* (financial resources from banks) at $p \leq 0.10$. For models based on the women-controlled HGEs subsample, networking capability also plays a statistically significant role in shaping the perceived accessibility of *fr6* (European Union funds; $p \leq 0.10$). Results also indicate that the factor 'motivation and qualifications' might play some role when shaping the perceived accessibility of financial resources and that men and women have different perceptions regarding the accessibility of different financial resources.

The significance of differences in regression coefficients (IDRE, 2018) for men- and women-controlled HGEs was tested (H4). The dummy *gender* variable (1–women, 0–men) and new variables, defined as the product of the gender variable and each of the three factors referring to the capital, were formed and named: *HC _1women, HC_2women,* and *NC_women.* Three groups of regression models were analysed, as presented in the second part of Table 7.3. Results indicate that regression coefficients that refer to the impact of networking capability (NC_women) on *fr1* (financial resources from suppliers and business partners) in women-controlled HGEs statistically differ from those of men-controlled HGEs. The same can be said for the factor 'motivation and qualifications' (HC_1women) in relation to financial resource *fr4* (financial resources from banks) ($p \leq 0.10$).

Due to the above-described results, hypothesis H4, stating that the impact of HGE human capital and network capability on the perceived accessibility of financial resources differs for men- and women-controlled HGEs, can also be partially accepted.

5.   DISCUSSION

Even though many scholars have highlighted the importance of HGEs (e.g., Birch, 1979; Henrekson and Johansson, 2010; Shane, 2009), the gap between men- and women-controlled HGEs, regarding their financing, remains a deficient and heterogeneous research scientific field. To obtain clearer insight into the relationship between EO, HGEs' capital, and the perceived accessibility of different financial resources, hypothesis H1 predicted an impact of HGEs' EO on the perceived accessibility of financial resources. According to our results, EO seems to play a statistically significant role in the perceived accessibility of five out of seven financial resource types. It seems that the risk-taking factor of EO plays the most important role. It seems that Slovenian HGEs that perceive higher risk levels also perceive better accessibility of different financial resources. As such, our results are partly consistent with previous research, supporting findings from Sahlman (1990) that higher risk will enhance the accessibility of financial resources like venture capitalist investments; however, at the same time, our results do not support findings in which a negative relationship was identified (e.g., for financial resources from banks) (Cowling et al., 2012). Since all included HGEs in our sample made a profit in the last year when they were listed as HGEs, investors seem not to differ between more and less risky HGEs as long as they have created profits. Results also support Shepherd's (1999, p. 627) thesis that venture capital investors prefer pioneers over followers, as proactiveness and competitive aggressiveness was found to be statistically significant for shaping perceived financial resource accessibility.

Hypothesis H2 predicted the existence of an impact of HGEs' human capital and networking capability on the perceived accessibility of financial resources. Results show that HGEs' human capital and network capability have an impact on the perceived accessibility to some financial resource providers. Among the three factors of HGEs capital, networking capability seems to have the most important role. Networking capability enhances strong ties with enterprises' suppliers and business partners (fr1), thus increasing the perceived accessibility of this financial resource. Networking capability also has a positive impact on the perceived accessibility of financial resources from European Union funds (fr6), thus supporting previous theory emphasizing that the structure of an enterprise's social networks will influence the quantity and quality of information they will receive (Shane, 2003, p. 49). HGEs with better networking capability will probably find it easier to deal with the application process and probably will avoid possible errors in the documentation when applying to receive resources. As such, our results support Ogoi's (2016, pp. 70–71) findings that inaccessibility of information could represent an obstacle in the financial resource acquisition process.

The results of testing H3, stating that the impact of EO on the perceived accessibility of financial resources differs for men- and women-controlled HGEs, confirmed that some such differences exist. Results partly support previous findings that women and men differ in terms of strategies and perceptions of enterprise funding in certain areas (Carter and Rosa, 1998), especially when analysing innovativeness (Runyan et al., 2006). On the other hand, the risk-taking factor that was found important in previous research (Charness and Gneezy, 2012) was not significant in the present research. Since our research results indicate that women and men do not differ with regard to the perception of HGEs' EO factors,[2] it is likely that any difference between women- and men-controlled HGEs with regard to the impact of HGEs' innovativeness on the accessibility of informal financial resources (fr7) can be attributed to a direct, gender-discriminatory effect (Verheul and Thurik, 2001) that may emerge from discriminatory investors preferring men- over women-controlled HGEs (negative regression coefficient for women-controlled HGEs). It may be expected that investors' attitudes and the possibility of gender-biased or even gender-discriminatory views toward financing HGEs are, to a certain extent, determined by cultural backgrounds and are difficult to modify (European Commission, 2015); however, at the same time, such values and attitudes can be, at least to a small extent, shaped by introducing entrepreneurial gender

Table 7.2   *Regression analysis results*

Independent variable	Women- and men-controlled HGEs (n = 125) Dependent variables							Men-controlled HGEs (n = 59) Dependent variables							Women-controlled HGEs (n = 66) Dependent variables						
EO factors	fr1	fr2	fr3	fr4	fr5	fr6	fr7	fr1	fr2	fr3	fr4	fr5	fr6	fr7	fr1	fr2	fr3	fr4	fr5	fr6	fr7
	Regression coefficients							Regression coefficients							Regression coefficients						
Constant	4.736	2.456	2.160	4.856	3.400	2.840	3.224	4.429	2.527	2.210	4.866	2.951	2.588	3.408	5.015	2.447	2.127	4.839	3.751	3.095	3.105
EO_1	.369 **	.062	.222 *	.122	.281	.169	−.243	.300	−.184	.202	.091	.519 *	.068	−.565 *	.577 ***	2.213	.165	.187	.204	.263	−.046
EO_2	.208	−.030	−.006	−.008	.130	.094	.011	.306	.037	.007	.170	.254	.218	.581 **	−.010	−.092	.032	−.328	−.085	−.046	−.855 ***
EO_3	.423 ***	.311 **	.380 ***	.601 ***	.478 ***	.528 ***	.133	.248 *	.484 *	.536 **	.538 **	.351	.671 ***	.387	.645 ***	.274	.240	.748 ***	.522 **	.461 *	.252
Model								Model							Model						
R	.320	.181	.289	.331	.273	.276	.127	.284	.252	.370	.301	.360	.373	.374	.423	.181	.193	.408	.249	.222	.374
Adjusted R square	.080	.009	.061	.088	.052	.053	−.008	.031	.012	.090	.041	.082	.092	.093	.139	−.014	−.009	.127	.017	.003	.078
F-value	4.617 ***	1.364	3.684 ***	4.974 ***	3.259 **	3.329 **	.664	1.610	1.243	2.901 **	1.830	2.731 **	2.970 **	2.983 **	4.500 ***	.703	.797	4.138 ***	1.364	1.072	2.826 **
HGEs capital factors	Regression coefficients							Regression coefficients							Regression coefficients						
Constant	4.736	2.456	2.160	4.856	3.400	2.840	3.224	4.407	2.462	2.198	4.977	2.951	2.568	3.314	4.928	2.450	2.204	4.875	3.808	3.177	3.233
HC_1	.063	−.047	−.146	.133	−.051	−.141	−.361 *	−.176	−.043	.012	.466 *	−.081	.073	−.155	.244 *	−.008	−.277	−.120	−.227	−.544 **	−.555 **
HC_2	−.028	.059	.155	−.064	.073	−.085	−.145	.075	.026	.063	−.137	.218	.064	−.195	−.048	.074	.201	−.109	.023	−.214	−.151

High-growth women's entrepreneurship

	Women- and men-controlled HGEs (n = 125)							Men-controlled HGEs (n = 59)							Women-controlled HGEs (n = 66)						
NC	.495	.255	.207	.156	.314	.599	.373	.900	.467*	.307	.498	.338	.456	.324	.170	.109	.179	.010	.322	.781	.459
	***					***	*	***			*		*							***	*
Model								Model									Model				
R	.270	.154	.201	.119	.161	.283	.215	.460	.241	.186	.336	.213	.244	.157	.183	.086	.270	.081	.173	.384	.283
Adjusted R square	.050	.000	.017	−.010	.002	.057	.022	.169	.007	−.018	.064	−.007	.008	−.029	−.013	−.041	.028	−.041	−.017	.106	.036
F-value	3.160	.983	1.699	.576	1.073	3.517	1.950	4.922	1.129	.656	2.329	.870	1.158	.460	.719	.155	1.619	.138	.641	3.570	1.803
	**					**		***			*									**	

Notes: Statistical significance: *** $p \leq 0.01$, ** $p \leq 0.05$, * $p \leq 0.10$.

Table 7.3   *Test of statistically significant differences in regression coefficients*

		Financial resource	Regression coefficient	t-value
H3	EO_1women	fr1	0.068	.205
		fr2	0.207	.640
		fr3	−0.235	−.851
		fr4	−0.210	−.619
		fr5	−0.523	−1.419
		fr6	−0.087	−.235
		fr7	0.365	.920
	EO_2women	fr1	−0.166	−.486
		fr2	−0.016	−.050
		fr3	0.136	.482
		fr4	−0.285	−.827
		fr5	−0.197	−.519
		fr6	−0.092	−.246
		fr7	−1.333	−3.439***
	EO_3women	fr1	0.243	.739
		fr2	−0.213	−.675
		fr3	−0.380	−1.424
		fr4	0.127	.396
		fr5	0.019	.051
		fr6	−0.254	−.713
		fr7	0.001	.001
H4	HC_1women	fr1	0.434	1.269
		fr2	0.044	.133
		fr3	−0.266	−.944
		fr4	−0.574	−1.685*
		fr5	−0.091	−.240
		fr6	−0.390	−1.041
		fr7	−0.235	−.0584
	HC_2women	fr1	−0.308	−.913
		fr2	−0.041	−.127
		fr3	0.117	.423
		fr4	−0.150	−.442
		fr5	−0.182	−.488
		fr6	−0.187	−.506
		fr7	0.125	.312
	NC_women	fr1	−0.695	−2.142**
		fr2	−0.353	−1.095
		fr3	−0.178	−.639
		fr4	−0.514	−1.515
		fr5	−0.134	−.356
		fr6	0.125	.346
		fr7	0.036	.088

Notes: Statistical significance: *** $p \leq 0.01$, ** $p \leq 0.05$, *$p \leq 0.10$.

equality elements into the educational system and by media attention toward gender equality in entrepreneurship. Since several studies have analysed the impact of entrepreneurial education and training on the entrepreneurial activity of individuals from different viewpoints and educational levels (Audretsch et al., 2002; Oosterbeek et al., 2010), the emphasis on gender equality for generating high-quality business ideas and rapidly growing businesses, in terms of entrepreneurial characteristics as well as the capacity for innovation breakthroughs, should become an integrative part of entrepreneurial education and training. According to the social cognitive theory of mass communication, media communications have an impact on social attitudes and behavioural intentions (Bandura, 2001). Also, Levie et al. (2010, p. 3) reported that media has an important role to play in raising the level of desirability and engagement regarding entrepreneurial activity; it may be expected that this includes personal attitudes of investors toward financing entrepreneurial activities as well. High-profile media stories about gender equality in terms of performance in running fast-growing businesses could also tap investors' perceptions and increase the desirability of enabling equal gender opportunities regarding their financial investments.

Hypothesis H4 stated that the impact of HGE human capital and network capability on the perceived accessibility of financial resources differs for men- and women-controlled HGEs. As the results suggest (Table 7.3), our research identifies statistically significant difference between genders, namely regarding the impact of networking capability on the perceived accessibility to *fr1* (financial resources from suppliers and business partners). Although women professional networks are typically smaller compared to their male counterparts (Barringer et al., 2005), in Slovenian HGEs this isn't the case. Contextualization of institutional context recommended by Welter (2011) helps us to explain these results. It is important to highlight that in recent years the Slovenian entrepreneurship policy intensively stimulated the integration of women into the entrepreneurship ecosystem through numerous associations, councils, societies and groups within different organizations and institutions. Another statistically significant difference between genders is in motivation and qualifications (human capital factor) and *fr4* (banks). Indirect[3] as well as direct effects were identified. These results indicate that, even though higher levels of motivation and qualifications are identified for women-controlled HGEs, lower levels of accessibility to financial resources from banks are perceived. There are many possible explanations why this disparity might emerge. One of the most probable reasons is that women are, on average, more reluctant than men to assume a position of debt (McCracken et al., 2015), as they rely more heavily on internal financial resources (Adema et al., 2014), thus also reflecting lower confidence in their own capabilities when acquiring financial resources (OECD, 2015, 2016). Other possible reasons include investors' discriminant behaviour, including non-economic discrimination based on investors' preferences or statistical discrimination based on information asymmetries associated with characteristics of a particular (i.e., female) demographic group (OECD, 2013, p. 134).

Economic policy measures aimed at overcoming the direct gender-discriminatory effect in financing HGEs identified in our research should be distinguished from measures designed to promote women's entrepreneurship.

To avoid possible non-economic and statistical discrimination in financing, women should be encouraged to become 'big dreamers' (Brush et al., 2014; OECD, 2016), as this would increase the demand of women-controlled enterprises for financial resources, as well as their motivation to grow. Change on the supply side (i.e., investors) is also necessary to overcome women's financial constraints. Change in the demand as well as the supply side could be achieved with positive role models (OECD, 2015, p. 92). Although Kwapisz and Hechavarría (2018) suggest that women are less likely to ask for external financing than men, we believe that highlighting successful women-controlled HGEs might help them to take risks and overcome traditional stereotypes. Positive change could also appear on the supply side, as financial resource providers will recognize that women-controlled enterprises are just as successful, and sometimes even more so, than men-controlled enterprises (Brush et al., 2014, p. 24). Previous research also suggests that women tend to have more obvious difficulties accessing venture capitalists' and business angels' investments (McCracken et al., 2015, p. 15). Because there are relatively fewer women among investors themselves (Brush et al., 2004a), policies should also strive to increase the representation of women among the overwhelmingly male investors' community, in order to prevent the formation of possible discriminatory behaviour.

5.1   Practical Implications

The suggested and above-discussed measures to promote women entrepreneurship and achieve higher levels of growth have been successfully used in many forms.

One example of a successful programme that enables women to be 'big dreamers' and thus increases their motivation to grow, comes from Ireland ('Going for growth in Ireland'). When launched, the programme had offered support groups led by successful women entrepreneurs and delivered quite outstanding results with relatively low costs—EUR 1500 per participant, while one cohort (60 women) of the 2013 programme cycle created 50 additional jobs in the following year (OECD, 2015, p. 14). Similarly, the initiative 'Frauen unternehmen' in Germany created a network of 'role model' women entrepreneurs who travel across the country to promote female entrepreneurship through various events. In Sweden the 'Women's Entrepreneurship Ambassadors Programme' was also implemented (OECD, 2016).

In addition to role models and motivation to grow, HGEs' access to financial resources should be promoted. An example of good practice comes from the Province of Trento in Italy where a special 'Seed Money Fund' was launched to support innovative and growing enterprises, primarily led by under-represented and disadvantaged groups, including women (OECD, 2015).

6.   CONCLUDING REMARKS AND SUGGESTIONS FOR FUTURE RESEARCH

Even though there are no formal or legal barriers that prevent equal access to financial resources for both genders, in the case of Slovenia several aspects of a gender gap were identified. The present research is important from the academic/scientific viewpoint for high-growth women's entrepreneurship. The developed research model presented in the chapter provides a foundation for researching a heterogeneous and deficient research area of HGE financing and enables analysis of gender differences regarding the influence of selected determinants on the perceived accessibility of various forms of financing. On this basis, policy recommendations aiming to support the financing of women-controlled HGEs can be formed.

Several enhancements of this research are possible. To enhance gender-gap understanding, an analysis of equally sized women- and men-controlled HGEs is recommended, as the research results revealed that women-controlled HGEs differ from men-controlled HGEs in both average capital acquired, and the average number of employees employed. Even though this is in line with previous findings (Coleman and Robb, 2014, p. 12) it could also mean that the identified differences regarding the perceived accessibility to financial resources are (at least to some extent) the consequence of differences in the characteristics of women-controlled companies that may be less desirable from the investors' point of view. A comparison between women- and men-controlled HGEs based on sector/industry would also provide an important extension to resolve any debates that could arise. Additionally, in order to verify the reliability of the self-reported perceived levels of growth determinants included in the study (EO, human capital, networking capability) and their influence on financial resource accessibility, an analysis based on objective measures and real usage of different financial resources is recommended.

Another possible option for future research is the expansion of additional international and longitudinal insights. As such, regional comparison should provide important insights; although the EU policy strives to unify the EU market as much as possible, extensive country as well as regional differences still exist (Močnik and Širec, 2016). Next, the development of a longitudinal study and inclusion of other growth determinants (as results indicate that there are several other factors influencing the perceived accessibility of financial resources) would be a significant improvement. Finally, we consider it to be of great importance to study in depth the relationship between HGEs' perceived (or real) access to different financial resources and HGEs' implemented long-term growth strategies.[4]

NOTES

1. Including net revenues from sales higher than 100 000 EUR for the last year, positive added value in the last year, added value from the last year higher than added value from the first year of the selected time period and higher than 21 000 EUR per employee, a positive cumulative net profit and an increase of employees in last year (AJPES, 2017).
2. An additional analysis of differences (based on the Mann–Whitney U test— variables representing factors of EO that are not normally distributed, $p \leq 0.05$) did not confirm statistically significant differences between men- and women-controlled HGEs in terms of average perception of EO factors (all $p > 0.05$).
3. An additional analysis of differences in the average perception of HGEs' capital factors (based on the Mann–Whitney U test—variables representing factors of HGEs' capital that are not normally distributed; $p \leq 0.05$) confirmed that statistically significant differences in the average perception of HGEs' capital factors between men- and women-controlled HGEs exist when analysing the factor 'motivation and qualifications' (mean rank men-controlled HGEs: 53.40; mean rank women-controlled HGEs: 71.58, $p = 0.005$) and when analysing the factor 'recognition and creativity', at $p \leq 0.10$ (mean rank men-controlled HGEs: 69.16; mean rank women-controlled HGEs: 57.49, $p = 0.072$). For the factor 'networking capability', statistically significant differences were not identified, and thus previous findings arguing that men and women have different networks (Watson, 2011, p. 537) cannot be confirmed for Slovenian HGEs.
4. The authors acknowledge the financial support from the Slovenian Research Agency (research core funding No. P5-0023).

REFERENCES

Adema, W., N. Ali, V. Frey, K. Hyunsook, M. Lunati, M. Piacentini and M. Queisser (2014), *Enhancing Women's Economic Empowerment through Entrepreneurship and Business Leadership in OECD Countries*, Paris: OECD Directorate for Employment, Labour and Social Affairs.

Agency of the Republic of Slovenia for Public Legal Records and Related Services (AJPES) (2017), 'Data about high-growth enterprises', accessed 10 July 2018 at https://www.ajpes.si/Letna_porocila/Informacije/Podatki_po_regijah.

Aggarwal, R., J.W. Goodell and L.J. Selleck (2015), 'Lending to women in microfinance: role of social trust', *International Business Review*, 24(1), 55–65.

Ajrouch, J.K., A.Y. Blandon and T.C. Antonucci (2005), 'Social networks among men and women: the effects of age and socioeconomic status', *The Journals of Gerontology: Series B*, 60(1), 311–317.

Allison, H.T., A.F. McKenny and J.C. Short (2013), 'The effect of entrepreneurial rhetoric on microlending investment: an examination of the warm-glow effect', *Journal of Business Venturing*, 28(6), 690–707.

Alsos, A.G., E.J. Isaksen and E. Ljunggren (2006), 'New venture financing and sub-sequent business growth in men- and women-led businesses', *Entrepreneurship Theory and Practice*, 30(5), 667–686.

Audretsch, B.D., R. Thurik, I. Verheul and S. Wennekers (2002), 'An eclectic theory of entrepreneurship', in D.B. Audretsch, R. Thurik, I. Verheul and S. Wennekers (eds.), *Entrepreneurship: Determinants and Policy in a European–US Comparison*, Boston/Dordrecht: Kluwer Academic Publishers.

Bandura, A. (2001), 'Social cognitive theory of mass communication', *Media Psychology*, 3(3), 265–299.

Barringer, R.B., F.F. Jones and D.O. Neubaum (2005), 'A quantitative content analysis of the characteristics of rapid-growth firms and their founders', *Journal of Business Venturing*, 20(5), 663–687.

Batjargal, B. and M. Liu (2004), 'Entrepreneurs' access to private equity in China: the role of social capital', *Organization Science*, 15(2), 159–172.

Beck, T. and A. Demirguc-Kunt (2006), 'Small and medium-size enterprises: access to finance as a growth constraint', *Journal of Banking & Finance*, 30(11), 2931–2943.

Bilau, J. and S. Sarkar (2016), 'Financing innovative start-ups in Portuguese context: what is the role of business angles networks?', *Journal of the Knowledge Economy*, 7(4), 920–934.

Birch, L.D. (1979), *The Job Generation Process*, Cambridge: MIT Program on Neighborhood and Regional Change.

Brown, E.T. (1996), 'Resource orientation, entrepreneurial orientation and growth: how the perception of resource availability affects small firm growth', Newark, NJ, Graduate School.

Brush, G.C., N.M. Carter, E.J. Gatewood, P.G. Greene and M. Hart (2004a), 'Gatekeepers of venture growth: a Diana Project report on the role and participation of women in the venture capital industry', Kansas City: Kauffman Foundation.

Brush, G.C., N.M. Carter, E.J. Gatewood and M. Hart (2004b), *Clearing the Hurdles: Women Building High-Growth Business*, Upper Saddle River, NJ: Financial Times/Prentice Hall.

Brush, C., P. Greene, L. Balachandra and A. Davis (2014), *The Diana Report: Women Entrepreneurs 2014: Bridging the Gender Gap in Venture Capital*, Wellesley, MA: Babson College.

Carter, S. and P. Rosa (1998), 'The financing of male- and female-owned businesses', *Entrepreneurship & Regional Development*, 10(3), 225–242.

Carter, S., E. Shaw, W. Lam and F. Wilson (2007), 'Gender, entrepreneurship, and bank lending: the criteria and processes used by bank loan officers in assessing applications', *Entrepreneurship Theory and Practice*, 31(3), 427–444.

Charness, G. and U. Gneezy (2012), 'Strong evidence for gender differences in risk taking', *Journal of Economic Behavior & Organization*, 83(1), 50–58.

Cho, J.H. and V. Pucik (2005), 'Relationship between innovativeness, quality, growth, profitability, and market value', *Strategic Management Journal*, 26(6), 555–575.

Clark, C. (2008), 'The impact of entrepreneurs' oral "pitch" presentation skills on business angels' initial screening investment decisions', *Venture Capital*, 10(3), 257–279.

Coleman, S. and A. Robb (2014), 'Access to capital by high-growth women-owned businesses', San Rafael, CA: National Women's Business Council. Accessed 16 July 2018 at http://awbc.org/wp-content/uploads/2014/10/Access-to-Capital-by-High-Growth-Women-Owned-Businesses-Robb-Final-Draft.pdf.

Covin, G.J. and W.J. Wales (2012), 'The measurement of entrepreneurial orientation', *Entrepreneurship Theory and Practice*, 36(4), 677–702.

Cowling, M., W. Liu and A. Ledger (2012), 'Small business financing in the UK before and during the current financial crisis', *International Small Business Journal*, 30(7), 778–800.

Daniels, C., M. Herrington and P. Kew (2016), *Entrepreneurial Finance*, special topic report 2015–2016, Global Entrepreneurship Monitor.

Davidsson, P. and F. Delmar (2006), 'High-growth firms and their contribution to employment: the case of Sweden 1987–96', in P. Davidsson, F. Delmar and J. Wiklund (eds.), *Entrepreneurship and the Growth of Firms*, Cheltenham, UK and Northampton, MA, USA: Edward Elgar Publishing.

Delmar, F., P. Davidsson and W.B. Gartner (2003), 'Arriving at the high-growth firm', *Journal of Business Venturing*, 18(2), 189–216.

Delmar, F. and C. Holmquist (2004), 'Women's entrepreneurship: issues and policies', Proceedings of the 2nd Organisation for Economic Co-operation and Development (OECD) Conference of Ministers Responsible for SMEs, Promoting Entrepreneurship and Innovative SMEs in a Global Economy, Istanbul, Turkey.

DeTienne, R.D. and G.N. Chandler (2007), 'The role of gender in opportunity identification', *Entrepreneurship Theory and Practice*, 31(3), 365–386.

Engel, D. and M. Keilbach (2007), 'Firm-level implications of early stage venture capital investment: an empirical investigation', *Journal of Empirical Finance*, 14(2), 150–167.

European Commission (2015), *Strategic Engagement for Gender Equality 2016–2019*, Luxembourg: Publications Office of the European Union. Accessed 30 July 2018 at https://ec.europa.eu/anti-trafficking/sites/antitrafficking/files/strategic_engagement _for_gender_equality_en.pdf.

Field, A. (2009), *Discovering Statistics Using SPSS*, 3rd edition, London: Sage Publications.

Freel, S.M. (2007), 'Are small innovators credit rationed?', *Small Business Economics*, 28(1), 23–35.

Gilbert, B.A., P.P. McDougall and D.B. Audretsch (2006), 'New venture growth: a review and extension global', *Journal of Management*, 32(6), 926–950.

Goodwin, R.N. (2003), *Five Kinds of Capital: Useful Concepts for Sustainable Development*, Medford, MA: Tufts University, Global Development and Environment Institute.

Grichnik, D., J. Brinckmann, L. Singh and S. Manigart (2014), 'Beyond environmental scarcity: human and social capital as driving forces of bootstrapping activities', *Journal of Business Venturing*, 29(2), 310–326.

Henrekson, M. and D. Johansson (2010), 'Gazelles as job creators: a survey and interpretation of the evidence', *Small Business Economics*, 35(2), 227–244.

Hughes, M. and R.E. Morgan (2007), 'Deconstructing the relationship between entrepreneurial orientation and business performance at the embryonic stage of firm growth', *Industrial Marketing Management*, 36(5), 651–661.

Institute for Digital Research and Education (IDRE) (2018), 'How can I compare regression coefficients between two groups?', SPSS FAQ, accessed 10 July 2018 at https://stats.idre.ucla.edu/spss/faq/how-can-i-compare-regression-coefficients -between-two-groups/.

International Finance Corporation (IFC) (2011), *SME Finance Policy Guide*, Washington, DC: International Finance Corporation. Accessed 13 November 2017 at https://

www.ifc.org/wps/wcm/connect/f3ef82804a02db409b88fbd1a5d13d27/G20_Policy
_Report.pdf?MOD=AJPERES.

Janssens, W., K. Wijnem, P. De Pelsmacker and P. Van Kenhove (2008), *Marketing Research with SPSS*, Harlow: Pearson Education.

Kwapisz, A. and D.M. Hechavarría (2018), 'Women don't ask: an investigation of start-up financing and gender', *Venture Capital*, 20(2), 159–190.

Landström, H. (2010), 'David Birch', in H. Landström (ed.), *Pioneers in Entrepreneurship and Small Business Research*, New York: Springer.

Levie, J., M. Hart and M.S. Karim (2010), *Impact of Media on EI and Actions*, University of Strathclyde, Aston Business School.

Lewellen, K. (2006), 'Financing decisions when managers are risk averse', *Journal of Financial Economics*, 82(99), 551–589.

Lukkarinen, A., J.E. Teich, H. Wallenius and J. Wallenius (2016), 'Success drivers of online equity crowdfunding campaigns', *Decision Support Systems*, 87, 26–38.

Lumpkin, T.G. and G.G. Dess (2001), 'Linking two dimensions of entrepreneurial orientation to firm performance: the moderating role of environment and industry life cycle', *Journal of Business Venturing*, 16(5), 429–451.

McCracken, K., S. Marquez, C. Kwong, U. Stephan, A. Castagnoli and M. Dlouhá (2015), 'Women's entrepreneurship: closing the gender gap in access to financial and other services and in social entrepreneurship', Brussels: European Parliament, Policy Department C, Citizens' Rights and Constitutional Affairs.

Miller, D. (1983), 'The correlates of entrepreneurship in three types of firms', *Management Science*, 29, 770–791.

Močnik, D. and K. Širec (2016), 'Growth aspirations of early-stage entrepreneurs: empirical investigation of South-Eastern and Western European countries', *Journal of East European Management Studies*, 21(3), 298–317.

Mu, J. and A. Di Benedetto (2012), 'Networking capability and new product development', *IEEE Transactions on Engineering Management*, 59(1), 4–19.

OECD (2007), 'Human capital: how what you know shapes your life', accessed 13 July 2018 at https://www.oecd.org/insights/humancapitalhow whatyouknowshapesyourlife.htm.

OECD (2013), *The Missing Entrepreneurs: Policies for Inclusive Entrepreneurship in Europe*, Paris: OECD Publishing.

OECD (2015), *The Missing Entrepreneurs: Policies for Self-Employment and Entrepreneurship*, Paris: OECD Publishing.

OECD (2016), 'Policy brief on women's entrepreneurship', Luxembourg: Publications Office of the European Union, accessed 17 July 2018 at https://www.oecd.org/cfe/smes/Policy-Brief-on-Women-s-Entrepreneurship.pdf.

OECD (2018), 'Enhancing SME access to diversified financing instruments', Discussion paper, Mexico City: SME Ministerial Conference. Accessed 21 July 2018 at https://www.oecd.org/cfe/smes/ministerial/documents/2018-SME-Ministerial-Conference-Plenary-Session-2.pdf.

Ogoi, J.H. (2016), 'Strategies for accessing credit by small and medium enterprises', Minneapolis, MN: Walden University.

Oosterbeek, H., M. van Praag and A. Ijsselstein (2010), 'The impact of entrepreneurship education on entrepreneurship skills and motivation', *European Economic Review*, 54(3), 442–454.

Penrose, E. (1959), *The Theory of the Growth of the Firm*, New York: John Wiley.

Runyan, C.R., P. Huddleston and J. Swinney (2006), 'Entrepreneurial orientation and social capital as small firm strategies: a study of gender differences from a resource-based view', *The International Entrepreneurship and Management Journal*, 2(4), 455–477.

Sahlman, A.W. (1990), 'The structure and governance of venture-capital organizations', *Journal of Financial Economics*, 27(2), 473–521.

Shane, S. (2003), *A General Theory of Entrepreneurship, The Individual–Opportunity Nexus*, Cheltenham, UK and Northampton, MA, USA: Edward Elgar Publishing.

Shane, S. (2009), 'Why encouraging more people to become entrepreneurs is bad public policy', *Small Business Economy*, 33(2), 141–149.

Shepherd, A.D. (1999), 'Venture capitalists' assessment of new venture survival', *Management Science*, 45(5), 621–632.

Sonfield, M., R. Lussier, R. Corman and M. McKinney (2001), 'Gender comparisons in strategic decisionmaking: an empirical analysis of the entrepreneurial strategy matrix', *Journal of Small Business Management*, 39(2), 165–173.

Tajnikar, M. (2006), *Tvegano poslovodenje: knjiga o gazelah in rastočih poslih* [Risk Management: A Book on Gazelles and Growing Business], Ljubljana: Faculty of Economics, Ljubljana University.

Talaia, M., A. Pisoni and A. Onetti (2016), 'Factors influencing the fund raising process for innovative new ventures: an empirical study', *Journal of Small Business and Enterprise Development*, 23(2), 363–378.

Tominc, P. and M. Rebernik (2006), 'Female entrepreneurial growth aspirations in Slovenia: an unexploited resource', in C.G. Brush, N.M. Carter, E.J. Gatewood, P.G. Greene and M.M. Hart (eds.), *Growth-Oriented Women Entrepreneurs and Their Businesses: A Global Research Perspective*, Cheltenham, UK and Northampton, MA, USA: Edward Elgar Publishing.

Uzzi, B. (1999), 'Embeddedness in the making of financial capital: how social relations and networks benefit firms seeking financing', *American Sociological Review*, 64(4), 481–505.

Verheul, I. and R. Thurik (2001), 'Start-up capital: does gender matter?', *Small Business Economics*, 16(4), 329–345.

Vidotto Farasson, D.J., H.A. Ferenhof, P.M. Selig and R.C. Bastos (2017), 'A human capital measurement scale', *Journal of Intellectual Capital*, 18(2), 316–329.

Watson, J. (2011), 'Networking: gender differences and the association with firm performance', *International Small Business Journal*, 30(5), 536–558.

Welter, F. (2011), 'Contextualizing entrepreneurship: conceptual challenges and ways forward', *Entrepreneurship Theory and Practice*, 35(1), 165–184.

Yong, G.A. and S. Pearce (2013), 'A beginner's guide to factor analysis: focusing on exploratory factor analysis', *Tutorials in Quantitative Methods for Psychology*, 9(2), 79–94.

8. Women's awareness of financial policy and their debt financing activities: evidence from China

Juan Wu, Yaokuang Li and Shakeel Muhammad

1. INTRODUCTION

Female entrepreneurship is widely acknowledged as a significant engine for economic growth and societal well-being (Kelley et al., 2017). Nevertheless, access to finance, especially external finance, has historically been regarded as a major obstacle facing women entrepreneurs, particularly women entrepreneurs with growth aspirations (Carter et al., 2015; Naidu and Chand, 2017; World Bank, 2011). As a consequence, how to strengthen women's access to external finance has become a common concern of scholars, practitioners and policy makers. Given the striking challenges that women entrepreneurs have suffered in equity financing (Becker-Blease and Sohl, 2007; Brush et al., 2014, 2018; Jennings and Brush, 2013), we focus this study on another type of external financing—debt financing—which is a more common and available source through which women can secure external finance (Constantinidis et al., 2006; Eddleston et al., 2016).

Prior research suggests that women entrepreneurs are less likely to utilize debt financing and tend to rely on lower levels of debt financing (Carter et al., 2007; Jennings and Brush, 2013); this phenomenon is attributed to three distinct explanations, namely, structural factors, supply-side discrimination, and demand-side debt and risk aversion (Carter et al., 2007; Coleman and Robb, 2009; Constantinidis et al., 2006). However, far fewer studies have discussed broader entrepreneurial ecosystems, such as government policies. An exception is the study of Iakovleva et al. (2013), who investigated government support programs and the availability of financial resources for women. They reported the existence of support programs while underlining women's lower utilization of these programs. Similarly, a report from the World Bank (2006) revealed that despite the growing number of implemented policies and programs, access to finance is still the single biggest obstacle facing women entre-preneurs. Both findings imply a phenomenon in which government policies are not adequately leveraged by women entrepreneurs, and Iakovleva et al. (2013) further pointed out that one important reason is that women entrepreneurs lack knowledge of government programs.

Therefore, building on the research of Iakovleva et al. (2013), this chapter aims to provide some insights for addressing women's debt financing obsta-cles by empirically examining the relationship between policy awareness and women's debt financing activities in the Chinese context. More specifically, we focus on a significant governmental financial policy that was implemented in June 2010 (hereafter called the 2010 policy) and use the dataset of the Chinese Private Enterprises Survey (CPES) of 2012. Based on the total sample of 293 women entrepreneurs, both logit and tobit analyses are employed to investigate how women's awareness of the 2010 policy affected their debt financing activities in 2011, including their utilization of debt financing and the extent to which debt financing was used. The findings suggest a positive relationship between women's policy awareness and their debt financing. That is, the more that women are aware of the 2010 policy, the more likely they are to use debt financing, and if they do, they tend to secure higher levels of debt capital. The study contributes theoretically by providing additional empirical insights into the debt financing barriers faced by women entrepreneurs from a broader entrepreneurial ecosystem perspective and practically by providing some significant implications for women entrepreneurs, the government and scholars.

The remainder of this chapter is structured as follows. Section 2 is related to the country context that has been studied. We briefly present the development of Chinese female entrepreneurship; profile women entrepreneurs, their firms, and their access to finance; and introduce several key government policies that aim to ease the financing constraints. The next section is the literature review pertaining to women's access to debt finance and the presentation of our hypotheses. Section 4 describes the methodology, which consists of the data, measurement and analysis methods that were used in the study. Then, we present the empirical findings in section 5. The chapter concludes in section 6 with the discussion, summary remarks and some theoretical and practical implications.

2.   CONTEXT

Women's entrepreneurship has emerged in China since the launch of the reform and opening-up policy in 1978. Previously, the basic Chinese economic system was unitary public ownership, and thus women's participation in eco-nomic activities occurred mainly through employment. After 1978, the prior economic system was changed, and female entrepreneurship was legitimized. In particular, along with the legalization of private firms and business activities in 1988 and the subsequent rapid development of the private economy in the 1990s, a large number of female entrepreneurs arose in all walks of life. With the advent of the twenty-first century, the number of women entrepreneurs has continued to increase, and currently women represent more than 30 percent of all entrepreneurs.[1] Moreover, businesses owned by Chinese women have out-performed others worldwide, and a number of women billionaires have topped the annual Hurun list of Self-Made Women Billionaires from 2010 to 2019.[2] As a consequence, Chinese female entrepreneurship is receiving growing attention across the world.

A survey on Chinese female entrepreneurship in 2017 indicated that the average age of women entrepreneurs is 45.9, and most are well educated and motivated by self-fulfillment. While women tend to start and operate small and medium enterprises (SMEs) in the service industry, they always achieve good and steady business performance. In addition, the capital of the founder is the most important financing source for women when establishing their enterprises, and nearly half (48.13 percent) of the start-up capital comes from the founders themselves, while only 9.5 percent comes from bank loans (Li et al., 2017). Nevertheless, the majority of women entrepreneurs regard a lack of financing as a major barrier to developing their businesses, and they tend to attribute their financing obstacles to the particular challenges suffered in their access to debt capital (China Association of Women Entrepreneurs, 2011).

The Chinese government has long been devoted to facilitating the access of SMEs to finance, and as a result, a number of policies have been introduced. Overall, gender blindness exists in governmental financial support, except for microcredit. However, given the limited amounts provided by microcredit financing, women have to seek general financial support beyond microcredit in order to compensate for their inadequate finance. The first law for supporting and promoting the development of SMEs in China was the 'SMEs Promotion Law'. It was implemented in January 2003 and clearly stipulated some details about financial support for SMEs. Then, accompanied by the international financial crisis and the subsequent decline of SMEs, the State Council issued other suggestions to expedite the process of the development of SMEs in 2009, including many proposals to eliminate financing barriers for SMEs. To ensure the smooth implementation of these suggestions, the People's Bank of China further promulgated a significant policy in collaboration with the China Banking Regulatory Commission, the China Securities Regulatory Commission and the China Insurance Regulatory Commission in June 2010, namely the 2010 policy we mentioned earlier. This policy aimed to resolve the financing difficulties of SMEs through improved financial services to support and promote SMEs' growth.

We focus this study on the 2010 policy because it is a significant finan-cial policy in China aimed at reducing the financing barriers of SMEs that includes and details a tremendous number of initiatives or suggestions on debt financing. For example, the 2010 policy suggested that at a higher level, financial institutions should adopt the improvement of financial services and the expansion of credit for SMEs as the key strategy for ensuring that the growth rate of credit for SMEs is higher than that of all loans. In addition, the policy recommended the establishment of a multilevel financial organization system for financing SMEs by improving the service awareness of financing SMEs of large banks, strengthening the service ability of medium and small commercial banks, and promoting the development of new rural financial institutions and microcredit companies that provide services for SMEs in rural areas. Furthermore, in concrete practice, financial institutions should optimize and minimize loan approval procedures, such as online approval, to increase their efficiency and ensure that qualified SMEs obtain credit services both quickly and simply; strengthen the innovation of financial products and credit modes (for example, pledged loans, factoring, supply chain financing and so on) to match the financial needs of SMEs, thereby increasing loan support for SMEs; and expand the issue scale of debt financing instruments (for example, short-term financial bills, small and medium enterprise collective notes, and so on) for SMEs. In conclusion, the examination of the relationship between women's awareness of the 2010 policy and their debt financing activities in our study is relevant and appropriate.

3.   DEBT FINANCING AND WOMEN ENTREPRENEURS

Access to external finance has long been cited as the key barrier for women to establish and grow their businesses (Carter et al., 2015). There are two main ways women can secure external finance: equity financing mainly through venture capital and debt financing mainly through bank loans. While venture capital is linked closely to entrepreneurship and innovation, women seem to experience striking challenges in the venture capital funding landscape (Brush et al., 2014, 2018; Jennings and Brush, 2013). As articulated by Brush et al. (2018), during the three years from 2011 to 2013, only 2.7 percent of compa-nies in the United States receiving venture capital funding had a female CEO, and 15 percent had at least one woman on the executive team. This striking disproportion is also observable in angel investment financing (Becker-Blease and Sohl, 2007). Debt financing is thus regarded as a more common and avail-able source for women to secure external finance in comparison with equity financing.

For debt financing, prior studies have predominantly adopted the male/ female comparative approaches, and some gender differences were initially reported; for example, women entrepreneurs are less likely to use external debt financing, and if they do, they tend to use lower levels of debt capital both in the start-up stage and in ongoing operations (Alsos et al., 2006; Coleman, 2000; Coleman and Robb, 2009, 2012). However, further evidence suggests that these differences are most often explained as a product of the structural dissimilarities between male- and female-owned businesses (Haines et al., 1999; Marlow et al., 2012; Mirchandani, 1999; Read, 1998; van Hulten, 2012). For example, women are argued to have greater likelihoods of starting smaller businesses with lower growth ambitions (Coleman, 2000; Isaksen and Kolvereid, 2005; Orhan, 2001). In addition, they tend to organize their enterprises as proprietorships rather than corporations in less asset-intensive industries, such as the service and retail industries (Carter et al., 2001; Cole and Mehran, 2009; Constantinidis et al., 2006). Nevertheless, the above explanations are considered insufficient because several quantitative studies report residual differences when controlling for a range of structural factors (Carter and Rosa, 1998; Fraser, 2005). Therefore, two other explanations have been provided by researchers: supply-side discrimination and demand-side debt aversion.

With respect to supply-side discrimination, two aspects can be discussed. The first is related to perceived discrimination. Cole and Mehran (2009) showed that women are more likely to be discouraged from applying for credit but are not more likely to be denied if they do apply. Moreover, Fabowale et al. (1995) suggested that there is a widespread sense of injustice among women business owners, and they feel that they are treated more disrespectfully by lending officers in comparison to male business owners. The second is related to actual discrimination. Fay and Williams (1993) observed gender discrimination through two experiments that proved that different evaluative criteria are employed by bank officers for male and female applicants and that women without higher education are less likely to have their debt applications approved. In addition, the robust evidence from Alesina et al. (2013) showed that women pay more for credit than men in Italy, even after controlling for a large number of characteristics of the type of business, the borrower, and the structure of the credit market. Similar findings were also provided by Muravyev et al. (2009), Coleman (2000), and Orhan (2001).

Another explanation is the higher levels of risk aversion among women (Powell and Ansic, 1997; Watson and Robinson, 2003). On the one hand, women's debt aversion is caused by their subjective attitudes toward the development of their enterprises. Women are argued to be disinclined to engage in fast-paced business growth and instead tend to deliberately adopt slow and steady expansion (Bird and Brush, 2002; Cliff, 1998). As a consequence, women are reluctant to take on financing capital with more risk, such as external loans. On the other hand, risk aversion is considered a quasi-psychological characteristic among women (Carter et al., 2007). As described by Iakovleva et al. (2013), women in Russia and Ukraine fear 'living on credit', which is regarded as a post-Soviet syndrome, and they prefer to seek help from family and friends.

In conclusion, existing research on women's debt financing has mostly concentrated on analyses of owner- and firm-related characteristics and gender discrimination from capital providers, and discussions of the broader entrepreneurial ecosystem, such as government policies, have rarely been included (for example, Coleman et al., 2018; Iakovleva et al., 2013). As one exception, Iakovleva et al. (2013) investigated government support programs and the availability of financial resources for women through qualitative analyses of 60 interviewers. In their findings, they underline that 'several support programs exist and funding is available for entrepreneurs. However, according to female interviewees, they do not actively use the programs or support. Either they do not know that such programs exist, or they perceive obtaining such support to be too complex and demanding' (Iakovleva et al., 2013, p. 323).

In practice, women seem to be naturally distanced from government and are always less likely than men to participate in political areas. According to the Global Gender Gap Report of 2017, only approximately 23 percent of the political gap has been closed worldwide. That is, the gap between women and men in politics is still very large across the world. In this sense, women are more likely than men to suffer information asymmetry on governmental issues. As a consequence, when a government support policy has been promulgated, because of information asymmetry, women are more likely than men to not leverage these policies well or even to lose the opportunity to leverage them. Thus, in this study, we assume that women's better awareness of the 2010 financial policy would be beneficial to their debt financing activities. In summary, we propose the following hypotheses:

H1: Women's utilizations of debt financing are positively related to their awareness of the 2010 policy.

H2: The levels of debt capital used by women are positively related to their awareness of the 2010 policy.

4.   METHODOLOGY

4.1   Data

We use a dataset from a national large-scale survey, namely the CPES conducted in 2012. The dataset is relevant and appropriate for our study for the
following three reasons. First, the data are strong because the CPES used the
stratified random sampling method from a list of Chinese privately owned
enterprises across 31 provinces/municipalities. Second, the data include rich
information both on owner- and firm-related characteristics. Prior research
documents the impact of each of these when studying women's access to debt
finance; consequently, we can control these factors and, as a result, better
examine the impacts of women's policy awareness. Third and perhaps most
importantly, the CPES not only investigated the debt financing activities of
entrepreneurs in 2011[3] immediately after the promulgation of the 2010 policy
but also asked the respondents to report the degree of their awareness of the
2010 policy in the subsurvey on the enterprise development environment.

   There are 5073 respondents in the dataset of the 2012 survey, including 827
women-owned business (WOBs) samples.[4] Furthermore, we cleaned up the
data through the following steps. First, respondents in the 2012 survey were
asked to choose no more than three industries in which their businesses were
mainly involved, from an industry list.[5] Consequently, many respondents gave
two or three industry choices. This means that there is no way for us to control
the effect of industry in our analyses. Therefore, we eliminated responses
with two or three industry options. Second, the 2010 policy was launched to
ease the financial barriers of SMEs, and thus the respondents from large-sized
enterprises were excluded.[6] Finally, we also excluded incomplete responses
in the database. In total, we obtained a final dataset with 293 WOBs in our
sample.

4.2   Measurements

For the dependent variables, two variables were used to measure women's debt
financing activities. First, a binary variable, debt usage, was used to indicate
whether women utilized debt financing in their enterprise's expanded production in 2011. Women who utilized debt financing were coded as 1 and those
that did not use debt financing were coded as 0. Second, a continuous variable,
debt ratio, was employed to measure the levels of debt capital women entrepreneurs used in 2011. We included the natural logarithm of the percentage
of debt capital with respect to the total capital for expanded production plus
one in the study. In terms of the independent variable, policy awareness was

measured by asking women business owners to report if they were aware of the 2010 policy. This variable was coded as 1 if the owner did not know the 2010 policy and as a 2 or 3 if the owner knew a little or a lot about the policy, respectively.

Finally, to ensure that the results were not unjustifiably influenced by owner- and firm-related characteristics, we included a number of control variables in the study. With respect to owner-related characteristics, we mainly controlled for the women's age, education, political ties, and business ties. Age was a continuous variable that was measured by the number of years from the owner's birth to the end of 2011. Education was a dummy variable measuring whether the respondents had acquired at least a college degree or not. Those who had acquired a college degree or higher education were coded as 1 and 0 otherwise. Moreover, given the important influences of social capital on debt financing (Claessens et al., 2008; Kuada, 2009; Yu and Pan, 2008), we also controlled for women's political connections and business connections. Political connections was measured by whether the women owners were People's Congress deputies or People's Political Consultative Conference members, while business connections was measured by whether the women owners were members of the Association of Industry and Commerce. Both variables were dichotomous, as owners with political or business connections were labeled as 1 and 0 otherwise. In addition, inspired by Frid et al. (2016), we included economic status as a control variable. It was measured by women's self-assessment of their economic status compared with others around them. Women who perceived their economic status as the highest were coded as 10, while those with the lowest economic status were coded as 1.

With respect to firm-related characteristics, six variables were included, namely, location, firm age, size, type, industry and growth aspiration. Location consisted of two dummy variables, eastern area and central area, which assumed a value of 1 if the WOB was located in either the eastern area or central area. If both variables were coded as 0, the WOB was located in the western area. Firm age was measured by the number of years from the firm's foundation to the end of 2011. Size was measured as the natural logarithm of the total number of employees at the end of 2011. In addition, prior research has also examined the effect of legal organization on external financing. For example, incorporated ventures may provide banks with a good signal related to their credibility and the formality of their operations and thus lead to greater utilization (or supply) of bank financing (Cassar, 2004; Storey, 1994). Therefore, we also included organization type as one of the control variables in the study. Similar to the operationalization of the location variable, it consisted of three dummy variables because four types of organizations were investigated in the survey, namely, sole proprietorship, limited liability company (LLC), partnership and company limited by shares. Industry was measured through a dummy variable that was coded as 1 if women established their businesses in the service sector. Growth aspiration was also a dummy variable that indicated whether women intended to grow their businesses in the following year of 2012. The variable was coded as 1 when women had growth aspirations and 0 otherwise. Table 8.1 summarizes the operational definitions of all the variables used in this study.

4.3   Analytical Strategy

In this study, we employed the following empirical strategy. On the one hand, given that the dependent variable, debt usage, was a dichotomous variable, binary logit analysis was the appropriate technique to employ. On the other hand, the other dependent variable, debt ratio, was a continuous random variable with nonnegative values and there were many actual zero values since a number of WOBs did not use debt financing during their enterprise's expanded production. This case fits the tobit model (Tobin, 1958). Consequently, we conducted both logit analysis and tobit analysis to test our hypotheses.

5.   EMPIRICAL ANALYSIS

5.1   Descriptive Statistics

The characteristics of the samples are summarized in Table 8.2. In 2011, a total of 99 (33.8 percent) women owners used debt financing in the expanded production of their enterprises. Moreover, the percentage of debt capital in the total capital amount for expanded production ranged from 0 to 100 percent, with a mean of 13.63 percent. Among the 293 usable responses, 65 women owners (22.2 percent) reported that they did not know the 2010 policy, while 166 (56.7 percent) and 62 (21.2 percent) women owners knew a little and a lot, respectively. In terms of the women's individual characteristics, their average age was 42.49 years, and 92 (31.4 percent) women owners possessed at least a college degree. There were 93 (31.7 percent) and 132 (45.1 percent) women owners who had either political connections or business connections. Women generally assessed their economic status as medium level, with a mean value of 5.26. With respect to firm-related characteristics, more than half (61.8 percent) of WOBs were located in eastern China. The largest firm had 1514 employees, while the smallest had only one person, and the average number of employees was 75.92. Of the WOBs, 73.4 percent were organized as limited liability companies, and 61.8 percent were established in the service industry. Surprisingly, 87.7 percent of women owners reported aspirations to grow their businesses in the subsequent year of 2012.

Table 8.1   *Definitions and measurements of the variables*

Variables	Definition / description	Values
Dependent variables		
Debt usage	Whether women used debt financing in their enterprise's expanded production in 2011.	Yes=1, No=0
Debt ratio	The levels of debt financing that women owners used in 2011. It is measured by the natural logarithm of the percentage of debt capital with respect to total capital for expanded production plus one.	Continuous variable
Independent variables		
Policy awareness	How much women owners are aware of the 2010 policy.	do not know=1, know a little=2, know a lot=3
Control variable (owner-related characteristics)		
Age	The number of years from the owner's birth to the end of 2011.	Continuous variable
Education	Whether women owners have acquired at least a college degree.	Yes=1, No=0
Political connections	Whether women owners are People's Congress deputies or People's Political Consultative Conference members.	Yes=1, No=0
Business connections	Whether women owners are members of the Association of Industry and Commerce.	Yes=1, No=0
Economic status	Women's self-assessment of their economic status in comparison with others.	Ordinal variable from 1=lowest economic status to 10=highest economic status
Control variable (firm-related characteristics)		
Location (Eastern area)	Whether women owners have established their businesses in the eastern area of China.	Yes=1, No=0
Location (Central area)	Whether women owners have established their businesses in the central area of China.	Yes=1, No=0

Variables	Definition / description	Values
Firm age	The number of the years from the firm's foundation to the end of 2011.	Continuous variable
Size	The natural logarithm of the total number of employees at the end of 2011.	Continuous variable
Organization type (Sole proprietorship)	Whether the WOBs are organized as sole proprietorships.	Yes=1, No=0
Organization type (Limited liability company)	Whether the WOBs are organized as limited liability companies.	Yes=1, No=0
Organization type (Partnership)	Whether the WOBs are organized as partnerships.	Yes=1, No=0
Industry	Whether women have established their businesses in the service sector.	Yes=1, No=0
Growth aspiration	Whether women intend to grow their businesses in the subsequent year of 2012.	Yes=1, No=0

5.2   Results

We used several diagnostic procedures to control for multicollinearity problems between the variables. Table 8.3 shows the Pearson correlations for our dependent, independent and control variables. The correlation coefficients between the independent variables are all below 0.80. Additionally, the variance inflation factors (VIFs) are also calculated for the independent variables to examine multicollinearity in the regression models. The VIF values are well below the threshold of 10.00 (Gujarati, 1995). As a result, multicollinearity is not a problem in the study.

First, logit analysis was used to determine the probability of women's debt usage in the year 2011. Table 8.4 depicts the estimates, t-values and the levels of significance. Overall, the model is significant with a p value of 0.000. For control variables, given all other variables remain unchanged, there are significant negative associations between women's age ($\beta = -0.0474$; $p < 0.05$), education ($\beta = -0.5853$; $p < 0.1$), industry ($\beta = -1.0714$; $p < 0.0000$) and their probability of using debt financing and significant positive associations between economic status ($\beta = 0.2204$; $p < 0.05$), firm size ($\beta = 0.3139$; $p < 0.05$), growth aspirations ($\beta = 1.5466$; $p < 0.05$) and their probability of using debt financing. For the independent variable, policy awareness, the results reveal a significant positive association between women's policy awareness and women's probability of using debt financing ($\beta = 0.6684$, $p < 0.01$), thereby implying that the

Table 8.2   *Characteristics of the samples*

		Freq.	%	Min. / Max. (Mean)
Debt usage	Yes	99	33.8	
	No	194	66.2	
Debt ratio*	—	—	—	0 / 100 (13.63)
Policy awareness	Do not know	65	22.2	
	Know a little	166	56.7	
	Know well	62	21.2	
Age	—	—	—	23 / 71 (42.49)
Education (College degree)	Yes	92	31.4	
	No	201	68.6	
Political connections	Yes	93	31.7	
	No	200	68.3	
Business connections	Yes	132	45.1	
	No	161	54.9	
Economic status	—	—	—	1 / 10 (5.26)
Location	Eastern area	181	61.8	
	Central area	62	22.9	
	Western area	45	15.4	
Firm age	—	—	—	0 / 22 (6.86)
Size*	—	—	—	1 / 1514 (75.92)
Organization type	Sole proprietorship	46	15.7	
	Limited liability company	215	73.4	
	Partnership	13	4.4	
	Company limited by shares	19	6.5	
Industry (Service)	Yes	181	61.8	
	No	112	38.2	
Growth aspiration	Yes	257	87.7	
	No	36	12.3	

Note: * indicates that the results were calculated using the original data rather than transformed dataa.

more women owners were aware of the 2010 policy, the more likely they were to utilize debt financing in their firm's expanded production. Thus, hypothesis 1 is supported. Furthermore, we also estimated marginal effects to make the results more tangible, that is, what is the probability that women used debt financing at the three different levels of policy awareness. Figure 8.1 presents the results. The average woman who did not know the 2010 policy had a 16.6 percent probability of using debt financing in her firm's expanded reproduction, while those who knew it a little and knew it a lot had 27.9 percent and 43.0 percent probabilities, respectively.

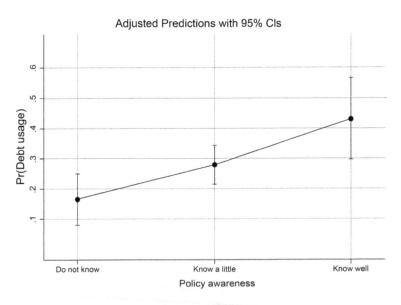

*Figure 8.1   Probability of women's debt usage at the three different
                 levels of policy awareness*

Then, we established a tobit model to examine the influences of policy awareness on the levels of debt capital used by women owners in 2011. Table 8.5 presents the results. The results show a significant positive association between women's policy awareness and the debt ratio ($\beta = 1.1730$, $p < 0.01$), implying that the levels of debt capital that women used in their firm's expanded production in 2011 were higher when women were better aware of the 2010 policy. As a result, hypothesis 2 is supported. With respect to the control variables, significant negative effects exist between age ($\beta = -0.0636$, $p < 0.05$), industry ($\beta = -1.9122$, $p < 0.01$) and debt ratio. That is, older women owners and those who have established their businesses in the service industry tend to use lower levels of debt capital in their expanded production. In addition, the results also show some significant positive effects. For example, women owners who perceived higher economic status ($\beta = 0.4237$, $p < 0.05$), operated larger firms ($\beta = 0.5361$, $p < 0.05$) and had growth aspirations ($\beta = 3.0520$, $p < 0.05$) used higher levels of debt capital in their firm's expanded production in 2011.

6. DISCUSSION AND CONCLUSION

Female entrepreneurship matters greatly for economic growth and societal well-being, but access to external finance has long been considered a key barrier preventing women from establishing and growing their businesses (Carter et al., 2015; Kelley et al., 2017). In this study, we provide additional insights on how to strengthen women's access to external finance through empirically examining the relationship between policy awareness and women's debt financing activities in the Chinese context. More specifically, we selected a significant financial policy that was issued to reduce the financial barriers of SMEs in June 2010 and focused on how women's awareness of this policy affected their debt financing activities in 2011. By employing both logit analysis and tobit analysis, our results show the significant positive impacts of women's policy awareness on both the utilization of debt financing and the debt ratios in their firm's expanded production. In other words, when women had better awareness of the 2010 policy, they were more likely to utilize debt financing and relied on higher levels of debt capital in 2011. Therefore, our findings empirically confirm that women's better policy awareness is beneficial to their access to debt financing, thus providing another effective way to reduce their external financing constraints so that they can better establish and grow their businesses.

In addition, with respect to owner-related characteristics, we find that older women owners were less likely to use debt financing and tended to use lower levels of debt capital when they did. This finding is consistent with Vos et al. (2007) and Frid et al. (2016). Contrary to several prior studies (Bates, 1990; Fay and Williams, 1993; Slavec and Prodan, 2012), our study also showed a marginally significant but negative relationship between women's education and their debt usage. In addition to providing lenders with a signal that the firm is less risky (Slavec and Prodan, 2012), high education reflects a better understanding and perception of financing alternatives (Wang, 2012). This finding implies that individuals with higher education are more likely to use more advanced financing patterns rather than debt financing. With respect to economic status, the results of the two estimations indicate a significant positive correlation between women's economic status and both their debt usage and debt ratio. That is, the higher that women perceived their economic status in comparison to others, the more likely they were to utilize debt financing, and they tended to rely more heavily on debt capital in their expanded production process. This finding is consistent with the prior work conducted by

Table 8.3   *Descriptive statistics and Pearson correlation matrix*

	Mean	SD	1	2	3	4	5	6	7	8	9	10	11	12	13	14	15	16	17
1. Debt usage	0.34	0.474	1																
2. Debt ratio	1.20	1.725	0.979	1															
3. Policy awareness	1.99	0.659	0.219	0.200	1														
4. Age	42.49	8.912	–0.027	–0.008	.061	1													
5. Education	0.31	0.465	–0.017	–0.019	0.133	–0.067	1												
6. Political connections	0.32	0.466	0.257	0.238	0.077	0.131	0.092	1											
7. Business connections	0.45	0.498	0.209	0.194	0.139	0.200	0.038	0.576	1										
8. Economic status	5.26	1.726	0.265	0.276	0.129	0.096	0.129	0.348	0.286	1									
9. Eastern area	0.62	0.487	0.013	0.013	0.062	0.046	–0.028	0.008	0.063	0.069	1								
10. Central area	0.23	0.421	–0.011	–0.008	–0.029	0.009	0.069	–0.005	–0.036	0.008	–0.692	1							
11. Firm age	6.86	5.060	0.080	0.063	0.042	0.364	–0.034	0.242	0.416	0.139	0.088	–0.089	1						
12. Size	3.14	1.515	0.323	0.308	0.144	0.284	0.151	0.494	0.525	0.402	0.075	–0.063	0.385	1					

	Mean	SD	1	2	3	4	5	6	7	8	9	10	11	12	13	14	15	16	17
13. Sole proprietorship	0.16	0.364	-.031	-.033	-.093	-.071	-.191	0.008	0.081	-.152	0.031	-.056	0.055	-.064	1				
14. LLC	0.73	0.443	-.027	-.037	0.096	0.075	0.141	-.004	-.106	0.109	-.140	0.107	-.040	0.056	-.716	1			
15. Partnership	0.04	0.206	-.049	-.035	-.097	-.051	-.003	-.111	-.029	-.090	0.169	-.117	-.024	-.094	-.093	-.358	1		
16. Industry	0.62	0.487	-.314	-.297	-.108	-.103	0.033	-.158	-.191	-.114	0.032	-.090	-.123	-.377	0.031	-.029	0.101	1	
17. Growth aspiration	0.88	0.329	0.201	0.195	0.168	0.063	0.074	0.144	0.130	0.261	-.016	0.030	0.055	0.170	-.153	0.104	0.030	-.038	1

Table 8.4   Logit analysis predicting the probability of debt usage

Variables	Coef.	Std. Err.	t	P > |t|
Policy awareness	0.6684	0.2486	2.69	0.007**
Owner-related variables				
Age	−0.0474	0.0230	−2.06	0.039*
Education	−0.5853	0.3128	−1.87	0.061[+]
Political connections	0.5415	0.3643	1.49	0.137
Business connections	−0.1181	0.3751	−0.31	0.753
Economic status	0.2204	0.1002	2.20	0.028*
Firm-related variables				
Eastern area	−0.2746	0.4016	−0.68	0.494
Central area	−0.1817	0.4550	−0.40	0.690
Firm age	−0.0010	0.0322	−0.03	0.976
Sole proprietorship	−0.6170	0.6562	−0.94	0.347
Limited liability company (LLC)	−0.8563	0.5700	−1.50	0.133
Partnership	−0.5440	1.100	−0.49	0.621
Size	0.3139	0.1340	2.35	0.019*
Industry	−1.071	0.3041	−3.52	0.000***
Growth aspiration	1.5466	0.6123	2.53	0.012*
Constant	−2.0773	1.3062	−1.59	0.112
Number of obs	293			
Log pseudolikelihood	−145.8338			
Pseudo R2	0.2218			
Prob > chi2	0.000			
Correctly classified	75.77%			

Notes: [+], *, **, and *** indicate significance at 0.1, 0.05, 0.01 and 0.001, respectively.

Frid et al. (2016), who examined the relationship between an entrepreneur's wealth and their access to external finance and found that low-wealth founders are less likely to obtain external funds and receive less amounts when they do. Surprisingly, political and business connections have no significant impacts on either the debt usage or debt ratio for women owners. This finding is contrary to the prior work on general business owners (Claessens et al., 2008; Faccio et al., 2006; Slavec and Prodan, 2012; Yu and Pan, 2008).

With respect to firm-related characteristics, there was no significant effect of firm age, location and organization type on women's financing activities. By contrast, we found that other firm characteristics, including size, industry and growth aspirations, had significant impacts on women's usage of debt

Table 8.5   Tobit analysis explaining the debt ratio

Variables	Coef.	Std. Err.	t	P > |t|
Policy awareness	1.1730	0.4091	2.87	0.004**
Owner-related variables				
Age	−0.0636	0.0321	−1.98	0.048*
Education	−1.0942	0.5942	−1.84	0.067[+]
Political connections	0.8860	0.6809	1.30	0.194
Business connections	−0.2428	0.6916	−0.35	0.726
Economic status	0.4237	0.1765	2.40	0.017*
Firm-related variables				
Eastern area	−0.5513	0.7554	−0.73	0.466
Central area	−0.4477	0.8625	−0.52	0.604
Firm age	−0.0260	0.0591	−0.44	0.660
Sole proprietorship	−1.1725	1.1266	−1.04	0.299
Limited liability company (LLC)	−1.6762	0.9474	−1.77	0.078[+]
Partnership	−0.6741	1.5954	−0.42	0.673
Size	0.5361	0.2436	2.20	0.029*
Industry	−1.9122	0.5776	−3.31	0.001**
Growth aspiration	3.0520	1.1777	2.59	0.010*
Constant	0.3608	2.4303	0.15	0.882
Left censored obs	194			
Uncensored obs	99			
Log likelihood	−352.1310			

Notes: [+], *, **, and *** indicate significance at 0.1, 0.05, 0.01 and 0.001, respectively.

financing and the debt ratio in their firm's expanded production. In detail, women owners who operated smaller businesses, established businesses in the service industry and were reluctant to grow them were less likely to use debt financing and rely on lower levels of debt capital in their expanded production. This finding is consistent with statements from Orhan (2001) and Constantinidis et al. (2006).

This research contributes to the existing literature in two ways. First, to the best of our knowledge, this is the first quantitative study investigating the impacts of women's awareness of a financial policy on their debt financing activities. This study adds additional empirical insights on how to promote women's debt financing activities to reduce their external financing constraints from a broader entrepreneurial ecosystem perspective, in contrast to the extensive study of owner- and firm-related determinants in prior research.

Second, as noted by Vita et al. (2014), there are very few studies of Chinese women entrepreneurs, and only two papers on Chinese women entrepreneurs were included among the 70 total papers in this review's literature dataset. Therefore, our study also helps to enrich the existing women's entrepreneurship research in the Chinese context.

In addition, our findings have some implications for women owners, the government and scholars. First, our study empirically confirms the positive influences of women's policy awareness on their debt financing activities and thus provides an alternative way for women to improve their lack of external finance. In addition to the focus on owner- and firm-related characteristics, better awareness of governmental policies will be helpful to alleviate women's financing difficulties by leveraging these policies so that they can better establish and grow their businesses. Therefore, women entrepreneurs should on the one hand pay more attention to government websites and other traditional media such as newspapers and television to directly receive information on government policies or programs; on the other hand, women should broaden their social networks by joining groups and organizations, such as women entrepreneur associations or incubators, to indirectly obtain such information. Second, our findings show the great importance of policy propaganda by governments. Thus, publicizing their policies or support programs widely may be an effective way for governments to improve women's financing constraints. More specifically, the government should combine both traditional media and new media (for example, the governmental website, blogging, WeChat and so on) to widely disseminate their policies and programs to increase women's awareness of them. Furthermore, some other activities, such as policy interpretation or relevant training, can also help women better understand the government policies and further leverage them. Third, our study also has some implications for scholars in the women's entrepreneurship terrain. Scholars need to be cautious when articulating their recommendations for a new policy since, in some cases, barriers faced by women entrepreneurs cannot be simply attributed to the lack of new policies but rather may be the result of the underutilization of existing policies, just as in our case.

As with any research, several limitations should be noted and present avenues for future research. First, one limitation of our study is the oversimplified measurement of the independent variable. Given the limitation of the national survey design, we only introduced three levels of policy awareness in our study, which are do not know, know a little and know a lot. Future research is needed to employ more systematic measurements for deeper investigations. Second, as mentioned earlier, there is gender blindness in Chinese governmental financial support, and thus we focused on a general financial policy (for both men and women) in our study. On the one hand, how does men's awareness of such general policies shape men's debt financing activities?

How do these effects differ between men and women? On the other hand, there are indeed a number of financial policies or programs in contexts other than China that are specific to women entrepreneurs, such as the Wells Fargo Women's Business Services program, and they do help a lot for women's access to finance (World Bank, 2006). So how does women's awareness of such gender-specific policies shape their financing activities, and how do the effects of general policies and gender-specific policies differ? All of the above topics are worthy of examination in future research. Third, we mainly explored the effects of the financial policy on debt financing activities, and additional analysis focusing on other financing patterns may help extend the insights presented here. Lastly, we only investigated the effects in the context of the Chinese economy, and further research is needed to explore whether our results hold in other countries.[7]

NOTES

1. China Women's Entrepreneurship Report 2018, presented at the Global Mulan Forum and China Business Mulan Annual Meeting 2018, accessed at http://www .iceo.com.cn/zt/2018_mulannh/.
2. Hurun Global Self-Made Women Billionaires List (2010–2019), accessed at http://www.hurun.net/CN/Home/Index.
3. Debt financing in the 2012 survey is distinguished from equity financing and founder's own capital. It includes (but is not limited to) secure debt finance from joint-stock commercial banks and small financial institutions (e.g., rural credit cooperatives, microcredit companies, etc.).
4. The survey distinguished between women-owned business and men-owned business according to the sex of the main investors. Thus, WOBs in the study refer to those enterprises whose main investors are women.
5. The industry list in the 2012 survey consisted of 19 industries: Agriculture, Excavation, Manufacturing, Electric and Gas, Construction, Transportation and Traffic, Information Services, Wholesale and Retail, Accommodations and Catering, Finance, Real Estate, Leasing, Research and Technology, Public Facility, Resident Service, Education, Health, Culture and Sport, and others. According to 'Industrial Classification for National Economic Activities', all but the first five industries are regarded as service industries.
6. To distinguish SMEs from large-sized enterprises in the study, the 'Provisional Rules on Criteria of Small and Medium Sized Enterprises', which was issued by the Ministry of Industry and Information Technology, the National Bureau of Statistics, the National Development and Reform Commission, and the Ministry of Finance in September 2011, was used as a reference.
7. We acknowledge using the data based on the Chinese Private Enterprises Survey (CPES), which was conducted by the Privately Owned Enterprises Research Project Team (member organizations include All-China Federation of Industry and Commerce, State Administration for Industry and Commerce, the China Society of Private Economy, and the United Front Work Department of CCP). Research Center for Private Enterprises at Chinese Academy of Social Sciences (PCPE-CASS) is the authorized organization that manages and issues the survey

data. We appreciate the data support from the above organizations. All errors and omissions are the sole responsibility of the authors. Furthermore, we also acknowledge the financial support from the National Natural Science Foundation of China [award number: 71272056].

REFERENCES

Alesina, A., F. Lotti and P. Mistrulli (2013), 'Do women pay more for credit? Evidence from Italy', *Journal of the European Economic Association*, 11(S1), 45–66.

Alsos, G., E. Isaksen and E. Ljunggren (2006), 'New venture financing and subsequent business growth in men- and women-led businesses', *Entrepreneurship Theory and Practice*, 30(5), 667–686.

Bates, T. (1990), 'Entrepreneur human capital inputs and small business longevity', *Review of Economics & Statistics*, 72(4), 551–559.

Becker-Blease, J. and J. Sohl (2007), 'Do women-owned businesses have equal access to angel capital?', *Journal of Business Venturing*, 22(4), 503–521.

Bird, B. and C. Brush (2002), 'A gendered perspective on organizational creation', *Entrepreneurship Theory and Practice*, 26(3), 41–65.

Brush, C., P. Greene, L. Balachandra and A. Davis (2014), *The Diana Report: Women Entrepreneurs 2014: Bridging the Gender Gap in Venture Capital*, Wellesley, MA: Babson College.

Brush, C., P. Greene, L. Balachandra and A. Davis (2018), 'The gender gap in venture capital: progress, problems, and perspectives', *Venture Capital: An International Journal of Entrepreneurial Finance*, 20(2), 115–136.

Carter, S., S. Anderson and E. Shaw (2001), 'Women's business ownership: a review of the academic, popular and internet literature', Report to the Small Business Service, Department of Marketing, University of Strathclyde, Glasgow, August.

Carter, S., S. Mwaura, M. Ram, K. Trehan and T. Jones (2015), 'Barriers to ethnic minority and women's enterprise: existing evidence, policy tensions and unsettled questions', *International Small Business Journal*, 33(1), 49–69.

Carter, S. and P. Rosa (1998), 'The financing of male and female-owned businesses', *Entrepreneurship & Regional Development: An International Journal*, 10(3), 225–241.

Carter, S., E. Shaw, W. Lam and F. Wilson (2007), 'Gender, entrepreneurship, and bank lending: the criteria and processes used by bank loan officers in assessing applications', *Entrepreneurship Theory and Practice*, 31(3), 427–444.

Cassar, G. (2004), 'The financing of business start-ups', *Journal of Business Venturing*, 19(2), 261–283.

China Association of Women Entrepreneurs (ed.) (2011), *Chinese Women Entrepreneurs' Development Report 2011*, Beijing: Geology Press.

Claessens, S., E. Feijen and L. Laeven (2008), 'Political connections and preferential access to finance: the role of campaign contributions', *Journal of Financial Economics*, 88(3), 554–580.

Cliff, J. (1998), 'Does one size fit all? Exploring the relationship between attitudes towards growth, gender, and business size', *Journal of Business Venturing*, 13(6), 523–542.

Cole, R. and H. Mehran (2009), 'Gender and the availability of credit to privately held firms: evidence from the surveys of small business finances', Working Paper, Federal Reserve Bank of New York—Research and Statistics Group.

Coleman, S. (2000), 'Access to capital and terms of credit: a comparison of men- and women-owned small businesses', *Journal of Small Business Management*, 38(3), 37–52.

Coleman, S., C. Henry, B. Orser, L. Foss and F. Welter (2018), 'Policy support for women entrepreneurs' access to financial capital: evidence from Canada, Germany, Ireland, Norway, and the United States', *Journal of Small Business Management*, https://doi.org/ 10.1111/jsbm.12473.

Coleman, S. and A. Robb (2009), 'A comparison of new firm financing by gender: evidence from the Kauffman Firm Survey data', *Small Business Economics*, 33(4), 397–411.

Coleman, S. and A. Robb (2012), 'Gender-based firm performance differences in the United States: examining the roles of financial capital and motivations', in K. Hughes and J. Jennings (eds.), *Global Women's Entrepreneurship Research: Diverse Settings, Questions and Approaches*, Cheltenham, UK and Northampton, MA, USA: Edward Elgar Publishing.

Constantinidis, C., A. Cornet and S. Asandei (2006), 'Financing of women-owned ventures: the impact of gender and other owner- and firm-related variables', *Venture Capital: An International Journal of Entrepreneurial Finance*, 8(2), 133–157.

Eddleston, K., J. Ladge, C. Mitteness and L. Balachandra (2016), 'Do you see what I see? Signaling effects of gender and firm characteristics on financing entrepreneurial ventures', *Entrepreneurship Theory and Practice*, 40(3), 489–514.

Fabowale, L., B. Orser and A. Riding (1995), 'Gender, structural factors, and credit terms between Canadian small businesses and financial institutions', *Entrepreneurship Theory and Practice*, 19(4), 41–65.

Faccio, M., R. Masulis and J. McConnell (2006), 'Political connections and corporate bailouts', *Journal of Finance*, 61(6), 2597–2635.

Fay, M. and L. Williams (1993), 'Gender bias and the availability of business loans', *Journal of Business Venturing*, 8(4), 363–376.

Fraser, S. (2005), 'Finance for small and medium sized enterprises: a report on the 2004 UK survey of SME finances', Coventry: SME Centre, University of Warwick.

Frid, C., D. Wyman, W. Gartner and D. Hechavarría (2016), 'Low-wealth entrepreneurs and access to external financing', *International Journal of Entrepreneurial Behaviour & Research*, 22(4), 531–555.

Gujarati, D. (ed.) (1995), *Basic Econometrics*, 3rd edition, New York: McGraw-Hill.

Haines, G., B. Orser and A. Riding (1999), 'Myths and realities: an empirical study of banks and the gender of small business clients', *Canadian Journal of Administrative Sciences*, 16(4), 291–307.

Iakovleva, T., M. Solesvik and A. Trifilova (2013), 'Financial availability and government support for women entrepreneurs in transitional economies: cases of Russia and Ukraine', *Journal of Small Business and Enterprise Development*, 20(2), 314–340.

Isaksen, E. and L. Kolvereid (2005), 'Growth objectives in Norwegian start-up businesses', *International Journal of Entrepreneurship & Small Business*, 2(1), 17–26.

Jennings, J. and C. Brush (2013), 'Research on women entrepreneurs: challenges to (and from) the broader entrepreneurship literature', *Academy of Management Annals*, 7(1), 663–715.

Kelley, D., B. Baumer, C. Brush, P. Greene, M. Mahdavi, M. Majbouri, M. Cole, M. Dean and R. Haevlow (2017), *Global Entrepreneurship Monitor 2016/2017 Report on Women's Entrepreneurship*, Wellesley, MA: Babson College.

Kuada, J. (2009), 'Gender, social networks, and entrepreneurship in Ghana', *Journal of African Business*, 10(1), 85–103.

Li, L., W. Zhong and Y. Wang (2017), 'The development of women entrepreneurs in China: current situation, problems and prospects: a questionnaire survey report of 2,505 women entrepreneurs', *Management World*, 11, 50–64.

Marlow, S., M. Hart, J. Levie and M. Shamsul (2012), 'Women in enterprise: a different perspective', Edinburgh: RBS Group.

Mirchandani, K. (1999), 'Feminist insight on gendered work: new directions in research on women and entrepreneurship', *Gender, Work & Organization*, 6(4), 224–235.

Muravyev, A., O. Talavera and D. Schäfer (2009), 'Entrepreneurs' gender and financial constraints: evidence from international data', *Journal of Comparative Economics*, 37(2), 270–286.

Naidu, S. and A. Chand (2017), 'National culture, gender inequality and women's success in micro, small and medium enterprises', *Social Indicators Research*, 130, 647–664.

Orhan, M. (2001), 'Women business owners in France: the issue of financing discrimination', *Journal of Small Business Management*, 39(1), 95–102.

Powell, M. and D. Ansic (1997), 'Gender differences in risk behaviour in financial decision-making: an experimental analysis', *Journal of Economic Psychology*, 18(6), 605–628.

Read, L. (ed.) (1998), *The Financing of Small Business: A Comparative Study of Male and Female Business Owners*, London: Routledge.

Slavec, A. and I. Prodan (2012), 'The influence of entrepreneurs' characteristics on small manufacturing firm debt financing', *Journal for East European Management Studies*, 17(1), 104–130.

Storey, D. (1994), 'The role of legal status in influencing bank financing and new firm growth', *Applied Economics*, 26(2), 129–136.

Tobin, J. (1958), 'Estimation of relationships for limited dependent variables', *Econometrica*, 26(1), 24–36.

van Hulten, V. (2012), 'Women's access to SME finance in Australia', *International Journal of Gender and Entrepreneurship*, 4(3), 266–288.

Vita, L., M. Mari and S. Poggesi (2014), 'Women entrepreneurs in and from developing countries: evidences from the literature', *European Management Journal*, 32(3), 451–460.

Vos, E., A. Yeh, S. Carter and S. Tagg (2007), 'The happy story of small business financing', *Journal of Banking & Finance*, 31(9), 2648–2672.

Wang, F. (2012), 'Empirical research on the relation between entrepreneurs' resource endowments and their cognition degree of financing schemes', *Systems Engineering*, 30(2), 36–43.

Watson, J. and S. Robinson (2003), 'Adjusting for risk in comparing the performance of male and female controlled SMEs', *Journal of Business Venturing*, 18(6), 773–788.

World Bank (2006), 'Women entrepreneurs and access to finance: global profiles', accessed December 5, 2018 at https://www.ifc.org/wps/wcm/connect/848d0f80488553a0afe4ff6a6515bb18/Women%2BEntrepreneurs%2Band%2BAccess%2Bto%2BFinance.pdf?MOD=AJPERES&CACHEID=848d0f80488553a0afe4ff6a6515bb18.

World Bank (2011), 'Strengthening access to finance for women-owned SMEs in developing countries', accessed November 28, 2018 at https://www.ifc.org/wps/wcm/connect/a4774a004a3f66539f0f9f8969adcc27/G20_Women_Report.pdf?MOD=AJPERES.

Yu, M. and H. Pan (2008), 'The relationship between politics, institutional environments and private enterprises' access to bank loans', *Management World*, 9, 9–21.

9. Where do we go from here? Summary of findings

Amanda Bullough, Diana M. Hechavarría, Candida G. Brush and Linda F. Edelman

Businesses that are able to scale and do so quickly are essential for economic prosperity, because they have a stronger positive impact on innovation, jobs, productivity and the community. While few dispute the fact that women's entrepreneurship is vital for economic and social development (Hechavarría et al., 2019), the reality worldwide is that female entrepreneurs are consistently found to have lower sales and slower employment growth, create fewer jobs, and be less profitable (Fairlie and Robb, 2009; Kelley et al., 2017; Orser et al., 2006). This reality has to change.

Even with all of this activity and progress, we still need more academic research on the facilitators and impediments that contribute to the growth of businesses that are owned by women entrepreneurs. The work that went into this book fostered a provoking conversation about topics on how public policy frameworks, along with programs and practices, are influencing the high-growth potential of women entrepreneurs. We developed this book and invited the authors of each chapter to contribute to more, quality knowledge around the programs, policies and practices that support high-growth entrepreneurship among women. Entrepreneurial training and curriculum (programs), entrepreneur-friendly legal and regulatory frameworks (policies), and behaviors, culture and institutional conventions (practices) are all important for fostering innovation and growth among women entrepreneurs.

Women-only programs, policies and practices represent one way to help women tackle the challenges around starting and running a new venture, which men do not face. Examples include skill building, training, technology, and finance that are supported by governments and the non-governmental sector and help to level the playing field so that women and men have equal opportunities for success with their businesses. Government interventions to boost the inclusion of women in high-growth entrepreneurship are frequently undertaken through partnerships with other organizations, like non-profits and non-governmental organizations. Public sector activity to coordinate among policies and agencies, support for equal access welfare benefits and tax incentives for entrepreneurs as well as waged earners, encouragement of diversity engagement in science, technology, engineering and math (STEM fields) are also important for high-growth women's entrepreneurship. Governments around the world have implemented women-friendly policies to support entrepreneurship and financing for business growth, including a reduction in discriminatory practices, increased access to loans and equity capital, loan guarantees, and education for women entrepreneurs (Henry et al., 2017; OECD, 2017).

As demonstrated throughout this book, programs, policies and practices must have unified and self-strengthening features that support high-growth entrepreneurship among women, which includes a positive entrepreneurial climate that promotes human capital development and readiness, monetary support, expansion opportunities, and a plethora of institutions and infrastructural mechanisms that support growth and innovation. The gendered nature of policies, laws and cultural expectations can be overt, as well as subtle and seemingly invisible, and nonetheless embedded in practices, rules and norms that are accepted as commonplace among men and women (Brush et al., 2018). Surmounting deep-seeded institutional impediments and realizing the growth-oriented capability of women leading their own businesses requires an ecosystem that supports women building productive business networks, equitable commercial and legal regulations, access to fair financial capital, and supportive cultural norms that facilitate growth-oriented women's entrepreneurship (Brush et al., 2018; Hechavarría and Ingram, 2018).

An integrated and sustained approach is needed on a global scale for stakeholder involvement and cultural change that positively influences entrepreneurial ecosystems that support the programs, policies and practices that promote diversity and inclusion. Such activity embodies the movement that will help to propel high-growth entrepreneurial activity for women. More specifically, administration, education, society and the media are needed for promoting women-led high-growth ventures. Examples include technology parks, tax incentives for investment, cultural and cluster initiatives, federal funding technology and science programs, and initiatives that provide training and mentorship.

In this book, the chapter authors conducted qualitative and quantitative research in a variety of contexts around the world, including Eswatini (Swaziland), Australia, China, Slovenia, Peru, and a global study of 43 countries. In Chapter 1, we identified key themes that emerged from these chapters, and we organized them into the following categories: the practice of building networks, programs and the support environment, and policies and regulations. These three themes became the supporting structure for our framework for policies, programs and practices that support high-growth women's entrepreneurship. This framework was presented as Figure 1.1 in the introduction chapter, and is provided again here as Figure 9.1 for convenience. The first component of our framework is the Practice of Building Networks, which includes creating and facilitating opportunities for women entrepreneurs to make connections and build social, professional and business networks. The second component of our framework is Programs and the Support Environment, which includes education and training, mentoring and incubators and accelerators that support high-growth women's entrepreneurship. In addition, the third component of our framework is Policies and Regulation, which includes the accessibility of financial resources, the regulatory environment, and financial policies and debt financing that support women's business growth potential.

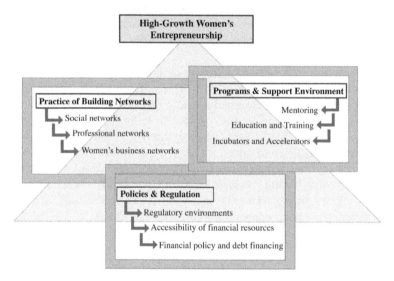

Figure 9.1   A framework for programs, policies and practices for high-growth women's entrepreneurship

What follows is a review and summary of the key recommendations that were proposed by the authors in each of the chapters in this book. This is again presented according to our framework for policies, programs and practices that support high-growth women's entrepreneurship. The following summary also follows the order in which each chapter was presented in the book.

THEME 1: THE PRACTICE OF BUILDING NETWORKS

Entrepreneurs benefit greatly from being socially adaptable and having a strong amount of social capital in order to achieve financial success (Baron and Markman, 2003). Yet, prior research has demonstrated that women tend to have smaller formal networks of business contacts, despite having more favorable feelings about networking (Dawson et al., 2011; Klyver and Grant, 2010). Widespread social networks and a positive reputation help entrepreneurs to build the network ties that are needed for access to cheaper resources and even to certain assets that might be completely inaccessible otherwise (Kuada, 2009). While both formal and informal networks, like friends and family, are important, prior research (Watson, 2012) has shown that it is the formal networks that are particularly important. Informal networks combined with formal professional networking and referrals can help entrepreneurs access the resources they need to start and grow their new ventures. Significantly, networks can help entrepreneurs to gain access to institutions such as banks and financial institutions, legal experts, and professional associations, which are critical for new companies and are likely areas in which the entrepreneur has little expertise.

In Chapter 2, Brixiová and Kangoye examined the role of social and professional networks. They looked at how friends and family, as well as other entrepreneurs, career advisors and teachers, may reduce gender gaps in access to formal financing and in entrepreneurial performance. Based on United Nations interview data in Eswatini (commonly known as Swaziland on the global stage), they demonstrated that networks are particularly important for women entrepreneurs in generating capital and sales. To overcome the challenge of women founding businesses, with lower levels of capital than men, and therefore growing smaller businesses, Brixiová and Kangoye recommend that policies aimed at women's entrepreneurship involve business education, and financial literacy training in particular, as well as activities that help women to build networks among other entrepreneurs and sources of financial capital. Their findings demonstrate that women who accept help from their professional networks have secured larger amounts of initial capital. They also find that women who participated in financial literacy training are more likely to utilize their professional networks to access external funding sources.

Prior research has shown that when entrepreneurs rely too exclusively on interactions with their informal networks, they run the risk of not accessing key resources they need for business success. In this way, informal networks can be more detrimental than helpful for business growth, if they are preventing an entrepreneur from stepping out of his or her comfort zone (Renzulli et al., 2000). Brixiová and Kangoye's results echo these findings and show that too much homogeneity and relying on relatives represent crucial weaknesses, which is what women entrepreneurs in Eswatini were found to be doing. The results suggest that policies towards women's entrepreneurship need to go beyond strengthening the business environment and include proactive steps such as building networks among women entrepreneurs and funders as well as financial literacy trainings. The chapter gave evidence on the positive role of networks in obtaining start-up capital and firm performance; further research is needed on the causal links, to identify mechanisms through which the network effects are achieved. For example, it would be useful to explore if gendered peer effects contribute to persistent gaps between men and women entrepreneurs in their choice of sectors of operation and funding sources.

In Chapter 3, Córdova and Huamán examined Peruvian women entrepreneurs showing how they created their own network for sharing information and knowledge and mentoring one another, in the absence of formal state initiatives and opportunities. Their findings show that entrepreneurial fortitude and business skills are insufficient for managing uncertainty and turbulence amidst institutional voids. The women in their study proved that they were proactive and resilient in taking advantage of the benefits of network-building. In addition, the network structure built by these women prompted the government to make their programs more accessible for female entrepreneurs. They recommend that the public sector take a leadership role in facilitating strategic resources for entrepreneurs and creating a stable business environment that supports opportunities for everyone. They argue that this should be done through state-based institutional intervention that is reinforced by regulations, and efficient legal and economic systems.

THEME 2: PROGRAMS AND THE SUPPORT ENVIRONMENT

The interconnected and reinforcing elements of an entrepreneurship ecosystem can make financial capital easier to secure by more people, and enable broader human capital development. A functioning entrepreneurial ecosystem also fosters new markets and opportunities, offers an array of institutional and infrastructural support, and influences a productive and innovative entrepreneurial culture for growth (Brush et al., 2018; Fetters et al., 2010; Hechavarría and Ingram, 2018). The most common hindrances to new business development, and to business growth, are talent acquisition, bureaucracy and lack of access to financial capital (Isenberg, 2014).

The added gender imbalance to the inherent barriers to many elements of the entrepreneurship ecosystem means that women lack equal access to support, resources and opportunities (Brush et al., 2018). Consistent diversity and bias training is one strategy for tackling these challenges and helping to create a more inclusive culture that embraces diversity initiatives and encourages awareness and skill development (Bezrukova et al., 2016). Women-only training programs represent another strategy to help women to build general business, entrepreneurial and leadership competencies that are important for growing businesses, in a way that gives women room to work through issues that affect them (Bullough et al., 2015).

In Chapter 4 Eversole, Birdthistle, Walo and Godinho examined the entrepreneurial ecosystem in two distinct regions of Australia. In doing so, they created a support ecosystem map that shows the elements of the ecosystem that are available for enterprising women. They found that a support ecosystem is present in both of the regions they examined—rural North West Tasmania and the city of Melbourne—including commonalities as well as localized variation. In both places, they found the support ecosystems to be strong in many respects, but ineffectively serving the needs of women entrepreneurs. Their mapping showed that women-led businesses start and stay small because of a lack of accessibility and appropriateness for women entrepreneurs in terms of mentoring and advice, training, finance, incubators and accelerators, and peer networks.

Both urban and rural regions were found to provide quality mentoring, coaching, education and training services, and women were reportedly pleased with these services. However, the women entrepreneurs they studied expressed an interest in more relational approaches to training that would offer in-depth conversations and exchanges, rather than a more transactional nature of providing information or advice. The women also reported that finding information about these services was difficult, and described feelings of a lack of a personal fit: few mentors with similar characteristics, feeling preyed upon as women, and cost and time constraints. Eversole, Birdthistle, Walo and Godinho's findings also highlighted the limited availability of financial instruments, and an absence of woman-specific financing options that would help women overcome a lack of collateral, and consider instead the viability of the business concept. The authors recommend training for investors and bank loan officers to remove overt gender bias, or at least limit the impact of unconscious bias.

Not surprisingly, Eversole, Birdthistle, Walo and Godinho found incubators and accelerators to be much more available in the urban setting than in the rural areas, and they note the gender-blind nature of this support industry that does not account for women-specific differences. Also effectively absent in rural areas, but prolific in urban municipalities was an abundance of peer networking opportunities, including some that are precisely focused on women entrepreneurs. Nevertheless, they highlighted one positive example of an organization that intentionally targeted women entrepreneurs by emphasizing an environment that purposefully provided relationship building and relational learning opportunities.

In Chapter 5, Cetindamar, James, Lammers, Pearce and Sullivan studied an Australian STEM (science, technology, engineering and math) program for women, called the Science in Australia Gender Equity (SAGE) program. More specifically, they examined how this program successfully stimulated its participants to become entrepreneurs with new technology companies. Their research into an institutional intervention in STEM education underlines the significance of a gender-inclusive atmosphere for STEM education and in the workplace. This in turn expands opportunities for women, and meaningfully influences academic and careers identities for women who increasingly see themselves in STEM fields, and as entrepreneurs. These authors recommend inspiring women from inside universities to consider entrepreneurial STEM opportunities, before they graduate or get disheartened, which has the potential to have a sustained, positive impact on increasing the numbers of female technology entrepreneurs. The focus should therefore be on complementary programs that might fortify the conduit between education in STEM fields and entrepreneurship. They further recommend: a clear focus of governmental policy on technology entrepreneurship, a life cycle approach to integrated education that encourages women and girls to enter STEM fields, scholarships and fellowships for women in STEM, mentoring and training for entrepreneurship, reducing or eliminating gender bias in tertiary STEM education and in the workplace, and increasing the representation of women in senior leadership positions.

THEME 3: POLICIES AND REGULATION

Prior research has shown that women experience greater challenges with regard to securing capital for their businesses than men. These challenges include gender bias in debt and in venture capital funding practices. The result is that women entrepreneurs secure lower levels of investment capital and smaller bank loans than their male counterparts (Balachandra et al., 2019; Kanze et al., 2017; Marlow and Patton, 2005; Wilson, 2016). With insufficient financial capital from investors and banks, and microcredit sometimes being the only option for women-led businesses (Armendáriz and Roome, 2008), it is not surprising that it is hard for women to succeed in high-growth businesses.

To help women overcome these hurdles, policies should incentivize organizations to market existing financial products directly to women, and design and set aside specific investment funds and loan products explicitly for women entrepreneurs. Putting policies in place to attract more female investors, and creating reserves led by women and intended for investment precisely in businesses founded and owned by women, may help to establish more balance in funds that are particularly meaningful for women entrepreneurs with growth-oriented businesses (Halabisky, 2018).

In Chapter 6, Boudreaux and Nikolaev suggest that the regulatory environment is the most critical aspect of the entrepreneurial ecosystem for understanding the differences in the growth aspirations of female and male entrepreneurs at the start-up stage. They used data from the World Economic Freedom Index and the Global Entrepreneurship Monitor in 43 countries to study these gender differences. Their research shows that as the quality of the regulatory environment improves, the gender differences in growth aspirations at the start-up stage begin to disappear. They found female entrepreneurs to have lower growth goals, until they saw improvements in credit market regulations in particular. Their findings also suggest that policies designed to enhance the quality of credit market regulations are even more important than improving labor market regulations or easing the costs of doing business, at least in terms of reducing gender differences in growth aspirations. The most significant way to improve credit market regulations is by purposefully removing (or at least limiting) discrimination in lending practices (Marlow and Patton, 2005; Muravyev et al., 2009), which has been found to be less of a problem in labor and business regulations (Djankov et al., 2002). Boudreaux and Nikolaev also recommend that policy makers work to improve the amount of private sector credit (as opposed to public sector credit) and reduce government control over interest rates.

In Chapter 7, Frešer, Širec and Tominc studied gender differences in perceived financial resources in Slovenian businesses. They too found overt discrimination against women from investors. To combat this, they recommend embedding gender fairness into entrepreneurship education, intensifying media coverage of women's entrepreneurship and gender equality from investors, and fostering an environment that attracts more women investors. These authors also argue that women should be encouraged to pursue a dream of launching and growing their own businesses, and be introduced to more female entrepreneur role models. One of Frešer, Širec and Tominc's key recommendations is for efforts to recruit more women into the whole business angel and investor community, in order to reduce discrimination and make financial capital easier for female entrepreneurs to know about and secure. In their chapter, they provide examples of successful programs in other parts of the world, one of which was in the form of entrepreneurial support groups in Ireland that were led by successful and experienced women entrepreneurs. The other program involved a network of female entrepreneurs who traveled around Germany to serve as role models for other women and to explicitly promote women's entrepreneurship at events. Finally, they made reference to an Italian program in which special feed funding was provided for innovative and growth-oriented businesses among underprivileged communities.

In Chapter 8, Wu, Li and Muhammad wanted to understand the relationship between policy awareness and women's debt financing activities. They investigated the implementation of a new financial policy in China that aimed to reduce obstacles to financing for small- and medium-sized enterprises. This 2010 policy included a large number of activities and recommendations on debt financing, with a significant level of detail for implementation. Wu, Li and Muhammad found that women's debt financing activity increased and they were more likely to secure higher levels of debt capital when they became aware of this financial policy. Wu, Li and Muhammad highlight the importance of policy propaganda by governments, and they recommend that governments market their policies and support programs widely through all forms of media (broadcast, social, internet, etc.). They also encourage women to proactively seek out information about programs and policies, to join networking groups, like women's entrepreneur associations and business organizations, and to utilize incubators for business support resources.

CONCLUSION AND SUMMARY RECOMMENDATIONS

Programs, policies and practices need to support the work of women entrepreneurs in order for them to create new jobs, add value to the economy, and build as much personal wealth and familial stability as possible. Progress has been made in recent years. Programs, policies and practices that are focused on women have been addressing the under-representation of women, embracing more women in the workforce, and enabling their economic freedoms. Enhanced visibility and access to finance, increased education and training, technological reinforcements, and facilitating the generation of business contacts and networks are some of the ways this has been accomplished. Additional NGO support, public sector involvement, university partnerships and more have accompanied many of these efforts.

That being said, women remain under-represented in entrepreneurial activity, invest less capital, exploit lower levels of financing, and grow their businesses less, compared to their male counterparts. To change these realities that continue to persist, and support high-potential female entrepreneurs in growing larger and more profitable businesses, the authors in this book have conducted research and made recommendations for important programs, policies and practices. We have summarized the findings of the research in this book into the following concise, albeit simplified, bullet points. In order to help women secure larger amounts of start-up capital and access external funding sources, reduce gender differences in growth aspirations, inspire women to consider entrepreneurial STEM careers, make more women aware of important financial policy, and increase women's debt financing activity, we recommend:

- Specific policies aimed at stimulating and supporting women's entrepreneurship.
- Specific financial products and options designed for women.
- Business education, and financial literacy training targeted specifically for women.
- Activities that help women to build professional networks among other entrepreneurs and sources of financial capital.

- Activities and programs to facilitate mentoring and access to role models.
- Public sector leadership roles aimed at facilitating strategic resources for entrepreneurs.
- Public sector leadership roles aimed at creating a stable business environment that supports opportunities for everyone.
- State-based institutional intervention that is reinforced by regulations, and efficient legal and economic systems.
- A focus on the viability of the business concept for financing as opposed to collateral.
- Gender and unconscious bias training for investors, bank loan officers, educators, managers and policy makers.
- Incubators and accelerators in rural as well as urban settings.
- Complementary programs connecting STEM education and entrepreneurship.
- Governmental policy to stimulate and support technology entrepreneurship.
- A life cycle approach to integrated education that encourages women and girls to enter STEM fields.
- Scholarships and fellowships for women in STEM.
- Removing barriers to increase the representation of women in senior leadership positions.
- More women entering the whole business angel and investor community, a quality regulatory environment, and credit market regulations in particular, by removing (or at least limiting) discrimination in lending practices.
- Explicit promotion of women's entrepreneurship at events.
- Government policies and support programs marketed widely through all forms of media.

In conclusion, high-growth women's entrepreneurship is important for global competitiveness. Worldwide, enduring, enhanced, and comprehensive programming and policy-making related to women's entrepreneurship need to be a focal point for all economic, societal and political actors. Women as a whole around the world present an astounding and under-tapped opportunity for economic and societal growth. A sustained and unified strategy for initiatives that support and encourage women's business capacity for high-growth business requires sweeping cultural change and efforts from all angles to accomplish this. Such efforts consist of initiatives and programs related to business management, mentorship, diversity and inclusion, the media, and influential economic, societal and political agents of progress.

REFERENCES

Armendáriz, B. and N. Roome (2008), 'Gender empowerment in microfinance', in S. Sundaresan (ed.), *Microfinance: Emerging Trends and Challenges*, Cheltenham, UK and Northampton, MA, USA: Edward Elgar Publishing.

Balachandra, L., T. Briggs, K. Eddleston and C. Brush (2019), 'Don't pitch like a girl! How gender stereotypes influence investor decisions', *Entrepreneurship Theory and Practice*, 43(1), 116–137.

Baron, R.A. and G.D. Markman (2003), 'Beyond social capital: the role of entrepreneurs' social competence in their financial success', *Journal of Business Venturing*, 18(4), 41–60.

Bezrukova, K., C.S. Spell, J.L. Perry and K.A. Jehn (2016), 'A meta-analytical integration of over 40 years of research on diversity training evaluation', *Psychological Bulletin*, 142(11), 1227–1274.

Brush, C., L.F. Edelman, T. Manolova and F. Welter (2018), 'A gendered look at entrepreneurship ecosystems', *Small Business Economics*, Online First.

Bullough, A., M. Sully de Luque, D. Abdelzaher and W. Heim (2015), 'Developing women leaders through entrepreneurship training', *Academy of Management Perspectives*, 29(2), 250–270.

Dawson, C., N. Fuller-Love, E. Sinnott and B. O'Gorman (2011), 'Entrepreneurs' perceptions of business networks: does gender matter?', *The International Journal of Entrepreneurship and Innovation*, 12(4), 271–281.

Djankov, S., R. La Porta, F. Lopez-de-Silanes and A. Shleifer (2002), 'The regulation of entry', *Quarterly Journal of Economics*, 117(1), 1–37.

Fairlie, R. and A.M. Robb (2009), 'Gender differences in business performance: evidence from characteristics of business owners survey', *Small Business Economics*, 33(4), 375–395.

Fetters, M., P.G. Greene, M.P. Rice and J.S. Butler (eds.) (2010), *The Development of University-Based Entrepreneurship Ecosystems: Global Practices*, Cheltenham, UK and Northampton, MA, USA: Edward Elgar Publishing.

Halabisky, D. (2018), 'Policy brief on women's entrepreneurship', OECD SME and Entrepreneurship Papers, No. 8, Paris: OECD Publishing. https://doi.org/10.1787/dd2d79e7-en.

Hechavarría, D., A. Bullough, C. Brush and L. Edelman (2019), 'High growth women's entrepreneurship: fueling social and economic development', *Journal of Small Business Management*, 57(1), 5–13.

Hechavarría, D.M. and A.E. Ingram (2018), 'Entrepreneurial ecosystem conditions and gendered national-level entrepreneurial activity: a fourteen-year panel study of GEM', *Small Business Economics*, Online First. https://doi.org/10.1007/s11187-018-9994-7.

Henry, C., B. Orser, S. Coleman and S. Foss (2017), 'Women's entrepreneurship policy: a 13 nation cross-country comparison', *International Journal of Gender and Entrepreneurship*, 9(3), 206–228.

Isenberg, D. (2014), 'What an entrepreneurship ecosystem actually is', *Harvard Business Review*, 5, 1–7.

Kanze, D., L. Huang, M.A. Conley and E.T. Higgins (2017), 'Male and female entrepreneurs get asked different questions by VCs – and it affects how much funding they get', *Harvard Business Review*, June 27.

Kelley, D., B. Baumer, C. Brush, P. Greene, M. Mahdavi, M. Majbouri, M. Cole, M. Dean and R. Haevlow (2017), *Global Entrepreneurship Monitor 2016/2017 Report on Women's Entrepreneurship*, Wellesley, MA: Babson College.

Klyver, K. and S. Grant (2010), 'Gender differences in entrepreneurial networking and participation', *International Journal of Gender and Entrepreneurship*, 2(3), 213–227.

Kuada, J. (2009), 'Gender, social networks and entrepreneurship in Ghana', *Journal of African Business*, 10(1), 85–103.

Marlow, S. and D. Patton (2005), 'All credit to men? Entrepreneurship, finance, and gender', *Entrepreneurship Theory and Practice*, 29(6), 717–735.

Muravyev, A., O. Talavera and D. Schäfer (2009), 'Entrepreneurs' gender and financial constraints: evidence from international data', *Journal of Comparative Economics*, 37(2), 270–286.

OECD (2017), *2013 OECD Recommendation of the Council on Gender Equality in Education, Employment and Entrepreneurship*, Paris: OECD Publishing. http://dx .doi.org/10.1787/9789264279391-en.

Orser, B.J., A.L. Riding and K. Manley (2006), 'Women entrepreneurs and financial capital', *Entrepreneurship Theory and Practice*, 30(5), 643–665.

Renzulli, L.A., H. Aldrich and J. Moody (2000), 'Family matters: gender, networks, and entrepreneurial outcomes', *Social Forces*, 79(2), 523–546.

Watson, J. (2012), 'Networking: gender differences and the association with firm performance', *International Small Business Journal*, 30(5), 536–558.

Wilson, J. (2016), 'Making loan decisions in banks: straight from the gut?', *Journal of Business Ethics*, 137(1), 53–63.

Index